7/00

Who Counts?

Who Counts?

The Politics of Census-Taking in Contemporary America

Margo J. Anderson
and
Stephen E. Fienberg

Russell Sage Foundation
New York

The Russell Sage Foundation

Library of Congress Cataloging-in-Publication Data

Anderson, Margo J., 1945–
    Who counts? : the politics of census-taking in contemporary America / Margo J. Anderson and Stephen E. Fienberg.
        p. cm.
    Includes bibliographical references and index.
    ISBN 0-87154-256-0
    1. United   States—Census—Methodology—History.   2. Census   undercounts—United States—History.
I. Fienberg, Stephen E.   II. Title.
    HA179.A53   1999
        304.6'0723—dc21   99-25035
                                                                                                                                        CIP

RUSSELL SAGE FOUNDATION
112 East 64th Street, New York, New York 10021
10 9 8 7 6 5 4 3 2 1

Contents

This book has its roots in a class that we cotaught, at Carnegie Mellon University in the spring of 1990, on social science and the decennial census. Much of the focus was on the 1990 census, which was then in progress, and most of the students participated in special parts of the enumeration process; we even had Census Bureau Director Barbara Bryant speak with the class.

Margo Anderson taught the first part of the course, and Stephen Fienberg the second, and so our teaching did not overlap. But the course planning turned out to be very enjoyable, especially when it led to interaction on topics on which we shared similar perspectives and those to which we brought very different knowledge bases to the table.

Two years later, we were both serving on a Committee on National Statistics panel dealing with planning for the 2000 census; much of the panel's discussion was rooted in the outcomes of and experiences from 1990. At times we found ourselves frustrated by the lack of a detailed narrative of the events surrounding the taking of the 1990 census and the controversy surrounding coverage evaluation and adjustment, especially a narrative rooted in the broader history of census taking in the United States and one informed on the technical details of the methods at the center of the adjustment controversy. A series of side conversations convinced us that our shared perspectives and differing backgrounds would allow us to write such a narrative, and thus began our effort on this book. By combining Margo's background as a social historian with a special interest in statistical methods and the history of the census with Stephen's background in the statistical methodology underlying census adjustment and his interest in the history of statistics, we felt that together we could write a narrative that neither of us could prepare on our own.

Early support came in the form of a grant from the Russell Sage Foundation and continued encouragement from staff officer Nancy Cunniff Casey, who allowed us considerable latitude as we wandered through the landscape of discussions surrounding the planning for census 2000 and tried to explore what lessons could be drawn from the 1990 experience. These wanderings led us to reformulate the plans for the book, actually several times, and to develop the policy-oriented perspective that ultimately guided us.

In terms of written documentation, the 1990 census was unique in census history, largely because of the files accumulated in conjunction with the 1991 report of the secretary of commerce on the decision not to adjust and the subsequent New York City lawsuit. Boxes of memorandums, reports, letters, and other materials thus fill our attics and offices, and these often allowed us to answer technical questions or resolve sequencing of events in a simple and direct fashion. In addition, through our work on the Committee on National Statistics panel, we acquired a regular flow of information both from 1990 and on the planning for 2000. We would like to thank the staff and other members of that panel for serving unwittingly as a sounding board for our ideas and our thinking on the events and issues surrounding the 1990 adjustment controversy.

We have benefited greatly from the Census Bureau's own voluminous documentation of the count, as well other analyses and memoirs of the 1990 census. Particularly relevant are the dense, thorough, though not terribly exciting official procedural history of the count and the more lively accounts by Harvey Choldin, *Looking for the Last Percent*, and Barbara Bryant and William Dunn, *Moving Power and Money*. We recommend their perusal to anyone wishing a comprehensive view of the 1990 census. In our treatment of the 1990 census, we have tried to analyze issues that these earlier treatments have not addressed and particularly to treat the relationship between the undercount adjustment litigation and the census process and the increasingly partisan perspectives on the decennial census and reapportionment process. As will be evident from what follows, we see the controversies surrounding the issue of adjustment for the differential undercount as part of a much larger set of questions about the relative distribution of political power and tax dollars triggered by census data. And we suggest that policy makers will need to keep the statistical and political issues and responsibilities sorted out. This turns out to be a difficult task. Our statistical colleagues often have the same difficulty.

In the process of assembling materials for the book, we conducted interviews with a number of key statisticians, both inside the Census Bureau and elsewhere in government, who were involved in either planning activities or in the evaluation of the adjustment methodology and the decision process on adjustment. In particular, we would like to thank Peter Bounpane, William Butz, Barbara Everitt Bryant, Hermann Habermann, C. Louis Kincannon, and John Thompson for spending time with us and often assisting us in other ways, as well. Other conversations of a more casual nature with several statisticians and others knowledgeable about the census and its history were equally important. In this regard we would like to thank Barbara Bailar, Patty Becker, Harvey Choldin, Connie Citro, Beth Osborne Daponte, Joe Eaton, Barry Edmonston, Eugene Ericksen, David Freedman, Bill Hobby, Howard Hogan, Richard John, Jay Kadane, Juanita Tamayo Lott, Terry Ann Lowenthal, Susan Miskura, Mary Mulry, Jeffrey Passel, David Pemberton, Martha Farnsworth Riche, Richard Rockwell, John Rolph, Representative Tom Sawyer, Ed Spar, Bruce Spencer, Duane Steffey, Katherine Wallman, Kenneth Wachter, Kirk Wolter, Donald Ylvisaker, and Alan Zaslavsky, all of whom were able to assist us in one way or another. Several people commented directly on an earlier draft of the book, and we are truly indebted to them for spotting holes, errors, and infelicitous phrases: Barbara Bryant, Connie Citro, Hermann Habermann, Jessica Heinz, Bill Hobby, Jay Kadane, David McMillan, Mary Mulry, Martha Riche, Ed Spar, and Katherine Wallman.

Stephen participated as an expert witness in the New York City lawsuit and testified on behalf of New York City in support of the procedures used by Census Bureau statisticians. Attorneys for both the New York plaintiffs and the Justice Department contacted Margo about providing testimony on the historical background of the census before the trial of the New York lawsuit. In the event, neither side asked her to testify. In the past year, we have both prepared declarations for submission with briefs filed by the City of Los Angeles as part of the litigation over the 2000 census and have participated in several professional meetings in which the 2000 census was the focus. Each time we attempted to complete the writing of the book, however, a new and potentially important event would occur, and we began to feel the need to revise in light of current events. With the recent Supreme Court hearing and the impeachment of the president by the House of Representatives, it seemed that we must choose an arbitrary ending point.

Earlier versions of some of the material that appears here were published in W. A. Wallace's *Ethics in Modelling* (Fienberg) and in the journals *Chance* (Fienberg, Anderson and Fienberg), *Society/Transaction* (Anderson and Fienberg), and the *Journal of Interdisciplinary History* (Anderson and Fienberg). Margo Anderson has published previous historical analysis on the census, particularly, *The American Cen-*

sus, and we have drawn from the arguments there. Although we have relied heavily on these previous writings, we have also spent time with original documentation wherever it was available. As a consequence, not only have we rewritten materials, but we have also updated technical details and discussion in many instances in light of subsequent developments.

The Department of Statistics at Carnegie Mellon has been especially hospitable to our efforts, with both colleagues and graduate students commenting on our work at various stages and supporting the preparation of the actual manuscript through its multiple revisions. Thanks also to colleagues in history and urban studies at University of Wisconsin–Milwaukee and the Woodrow Wilson International Center for Scholars for comments and a supportive research environment. We owe special thanks to Howard Fienberg, Joyce Fienberg, Leslie Persichetti, and Heidi Sestrich for work with various parts of the manuscript.

Finally, our families have lived through many years of discussions about census adjustment and census politics and have encouraged our research and collaboration. We are indebted to them for their support for close to a decade.

December 24, 1998

Prologue

E very ten years, the federal government, through the auspices of
the United States Bureau of the Census, counts the American population and reports the results to Congress. Congress, state legislatures, and local representative bodies then use the census results to
undertake the decennial process of reapportioning themselves in light
of population growth and change. New census numbers also trigger
changes in legislative formulas that allocate tax revenue among the
various levels of government through revenue-sharing and grant-in-
aid systems. Government policy makers, scholars, the media, and the
private sector also eagerly await the census results each decade and
use the information for myriad public and private purposes.

The census and reapportionment process is one of the oldest and
most venerable parts of the American political system. The framers of
the federal Constitution wrote the census mechanism into the political
system in 1787. The nation began counting its population in 1790 and
has continued to do so regularly each decade since. On the face of it,
counting the population is a simple matter of collecting information
on the characteristics of members of each household and aggregating
it from the household to the block, to the census tract or local neighborhood, to the town or municipality, to the county, and finally to the
state and the nation. Census data are as familiar as an old shoe; we
look up population figures in almanacs, we expect to see population
signs at city limits, and we rate our communities by how populous
they are. The instrument has served the country well.

Nevertheless, for the past generation, the census, as well as the
Census Bureau, has come under a cloud. The bureau has had to defend
its ability to count the population precisely, accurately, and, recently,
efficiently. Congress, local government officials, and the public have

increasingly complained that the census is not as accurate as it should be and thereby fails to provide a proper and legitimate basis for legislative apportionment and funding allocations. It counts some groups in the population more accurately than others, and this "differential undercount"—especially of minorities and poor, inner-city residents—undermines legislative apportionments and policy based upon the numbers. If not rectified, critics argue, a flawed census will damage the very fabric of the polity.

From the perspective of many state and local officials, federal officials have failed to respond to the challenges to count more efficiently. Accordingly, coalitions of state and local officials and private parties have sued the Census Bureau each decade since 1970, challenging the methodology and results of the census. Although the government has by and large prevailed in court, these lawsuits have become more elaborate each decade and more damaging to the legitimacy of the census. A coalition of city and state governments, led by New York City, sued the bureau before the 1990 census count. Filing in November 1988, they claimed that even before the census took place, the bureau knew that the 1990 census would be plagued by a differential undercount, and they asked the court to institute new procedures for counting so as to improve the enumeration. The story of the New York lawsuit, as it came to be called, forms a core theme of this book. We trace its history from the initial filing to its final resolution before the United States Supreme Court in March 1996.

Lawsuits are the most visible evidence of the controversies surrounding the capacity of the census to count fairly and efficiently. Since the latter half of the 1980s, however, a second major census controversy has surfaced in disagreements between Congress and the executive branch over the proper methods and goals of the decennial census. Since the late 1980s, census controversies have become partisan: a Democratic Congress lambasted the policies of Republican officials in the Commerce Department and Census Bureau, and since 1994, a Republican Congress has viewed the Clinton administration's census policies with equal suspicion. Partisan politics have increasingly plagued discussions of census accuracy, efficiency, and innovation. The plans for the 2000 census are embroiled in a complex set of negotiations between the legislative and executive branches of government and have reached to the third, judicial, branch. In the chapters that follow, we frame and discuss these controversies as they have emerged in discussions of adjustments for undercounts.

Parallel to these political controversies, and related to them, are two technical controversies surrounding counting. The first is the challenge to traditional census practices that advocates of dual-systems estimation have framed: the bureau can do a better job of counting the population, they claim, and the federal government, in failing to use the technique, violates the constitutional requirements for a "one person, one vote" legislative apportionment system. As later chapters indicate, the new methods pose conceptual challenges to the "traditional" census and have themselves become entwined in the debates about the relative obligations and responsibilities of Americans to stand up and be counted each decade. Changing to the new methods, advocates of the traditional methods suggest, would fundamentally undermine the legitimacy of the two-centuries-old census instrument.

The second technical controversy involves the appropriate methods for classifying the racial and ethnic characteristics of the American population. Statistical Policy Directive 15, promulgated by the Office of Management and Budget in the executive branch, defines the official categories and methods to be used to classify data on race and ethnicity for the federal statistical system. Developed initially in 1977 to standardize the disparate practices within the federal government, the directive was revised in 1997 after a four-year review process and is now known as "Standards for Maintaining, Collecting, and Presenting Federal Data on Race and Ethnicity." That process provides a unique window on the politics of counting and classifying and on the impact of the nation's changing demographics on statistical policy.

Myths in the Making

To provide the flavor of the issues surrounding census taking in the late 1990s, we open with recent commentary on past censuses and the plans for the decennial census in 2000. The 2000 census has become the subject of intense partisan and methodological controversy. Many of the statements of congressional leaders, public officials, and political commentators and reporters in the print media about census taking and statistical sampling in the past are, in fact, myths about past censuses rather than historical statements about what the census has been or descriptions of the census plans for 2000. Census politics burst into the national news in the summer of 1997, when Republicans in the United States House of Representatives attached to the flood relief bill for the Dakotas a rider banning the use of sampling in the 2000 census. President Bill Clinton vetoed the flood relief bill and, after several more months of negotiation and politics, Congress and the president compromised on language in the appropriations bill. That compromise created a Census Monitoring Board to monitor plans for and administration of the 2000 count and effectively put off the resolution of the sampling dispute to 1999 and beyond.

The Census Bureau and the Clinton administration promoted the 2000 plan as thoughtful and innovative, falling well within the time-honored tradition of census enumeration. Republican congressmen and a number of state and local officials conjured up visions of impending disaster, political manipulation of the count, and general incompetence within the Census Bureau officialdom. Newt Gingrich, Speaker of the House, and the Southeastern Legal Foundation filed separate lawsuits in federal court against the Clinton administration in an effort to block key aspects of the 2000 census plan. (*U.S. House et al. v. Dept. of Commerce et al.* 1998; *Glavin, Barr, et al. v. Clinton et al.* 1998; *Dept. of Commerce et al. v. House et al., Clinton v. Glavin* 1999). The cases were argued before the Supreme Court in November 1998. We present a selection of these myths by way of introducing our story.

MYTH 1
The census is an actual physical head count of each person. Figure 1.1 gives this myth in cartoon form. "The First Congress directed federal marshals to locate every person who could be found, and to count each person they identified."[1]

MYTH 2
"The decennial census has been conducted as an 'actual enumeration' by counting the national population in every census in the history of this country."[2]

MYTH 3
The "actual enumeration" has been highly successful at counting the population: "The 1990 census accurately counted 98.4 percent of the population."[3]

MYTH 4
The Constitution requires that each decade, the federal government take a census and reapportion 435 seats in the House of Representatives and 535 votes in the electoral college among the states. The Census Bureau and the commerce secretary tell Congress how to reapportion itself each decade.

Figure 1.1

THE FAMILY CIRCUS®   By Bil Keane

"Daddy's going to fill out the census questionnaire so we all hafta stand still while
he counts us."

Source: Bil Keane, *The Family Circus.* Reprinted with permission of the author.

MYTH 5

By using sampling, the Commerce Department and the Census Bureau
are attempting to violate the Constitution by not counting everyone:

> Defendants [U.S. Department of Commerce] have adopted a program
> for conducting the 2000 census that abandons any attempt to locate
> all persons who can be found and count them. Instead, Defendants
> will estimate the population using statistical methods commonly re-
> ferred to as sampling. Defendants' census totals will include millions
> and millions of people who are simply deemed to exist based upon
> computations of statisticians advising the Census Bureau. The totals
> used for apportionment may vary dramatically depending upon
> which of a number of demographic and statistical assumptions De-
> fendants choose to make.[4]

MYTH 6

The Commerce Department plan will manipulate the census totals for
the benefit of Democrats: "Census Sampling Would Favor Democrats."[5] The 2000 census results "will guide the reapportionment process in which congressional district lines are redrawn to conform to
population shifts. Statistical errors in the count, accidental or deliber-
ate, could result in as many as 24 GOP seats being lost, according to

election strategists." *Human Events* quotes the analysis of the Statistical Assessment Service, which claims that sampling has "potential for political corruption: 'This also creates a powerful political temptation for the party in power to skew the sample adjustment its way. The ability to "create" or "eliminate" millions of strategically placed citizens with the stroke of a pen introduces a potent and disturbing new political weapon,' they said."

MYTH 7
Sampling is unconstitutional; the federal courts decided during the 1990 census lawsuits that sampling in the census is unconstitutional: "The fact remains that sampling is a risky scheme of dubious constitutionality."[6]

MYTH 8
Sampling or statistical estimation is not scientific. According to William Safire, "Sampling is no science."[7]

MYTH 9
The framers of the Constitution were familiar with methods of statistical estimation and rejected their use in the census: "Even though [Thomas] Jefferson [secretary of state and the official in charge of the 1790 census] 'was familiar with methods of statistical estimation, having used them effectively in his 1782 survey of Virginia's population, he did not adjust the 1790 census numbers despite his knowledge that the "omissions . . . ha[d] been very great."[8]

MYTH 10
The proposal to adjust the census in 1990 was rightly rejected by the secretary of commerce because the methodology was fundamentally flawed and fraught with error: "A computer programming error . . . overstated the undercount by a million people and probably would have given a congressional seat to Arizona that belonged to Pennsylvania."[9] "[E]xperts believe that processing error accounts for 80 percent of the estimated undercount."[10]

And now everyone is confused. Recent censuses have been portrayed as both the most reliable—"[T]he 1980 and 1990 censuses are believed to have been far and away the most accurate on record, accounting in net for 98.8 percent and 98.2 percent of the population, respectively"[11]—and the least—"Census Bureau officials estimate the 1990 undercount was the largest in the census' 200-year history" (*Philadelphia Inquirer*, May 7, 1998).

A Brief Version of Our Argument

Federal officials have taken a decennial census of the U.S. population every ten years since 1790, as mandated by Article I, Section 2, of the 1787 Constitution and the enabling legislation for taking the census. The officials in the executive branch in charge of taking the census have traditionally counted the population by establishing procedures to contact the head or reference person of every household in the country, either in person or by mail. They will do so again in 2000. The head or reference person in each household is responsible for reporting the population in that household and either mailing the form back to the federal government or responding to an enumerator. At no point in the nation's history has there been a physical count of each person in the country. The officials in charge of gathering the information from all the households in the country aggregate the results by localities and states and forward them to Congress. Congress, in turn, sets in motion a procedure to reapportion the seats in the House of Representatives and the votes in the electoral college on the basis of the reported census results. Congress determines the apportionment method, the size of the House of Representatives, and the dates by which the census results should be reported. Since 1910, Congress has maintained the size of the House of Representatives at 435 members. Before 1910, the House size generally changed after each census. Congress, over the course of the nation's history, has employed a number of different apportionment formulas. The current method of equal proportions has been in use since 1940.

Federal officials who oversee the census and Congress have always been aware of problems with the accuracy of the census. These problems include undercounts, overcounts, and erroneous enumerations. Since 1940, the Census Bureau has conducted evaluation studies based on probability samples of subsets of the population to measure the level of accuracy of census results, in terms of both coverage errors—that is, underenumeration and overenumeration—and content error—that is, incorrect information on the characteristics of the population. The often reported statistic of the net undercount, 1.8 percent in 1990, represents, at the national level, the net undercount after undercounts are subtracted from overcounts and erroneous enumerations. It does not mean that 98.2 percent of the 1990 population was counted accurately. The evaluation studies of census coverage have themselves improved over the past twenty years, incorporating new measures of accuracy, including measures of gross error in the census—that is, the sum of overcounts, undercounts, and erroneous enumerations. These studies reveal that the level of gross error is substantial, in the range of 10 percent of the total population counted, and that the 1990 count had more gross error than did the 1980 census (see, for example, U.S. General Accounting Office 1991; and Ericksen and Defonso 1993).

The 2000 census plan proposes to employ some time-honored methods of counting and some innovations that have never been used in the history of the decennial census. The time-honored methods include the use of a mail census as the primary means of contacting households. The mail census was first used in 1970. In that year, about 60 percent of American households received their census forms in the mail and were instructed to fill them out and mail them back to the Census Bureau. In 1980 and 1990, more than 90 percent of households were contacted by mail. For the parts of the country that cannot be reached by mail, the Census Bureau uses enumerators to canvass a particular geographic area. This method was the fundamental enumeration procedure from 1790 to 1960. The 2000 census plan proposes collecting additional detailed information on the population through the use of a long-form sample in conjunction with the short-form complete count (long-form sampling began in 1940). The Census Bureau will evaluate the quality of coverage of the count with a postenumeration sample survey, a procedure begun in 1950 and used in one form or another ever since.

The Census Bureau has traditionally used enumerators to contact households that do not return the mail census form in a timely manner, in the counting phase known as nonresponse follow-up. The new methods envisioned for 2000 included sampling for nonresponse follow-up. It is this new procedure that has generated some of the most heated objections in Congress. Census officials know from past experience that residents at about one-third of the addresses will forget to fill out and mail back a census form, will ignore the form, or will perhaps not receive it in the first place. The Census Bureau follows up on these addresses to retrieve the census information, sending an enumerator to the address. This phase of the count starts in late April and is designed to retrieve information from the households that have not yet responded. In 1970, 1980, and 1990, nonresponse follow-up was conducted for all households that did not mail back their census forms. The evaluation results of the last two censuses indicate that the quality of the data collected by enumerators from nonresponding households got much poorer the longer it took the enumerators to collect it. That is, responses gathered from households in June or later were significantly more error filled than those collected in April and May. Thus, the Census Bureau concluded, a higher-quality sampling process for nonresponse follow-up would produce better data than 100 percent follow-up because the process could use better-trained employees and be done more quickly. The census plan guarantees that 90 percent of the households in each census tract will be counted directly by mail or personal visit; inferences for the residual nonresponders will be derived from the sampled nonresponse follow-up households. The opponents of sampling for nonresponse follow-up, as noted previously, claim that the Census Bureau has given up the effort to contact everyone and will make up people, a process that could be manipulated to the benefit of Democrats.

The other significant and controversial innovation of the 2000 census plan is the integration of the postenumeration survey (PES) process into the traditional enumeration. In 1990, the Census Bureau took a postenumeration survey and produced adjusted census counts on the basis of the survey results. But the 1990 census did not fully integrate the PES and the traditional enumeration to produce adjusted census counts on the basis of dual-systems estimation. Rather, the bureau released the results of the April, or traditional, enumeration in December 1990 and then released adjusted results in June 1991. There followed eight years of litigation on the quality and legality of the two sets of figures; hence, the 1990 experience echoes through the current plan. This decade, the Census Bureau had been proposing a one-number census—that is, procedures that would have produced a final census count that could not easily be disaggregated into the traditional enumeration and the adjustments made on the basis of the results of dual-systems estimation. Again, critics charged, the adjustment process would be subject to political manipulation—making up people.

In the chapters that follow, we evaluate the claims that the census must be a traditional enumeration and that the census does not count the population as well as it could or should. We begin in chapter 2 with basic historical background on census taking and the discovery of the differential undercount in the mid-twentieth century. Chapter 3 explores the controversies surrounding the undercount in the 1970 and 1980 censuses. Chapter 4 explicates the technique of dual-systems estimation and its application to census taking. Chapter 5 discusses the technical developments in census taking in the 1980s, the preparations for 1990, the emerging controversy between the Commerce Department and the Census Bureau over plans for 1990, and the

beginning phases of the New York lawsuit. Chapter 6 addresses the
administration of the 1990 census and the July 1991 Commerce Department decision not to adjust for the differential undercount. Chapter 7 traces the litigation that resumed after the Commerce Department's decision, from a district court trial to the Supreme Court.
Chapter 8 traces the process of the revision of Statistical Policy Directive 15 and its impact on census taking. Chapter 9 examines the proposed census design for 2000 and the current state of the controversies
surrounding the decennial. We conclude with an epilogue evaluating
the future. It is to the story of these controversies that we now turn.

Chapter 2

The History of the U.S. Census and the Undercount

In the summer of 1787, slightly more than a decade after the thirteen colonies had declared their independence from Great Britain, several dozen men met in Philadelphia to try to improve the existing American national government structure. War had ended in 1783, and the infant nation had returned to peace. Yet severe political and economic problems plagued the country. The Articles of Confederation, finally ratified in 1781 as the framework for the national government, had not been functioning well for a number of years. By the late 1780s, the states were willing to send delegates to discuss amendments. There were many different proposals about what to do, and although these men had the common experience of the Revolution to unite them, they also had sectional, political, religious, and local interests to divide them.

The men who gathered in Philadelphia thus faced a delicate and complex set of political questions. On the one hand, they had to empower a national government to deal with recurring problems arising from the unique historical development of the United States. The governments of the individual colonies had had few connections with one another prior to independence; they did not easily merge into a United States and, in fact, often looked jealously upon one another. One set of issues revolved around replacing the functions the British had served during the colonial era: national defense, diplomacy, trade policy, taxation, the opening of new land, and the creation of new colonies. On the other hand, the national government had to respect the autonomy of the individual states, recognize and mediate differences among the states and their citizens, and develop mechanisms to apportion power and tax burdens among the constituent elements of the United States. Revising the national government or devising a new one would be no easy matter. Several prior efforts had failed. Contemporaries might well have expected the men to disband with little accomplished at the end of the summer. We know now that that did not happen, that their deliberations resulted in a fundamentally new and breathtakingly radical governmental structure, which we have lived with ever since. The Constitution created three branches of government—executive, legislative, and judicial. (The Articles of Confederation had mandated a one-house congress and no executive branch.) The legislature was bicameral, with the lower house apportioned among the states according to population and elected by the people, the upper house apportioned among the states and elected by the state legislatures. The executive branch was headed by a president elected by the people through the mechanism of the electoral college. The new system increased the power of the national government considerably, yet it was also full of checks and balances to guarantee the powers of the states and citizens and to protect against the kind of tyranny the Crown had exercised.

The complex and relatively explicit structures, the detailed enumeration and delegation of powers, the checks and balances—all were mechanisms to foster both national unification ("a more perfect union") and the rights of the individual states. So also was the institution of a decennial census to measure the relative strength of the various elements of the population and hence to periodically readjust the relative power of the states and local areas in the national government. Article I, Section 2, of the Constitution created the House of Representatives and defined its membership and capacities. Paragraph 3 of Section 2 specified that the representatives and direct taxes were to be "apportioned among the several States which may be included within this Union, according to their respective numbers." This simple language provided the solution to one of the fundamental political controversies of the revolutionary era: namely, how to allocate representation fairly in legislative assemblies. Before the Revolution, the colonists had protested their lack of representation in the British Parliament. The newly united thirteen colonies had also struggled over the problem of the equitable distribution of the burdens and resources of the national government among large and small states. Critics had charged that the Articles of Confederation were an unsatisfactory grounding for a national government precisely because states had voted as units, regardless of their disparate wealth or populations. The 1787 Constitution allocated representation in the House according to population and in the Senate by state. Since direct taxes were also to be allocated according to population, the large states would gain House representation but incur a higher potential tax burden to the federal government. The strength of each state in the electoral college was to be determined by summing the state's Senate and House members. Finally, the census was to be taken every ten years, because the framers were well aware that populations—and especially the American population—grew and shifted over time.

The logic of the census system flowed from the experience and conceptions of the framers. The Founding Fathers debated other methods of allocating political power and tax responsibility during the Philadelphia convention. They discussed apportionments based on land assessments, other measures of wealth, and population. They agreed that theoretically, political power should be allocated on the basis of population and that tax responsibility should be based on wealth. Everyone agreed, however, that population was much easier to measure than wealth and that the wealth of states was highly correlated with population. Thus, population would be the apportionment measure. The new census and apportionment mechanisms of the federal Constitution were thus a crucial piece of the "Great Compromise" between the large and small states that made a national government possible. The periodic changes that had to take place to account for population growth and change were assigned to an automatic decennial routine, separated from the cycles of more frequent elections for House, Senate, and the presidency—which were also designed to shift power among the constituent elements of the population.

But there was one fly in the ointment that would come back to haunt the framers in future years and that is of particular relevance to us here. That was the question of defining exactly who was part of the "population" deserving the right to political participation in the society and owing responsibility to pay taxes to the state. The fundamental thrust of the discussion in the Constitutional Convention was to use the most expansive rule possible, including, for example, women, children, and the poor in the count, though they neither voted nor were necessarily responsible as individuals for taxes. The rub came when the framers considered how to treat slaves and Indians. Should the southern states, for example, be granted political representation for their slaves? At the time, southerners considered slaves property for purposes of tax assessments but did not count slaves when they apportioned their state legislatures. The double rule of using the same measure for representation and taxation broke down logically for slaves. Furthermore, they needed to consider whether Indians, who were generally considered outside the purview of the American polity and as members of foreign states, should be counted for representation and taxation.

The solution to these dilemmas was to hedge the universal rule of counting the population for apportionment with two provisos. The census clause in Article I, Section 2, paragraph 3, continued: the "respective Numbers [of the population] . . . shall be determined by adding to the whole Number of free Persons, including those bound to Service for a term of Years, and excluding Indians not taxed, three-fifths of all other Persons." The three-fifths compromise required the census to count slaves separately so they could be considered, for apportionment, as three-fifths of a free person. The second proviso eliminated "Indians not taxed" from the census altogether. Only people who came to be called "civilized Indians" were to be included in the decennial census count and, hence, in the apportionment totals. The important point to be made about these constitutional provisions was that they defined the population to be included or excluded, counted as whole people or as three-fifths of a person, according to the person's civil status. To avoid ambiguity, the Constitution even clarified that unfree indentured servants, that is, "those bound to Service for a term of Years," were to be included in the category "free Persons." Nowhere did the Constitution mention a racial classification, and in fact, the framers used the ambiguous "other persons" to define "slaves." But very quickly, as we shall see, in popular discourse and in the variable names listed on the census form, the racial attributes "White," "Black," "colored," and "Indian" replaced the civil statuses of free, slave, and "Indians not taxed."[1]

Demographic History

Today, representative democracy is a generally accepted principle, and nations around the world take periodic censuses. A census seems a fairly obvious tool to use to apportion political power among a set of constituencies. Yet the United States was the first nation in the world to institute a regular population count to apportion political power. The principles that political power was a function of population and that population could be measured were truly innovative in the eighteenth century and proved to be lasting only as they were implemented in the nineteenth and twentieth centuries.

Moreover, the census might well have been a rather minor constitutional innovation were it not for the extraordinary demographic character of the American population. The United States has had one of the most heterogeneous and demographically dynamic populations in the history of the world. In the past three centuries, the land that became the United States has seen rapid population growth, major migrations, and sharp demographic transitions—all in the context of a racially and ethnically heterogeneous population. In 1700, about 250,000 people lived in the colonies; by the time of the Revolution the population exceeded 2 million. The first census counted 3.9 million people, and the current population is more than a quarter billion (see table 2.1). The current land area of the country is four times the size of the nation in 1790; the population is almost sixty times larger. In 1850, the country was 85 percent rural; now it is 74 percent urban. From 1700 until the Civil War, the American population grew at the rate of 30 to 35 percent a decade. From 1860 to 1910, it grew about 24 percent a decade; since then it has grown about 13 percent a decade. The median age of the population has increased greatly. In the early nineteenth century, it was around sixteen, reflecting the high birthrates and shorter life expectancy of the times. Now, it is around thirty-four. In the early nineteenth century, a child could expect to live to about the age of forty; now, a child will live for about seventy-five years.

The population of the United States was and remains racially and ethnically diverse. At the first census in 1790, about a fifth of the population was African or African American and primarily slaves. The larger majority was free and "White"—primarily from the British Isles. Although slavery ended during the tumultuous Civil War of the mid-nineteenth century, racial distinctions continue to be major social markers in American society. Currently, about 12 percent of the population is Black.

Between 1820 and 1980, fifty million immigrants came to the United States in search of jobs and a new life; during the years of the major European migrations of the late nineteenth and early twentieth centuries, 13 to 15 percent of the population was foreign born; currently 9.6 percent are foreign born. Approximately 1.4 percent of the current United States population is estimated to be undocumented immigrants. Today, 11 percent of the population is of Hispanic origin. This is a diverse population made up of recent immigrants and Americans of Hispanic ancestry. Finally, the American population was and is regionally heterogeneous. For example, currently 74 percent of the

Table 2.1 Resident Population of
the United States

Year	Population
1790 (Aug. 2)	3,929,214
1800 (Aug. 4)	5,308,483
1810 (Aug. 6)	7,239,881
1820 (Aug. 7)	9,638,453
1830 (June 1)	12,866,020
1840 (June 1)	17,069,453
1850 (June 1)	23,191,876
1860 (June 1)	31,443,321
1870 (June 1)[a]	39,818,449
1880 (June 1)	50,155,783
1890 (June 1)	62,947,714
1900 (June 1)	75,994,575
1910 (April 15)	91,972,266
1920 (Jan. 1)	105,710,620
1930 (April 1)	122,775,046
1940 (April 1)	131,699,275
1950 (April 1)	151,325,798
1960 (April 1)	179,323,175
1970 (April 1)	203,302,031
1980 (April 1)	226,542,199
1990 (April 1)[b]	248,709,873

Source: U.S. Bureau of the Census 1996c.

[a]Revised to include adjustments for underenumeration in southern states.
[b]Unadjusted.

population is urban. However, in thirteen states, more than 80 percent
of the population is urban; in another seven states, the population is
more than 50 percent rural. Populations in seven states (all in the
South) are more than one-fifth Black, and in twenty-three states the
Black population is less than 5 percent. Overall, 9.6 percent of the
population is foreign born; yet the populations of New York, New
Jersey, Florida, California, and Hawaii are 10 to 15 percent foreign
born. In another twenty-four states, the population is less than 3 percent foreign born.[2]

These dramatic patterns make the decennial census and its apportionments major social, political, and intellectual events. Americans

are used to substantial demographic changes each decade and look to the census for their evidence. Census-based apportionments are supposed to take some difficult questions about the distribution of political power and economic resources off the immediate legislative agenda and consign them to predetermined allocations. Yet because so much is at stake, the census also runs the risk of being politicized. The census numbers are subject to intense scrutiny and analysis as each decade Congress, state legislatures, and other governmental bodies redistribute legislative seats, tax revenue, and grants-in-aid on the basis of the population-based apportionment formulas. By definition, for every gainer in the apportionment game, there must be a loser; legislators can soften the pain for the losers by shifting relative, but not absolute, power or revenue. Nevertheless, ultimately relying on the census leads to a zero-sum reapportionment game, which, though necessary, is still politically delicate and sometimes painful. Americans have not always agreed on whether the demographic changes in the population are good or bad, implying "progress" and "manifest destiny" or "degradation" and "race suicide." Accordingly, the development of the census itself as a more elaborate and more scientific count each decade is intimately bound up with the political and social history of the nation.

The Development of a Census Instrument, from 1790 to 1840

From a late-twentieth-century perspective, we know that a host of methodological issues are involved in taking a successful census, and another host of methodological issues are involved in devising a "fair" system of apportionment. From our perspective, the history of successful census taking turns on the achievement of an accurate count, given the technical capabilities of the government at the time, and thus the willingness of Americans to see the census as a legitimate and essential part of the federal governmental machinery.

The same men who wrote the Constitution discovered as much when they found themselves as legislators and officials in the new federal government. One of their first tasks was to write a bill to take the 1790 census. James Madison proposed a rather elaborate census, which included questions classifying the population by age and sex and a census of occupations, instead of the simple count of the free and slave population required by the Constitution. Congress rejected Madison's proposal and settled on a more modest scheme. The first census law mandated the secretary of state to charge the U.S. marshals to count the population in six simple categories. For each household, the enumerator listed the name of household head; the number of free White males under sixteen; the number of free White males sixteen and over; the number of free White females; the number of free colored; and the number of slaves. Even this simple count took eighteen months to complete as the difficulties of counting the population in rural America emerged. The first census recorded 3.9 million people. President George Washington thought the count was too low; but it was credible enough to be used for apportionment, and so Congress took up the second phase of the decennial census process: reapportionment.

At this point, as Michel Balinski and H. Peyton Young (1982) have indicated, another set of issues emerged. The Constitution was silent on the method of apportionment. Soon, Treasury Secretary Alexander Hamilton and Secretary of State Thomas Jefferson, the two leaders of the emerging political factions in the new government, came to be identified with two different methods of apportionment. Both methods were mathematically valid, but they had different effects on the distribution of seats in the House. A long debate ensued before Congress passed Hamilton's bill. George Washington sought advice from both men and vetoed the bill (using the presidential veto for the first time). At this point, everyone recognized that a constitutional crisis lurked behind the arcane issues of the census. If the legislators were not able to "constitute" Congress, there would be no government. Some weeks later, Congress passed a second bill, one that favored Jefferson's method. George Washington signed it, and all parties put the issue behind them for the decade.

The lessons the framers took from their initial experience with the census and apportionment were several. First, the census, and hence the new constitutional process, "worked." Furthermore, the framers recognized, there were questions of fairness inherent in the census and apportionment mechanisms, which the Constitution did not address. Third, it was perhaps best not to tinker with the process. The methods of the 1790s were thus used for the next fifty years, with minor modifications. Neither Congress nor the president saw the need to do much to improve the process. Contracts for the few clerical jobs involved in overseeing the census in Washington were given to political supporters of the administration; in a period of increasingly partisan politics, the most exciting facet of the census process was the congressional debate over the printing contract award. Over time, though, both the possibilities and the problems with the census began to capture the attention of politicians and the mathematical tinkerers of the early republic. After a few decades, one could calculate growth rates for the nation, the states, and local areas. Almanacs reprinted the latest figures. Congress could ponder the changing structure of the various states and factions in Congress. The data seeped into the political discourse of the nation. Their use, in turn, led to further curiosity about the character of the population. Each decade, Congress refined the age and sex breakdowns in the census and added a few new questions. By 1840, the six simple questions of 1790 had expanded to seventy or more. And, more ominously, the growing sectional split between North and South echoed through the decennial census and apportionment process. The free states grew faster than the slave states, and hence free-state representatives increasingly dominated the House. Votes in the electoral college similarly tilted toward the North. Southerners watched these trends with great fear and began to articulate positions that would allow them to opt out of a government dominated by hostile northerners or to devise mechanisms—such as the creation of new slave states—to restore their strength in the House and electoral college.

Census Accuracy: Sectionalism and the 1840 Census

At the time of the 1840 census, these trends were juxtaposed as the first major controversy over census accuracy erupted around the reported differential rates of insanity for free Blacks and slaves. The 1840 census included questions asking how many members of the household were "insane and idiotic." "White" and "colored" insane and idiotic were to be separated. The numbers were duly summed in the published census results and reported by states. Southern papers reported the data and noted that the rates of insanity for Blacks were much higher in the North than in the South. They concluded that freedom drove Blacks insane and argued that slavery was therefore the appropriate civil status for the Black population. Needless to say, antislavery leaders in the North objected strenuously and began to look at the data on which these assertions were based to find mistakes. Northerners initially accused Secretary of State John C. Calhoun of fabricating the data. Calhoun denied this but refused to authorize an independent inquiry into the issue. Edward Jarvis, a young Boston physician, pointed out that the data had to be in error, because the census reported insane free blacks in some Massachusetts towns that had no Black population (Cohen 1982).

The controversy raged for several years. John Quincy Adams pressed for a congressional investigation. The data were never changed, but the debate had several effects on the future of statistics and the census. First, Congress recognized that the accuracy of the census could be challenged. Second, Congress recognized that the challenge could be congruent with other political controversies—in this case, the debate about the future of slavery. Thus, the very system designed to depoliticize the apportionment of power in the United States could itself become part of the controversy. Third, Congress decided that the solution to these problems was to reform the census—that is, to take a better census in order to avoid errors in the data. To take a better census, Congress had to turn to experts who could suggest improvements. The 1850 census would be a much more ambitious undertaking, guided by the advice of statisticians who could guarantee that the 1840 problems would not recur.

Reforming the Census: From 1850 to 1890

In 1850, in the midst of the contentious debates about the future of slavery in the territories, Congress undertook a major overhaul of the census law and, in so doing, restored confidence in the census process. Before 1850, the census used the family as the unit of interest and reported few data on persons. The change to a focus on individuals in census taking was strongly influenced by the work Lemuel Shattuck— one of the American Statistical Association's founders, who had earlier conducted the Boston census of 1845—as well as that of Adolphe Quetelet, who helped to organize the 1846 Belgian census.

The United States instituted an individual-level census; created a large, but temporary, census office to tabulate the data; and embarked on a marked expansion of the publications from the census. The office, housed in the new Department of Interior, grew rapidly. In the mid-nineteenth century, the Census Office employed about 10 percent of the federal employees in Washington when the census processing was in full force—testimony to both the elaborate scale of the census and the relative lack of other federal government activity at the time. There was a good deal of grumbling in the press and in Congress about this rapid expansion, but because the patronage jobs the office dispensed proved to be advantageous to politicians, they were not anxious to curtail appointments. In the years that followed, patronage continued to be a central feature of census taking, but the size of the census staff never returned to the pre-1850 scale.

The American population rose from twenty-three million in 1850 to fifty million in 1880. Congress called upon the Census Office to collect and publish more data on the demographic, social, and economic character of the population. The 1850 census-reform law had created six schedules for the statistics of population, mortality, agriculture, manufacturing, and social statistics. The data derived from these schedules were tabulated and published as separate census volumes and summarized in a shorter abstract or a compendium. Surprisingly, perhaps, the Civil War itself did not disrupt either the 1860 or the 1870 censuses. The counts were taken, tabulated, and published during the war and Reconstruction, though we know now that the 1870 field enumeration in the South was poor. Nevertheless, at the time, the census again seemed to be the instrument that documented national growth and development, not sectionalism and fragmentation. The former Civil War general and Mugwump Republican Francis Amasa Walker replaced the Free Soil Whig Joseph C. G. Kennedy as census superintendent in 1870, and Walker became the key census innovator of the post–Civil War era.

Once the Washington Census Office existed, Congress, interested public officials, and the clerks responsible for the census recognized the weaknesses of the U.S. marshals and their assistants as the field staff for taking the census. Up to this point in time, the marshals had been in charge of all field operations, including mapping their districts and appointing sufficient assistants to actually do the canvass. Needless to say, the accuracy of the enumeration relied heavily on the abilities of the marshals—who otherwise worked for the attorney general's office, not the Interior Department, which oversaw the census. The census superintendent had no real bureaucratic control over the marshals. Sloppy work, late work, or incomplete work was hard to correct. There was no training, no means for teaching someone how to take the census except by the detailed instructions issued from Washington. One wonders how frequently the fine print was read. Furthermore, marshals were assigned according to the needs of the attorney general, not the needs of the census, and the marshals and everyone else complained of uneven work loads. In 1870, a marshal in New York supervised assistants who counted more than two million people. Another in South Florida supervised assistants who canvased an underpopulated frontier area with only sixty-five hundred people but with many smugglers.

The first efforts at changing the census field staff occurred during Reconstruction. They were initially a side effect of a congressional debate about the impact of the abolition of slavery on the census and apportionment. The Republican congressman James Garfield, of Ohio, began an investigation of census legislation to see what other changes in census law might be necessary. His committee worked in the summer of 1869 and eventually proposed a wide-ranging reform of the census machinery, including the creation of a field staff—supervisors and enumerators—appointed by and responsible to the census superintendent. Garfield's bill passed the House but failed in the Senate in early 1870 because of the field-enumeration provisions. Marshals were appointed by senators; Garfield's supervisors would be allocated by House districts and presumably appointed by House members. In a day when patronage meant so much in Washington, the patronage shift was enough to kill the bill, and the 1870 census was taken under the old system. Francis Walker ran the 1870 census as efficiently as he could from Washington, all the time pointing out the limitations of a system that used U.S. marshals as the field staff.

Walker and Garfield also recognized that they would have to do a bit more political homework to get a bill passed for the 1880 census. Walker expanded the 1870 clerical staff considerably, but he made sure he stayed within the limits of the budget for the 1870 census; he ran the office efficiently and even disbanded it three years into the decade to avoid charges of boondoggling. Late in the 1870s, he and Garfield came back with a revised census bill. Under the new bill, field-staff supervisors and enumerators reported to the census superintendent. However, the supervisors were also appointed by the president, with the advice and consent of the Senate. In 1879, the bill passed relatively easily. Whereas the field enumeration in 1870 had been run by about 65 marshals, in 1880 there were 150 supervisors. No enumeration district was to be larger than four thousand people. The time for the enumeration was shortened from six months to two weeks in cities and one month in rural areas. Walker hired Henry Gannett, from the Geological Survey, to be census geographer. Gannett systematically mapped the country for the census, set up a Geography Division in the Census Office, and began the collection of a complete set of accurate maps of minor civil divisions around the country. This alone was a major administrative and technical innovation, since the Geological Survey was still in its infancy and many parts of the country west of the 100th meridian were not mapped at all. The superintendent was beginning to exert more precise control over the conduct of the census in the field, but these efforts still left much to be done in the future: Correspondence was still by and large written in longhand, with letterpress copies for office records. The Geography Division and what we would now call the Field Division (then the Division of Supervisors' Correspondence) were separate entities and remained so. As in the past, the major control the central office had over supervisors and enumerators was financial. Before enumerators could be paid, their returns had to be certified as complete and error free by the supervisor and the Washington office. Communication back to the field was still extremely slow. Only rarely did an official from Washington visit the field.

Walker was the first census superintendent to confront complaints of local officials about census undercounts. The most spectacular of the challenges involved New York and Philadelphia. In 1870, both cities demanded and got recounts; in both cases, the second count came in about 2 percent over the first. Indianapolis also complained in 1870 when the census did not show its population at fifty thousand. A second count was done there, too—but the city boundaries were expanded considerably to increase the population by 19 percent. The complaints continued in later years: in 1890, New York City (a Democratic city) again complained that its population had been undercounted and blamed the Republican administration in Washington and the local supervisor; 2 percent of the enumerators were assigned to reenumerate districts "where the original work had been improperly done" (Holt 1929, 29). These partisan challenges to census accuracy led to much political verbiage but did not affect the process of census taking or fundamentally undermine the instrument itself.

The Census at the Turn of the Twentieth Century

The process of growth that had begun in 1870 led to a radically different census by 1900. At the same time, reapportionment, which had dominated public attention toward the census through much of the nineteenth century, receded as a controversial public issue. Before the Civil War, easterners had conceded the shift in political power to the growing areas of the West. After the Civil War, southerners conceded that their demographic decline would lead to a smaller role in Congress. Ironically, this decline was eased somewhat by the elimination of the three-fifths rule. Southern states received a boon of additional representation when the four million slaves were freed. In the postbellum era, Congress "solved" the problem of differential population growth by increasing the size of the House at each census. In the 1860s, Congress had 243 members; by 1910, there were 435. During that period, no state lost a seat through reapportionment. As the science of statistical data collection grew, census officials concentrated on improving their capacity to collect, process (classify and tabulate), and publish data.

The 1900 census was something of a high point for the expanding census. Congress, about to make the agency permanent, was willing to recognize that taking the census required special expertise. The 1900 census law authorized the appointment of an assistant director, "who shall be an experienced practical statistician," and five chief statisticians, "who shall be persons of known and tried experience in statistical work." William Merriam, the 1900 census director, was a Republican political appointee in the older tradition, but the list of statisticians, including Walter Willcox, S. N. D. North, Joseph Hill, Wesley Mitchell, and Allyn Young, read like a Who's Who of early-twentieth-century statistics and social science. They, among other 1900 census officials, all served as president of the American Statistical Association in later years. Many commentators at the time—surveying the growth of statistical activity throughout the federal government— even saw the Census Office on its way to becoming a true central statistical bureau, on the European model.

The Census Bureau became a permanent federal agency in 1902, located in the new Department of Commerce and Labor, but Congress did not see fit to centralize the federal statistical system. The new permanent Census Bureau, though now charged with collecting data on a wide variety of topics throughout the decade, fell upon difficult political times by 1910. Bureau leaders continued to press for centralization of federal statistical activities under the banner of an expanded Census Bureau. But statisticians in other federal agencies resisted the bureau's goals of consolidating all federal statistical programs in one agency. Between 1900 and 1910, it became clear that officials of the Bureau of Labor Statistics, and statisticians in other cabinet offices, such as the Departments of Agriculture and Treasury, saw things differently. Their statistical programs had also grown in the last thirty years of the nineteenth century, and they were integrated into the larger administrative functions of their agencies. These officials saw no reason to transfer their data collection and publishing activities to an agency in another cabinet department.[3]

When younger statisticians recognized that the Census Bureau was not going to become a true central statistical bureau, they saw it as a less attractive place to look for a career. Furthermore, the bureau did not continue to develop a job hierarchy. There were few mid-level jobs and fewer long-term possibilities for promotion. The overwhelming number of positions were clerical; positions contracted rapidly after the decennial census buildup. Innovation in statistics in this period generally began to shift from government agencies to the new research universities, with their laboratories and consistent research agendas. Finally, the arrival of the Wilsonian Democrats in 1913 prompted even more staff turnover in this traditionally Republican agency. Thus, the Census Bureau settled into a permanent routine existence as one of many bureaus within the Department of Commerce. (The Labor Department got separate cabinet status in 1912.) The decennial census, though still the major activity of the agency, competed with new statistical initiatives in other areas: manufacturing statistics, cotton statistics, vital statistics, special analytic studies, and contract work for congressional interests such as the Immigration Commission.

World War I created new data needs that reinforced these administrative trends. American entry into the world war severely challenged the federal government's ability to produce information for the war effort. The limitations of the uncoordinated prewar statistical system were quickly obvious to Congress and the administration. The nation needed accurate estimates of manpower, manufacturing capacity, agricultural strength, and naval and shipping capacity. Different agencies produced different numbers; eventually, President Woodrow Wilson consolidated the nation's efforts under Edwin Gay's Central Bureau of Planning and Statistics. Many former census officials, including a number of the chief statisticians from 1900 and 1910, returned to work on the statistical war effort. By the end of World War I, these efforts led to improvement of the situation in the Census Bureau and the development of something of a formal advisory and lobbying arm among professional statisticians. Longtime census officials proposed the creation an advisory committee composed of statistical experts—three each appointed by the American Statistical Association and the American Economic Association. Often composed of former census officials or university faculty who were strong supporters of the Census Bureau, this committee began to meet in 1919 and, in various forms including separate committees, has met several times each year ever since. Advising the bureau on policy, questionnaire design, and other aspects of statistical innovation, the Advisory Committee has become a tangible institutional link between the Census Bureau and the growing professional statistical community.

These trends continued during the 1920s, as the Census Bureau became a key agency in Herbert Hoover's Commerce Department. The Advisory Committee became a kind of unpaid policy board and fit well with Hoover's theories of the way the private sector and voluntary organizations could foster the "associative state" and expand bureau programs without the heavy hand of government planning. In the 1920s, the bureau focused especially on business statistics, developing the Survey of Current Business and the Census of Distribution. There was little talk of creating a central statistical bureau. Nor did the organizational structure within the bureau change much. Census monographs were contracted out or subsidized by private organizations. Innovations in the field of statistics increasingly took place in university settings rather than within government, as had occurred in the nineteenth century.

The chief controversy surrounding the census during the 1920s concerned the failure of Congress to reapportion itself after the 1920 census. For the only time in the nation's history, Congress could not muster a majority to pass a reapportionment bill. The roots of the problem were several. First, Congress had decided in 1910 to stop the growth in the size of the House. Thus, the 1920 reapportionment would be a true zero-sum game: one state's gain would be another state's loss. Second, several mathematicians produced competing apportionment methodologies, which had the effect of producing different allocations for key states. Third, the demographic trends evident in the 1920 census results were not to the liking of the Republican majority in Congress. The census results showed major shifts in population to the cities, to the far West, and to places in the country populated by immigrants. The census, critics held, had to be wrong. Leaders proposed, and failed to pass, bill after bill until, by the late 1920s, key congressional leaders proposed an automatic mechanism to go into place after the 1930 census. This bill passed Congress with another provision, which removed the mandate—present in every apportionment bill since 1840—that required congressional districts to be compact, contiguous, and, as nearly as possible, equally sized within states. Congress, in other words, reapportioned power among the states but quietly acquiesced to rural malapportionment within states. States with growing urban populations would gain in the number of seats, but those seats would not necessarily be allocated to urban districts. It was a practice that would lead to the reapportionment revolution forty years later and have a major impact on census taking.

Revitalizing the Census: The Depression and the War Years

In the late 1920s, though, reapportionment seemed a relatively unimportant issue to most statisticians and even to many bureau officials. The advice of professional statisticians became increasingly important in the twentieth-century Census Bureau, to the point that statisticians saw themselves as a lobbying group that pressured the bureau to collect and publish this or that kind of data. Nevertheless, despite these changes, the agency and the census instrument were still political tools. Their fortunes and challenges were intimately connected to broader political and social trends in the nation. Thus, just as political historians mark the coming of the Great Depression as a major point of change in our national history, so, too, the Great Depression dramatically changed the census and the American statistical system. The 1930 census was taken less than six months after the crash of the stock market. As the depression tightened its grip on the nation, the Census Bureau found itself drawn into a contentious debate about the scope and character of unemployment and thus the causes of the economy's slide. The bureau leadership was sympathetic with President Herbert Hoover's stance toward unemployment, and thus the bureau figures from the 1930 census and a special 1931 census of unemployment put the best face on what clearly was a dramatic rise in unemployment nationally. Democratic claims that the depression was deepening were overstated, census officials claimed. Unemployment always existed—especially during the winter and early spring months when the census was taken.

As it turned out, Hoover's evaluation of the depth of the depression and the appropriate way to cope with it was soundly rejected by the voters in 1932. In the spring of 1933, Franklin Roosevelt's New Dealers came to town intent on remaking American government and society and ending the depression. The Census Bureau came in for particular scrutiny as one of Hoover's favorite agencies, and—with the exception of the Wilson years—as a longtime Republican stronghold. Director William Mott Steuart resigned and was replaced by William Lane Austin. Assistant Director Joseph Hill, who was in his seventies and had first worked on the census in 1900, was transferred to a newly created "research" position. American Statistical Association president Stuart A. Rice replaced Hill as assistant director. Rice, a sociology professor at the University of Pennsylvania at the time, intended to stay in government for a year or so. He ultimately remained as a major figure in the federal statistical system until 1954—at the Census Bureau, then on the Central Statistical Board, and finally in the Division of Statistical Standards in the Bureau of the Budget (now the Office of Management and Budget).

Revitalizing the Census Bureau in the mid-1930s was no easy task. Throughout the 1930s, committees of statisticians, economists, and other academics—most notably the Committee on Government Statistics and Information Services—investigated bureau practices and found them wanting. Officials from Roosevelt's alphabet agencies called upon the bureau to provide data on the socioeconomic situation of the population. Congress built the grant-in-aid system to allocate tax money from the federal to state and local governments, and they sought population data on poverty, income distribution, and migration. Yet the Census Bureau of the early 1930s had yet to devise a credible measure of unemployment, had no data on income, and did not measure poverty. The New Dealers persevered and, by the end of the decade, Congress had proposed the introduction of sample surveys to measure unemployment, reorganized the agency's bureaucratic structure, increased the statistical training of employees, built a research unit, and analyzed and revamped classification systems. Many of these innovations became part of the 1940 census. The sixteenth census, in 1940, included the use of a sample long form for the first time, a housing census, and evaluation studies to systematically measure the level of accuracy of the enumeration, tabulation and coding procedures, coding bias, and sampling error.

Among those who worked on the probability sampling-based trial Census of Unemployment at the Census Bureau were Calvert Dedrick, Morris Hansen, Samuel Stouffer, and Frederick Stephan (Anderson 1988; Duncan and Shelton 1978). Hansen was then assigned, with a few others, to explore the field of sampling for other possible uses at the bureau and went on to work on the 1937 sample Census of Unemployment. After working on the sample component of the 1940 decennial census (under the direction of W. Edwards Deming), Hansen worked with others (for example, Jerome Cornfield, Lester Frankel, William Hurwitz, and J. Steven Stock) to redesign the unemployment survey based on new ideas on multistage probability samples and cluster sampling (Hansen and Hurwitz 1942a and 1942b).

The Discovery of the Undercount

It was as part of the general trend in statistical innovation at the Census Bureau that statisticians began their first systematic estimates of census undercount. Ever since George Washington had complained in the 1790s, officials had been concerned about undercounting the population. And ever since local officials had objected to their census counts in the 1870s, census officials had tried to improve the count to minimize errors. Much administrative reform of census procedures had been aimed at minimizing undercounts, overcounts, miscounts, padding, or curbstoning. But the growth of other large-scale administrative data systems—vital records and public health data, in particular—and the development of the disciplines of demography and statistics prompted a new set of questions. On the one hand, these other data systems sometimes generated alternative estimates of the population or segments of it. On the other, demographers and statisticians needed census counts for the denominators for their rate calculations or as sampling frames for other studies. Accordingly, both the professional community of statisticians and demographers and census officials began to conceive of precisely measuring the undercount for particular segments of the population.

The issue began to be framed after a somewhat serendipitous natural experiment in 1940. The selective-service registration of October 1940 allowed demographers to compare the April 1940 census counts of men of draft age (twenty-one to thirty-five) with the counts of men who registered for the draft. Daniel O. Price (1947) reported that nationally the 1940 census had underreported about 2.81 percent of the men in the age cohort (the draft registration recorded some 453,000 more men than did the census). More significant, though, was the finding that the level of the undercount varied by region and race. Some 13 percent of the Black men of draft age were missed in the census. Nationally, 229,000 more Black men registered for the draft than would have been expected from the census estimate. Price also demonstrated that the Black men registered for the draft in dramatically higher numbers in urban states than would have been expected from the April census counts. He could not, however, determine whether such men had migrated to an urban area between the time of the census and the registration date or, rather, the census had done a poorer job of counting urban residents. Price concluded his article by discussing some of the implications of his findings, particularly that the standard indicators of vital rates, such as death rates, would have to be recalculated in light of these data.

Additional studies followed in later years. In 1955, as part of the general project to develop a definitive demographic analysis of the American population, Ansley Coale (1955), published a revision of census figures by age, sex, and color for 1950. Coale's elaborate iterative technique used age-cohort data by race and sex from the 1930, 1940, and 1950 censuses to estimate the size of each cohort for each year, adjusted by aging the population forward each decade and correcting for deaths and immigration. Coale estimated a net census undercount of about 3.6 percent. He also concluded that the census undercounted "nonwhites" dramatically—by 12 to 13 percent in 1950. Again, because his "revisions" were in service of his larger demographic project, he ended his analysis by producing revised data by race, sex, and age for use by demographers. In the 1950s, the Census Bureau also began evaluation studies of undercounts as part of its larger evaluation program. One research thrust employed the "demographic analysis" methods, as the techniques used by Coale and Price came to be called: Information from earlier censuses and other population data sources were compared with the aggregate population counts for particular cohorts of the population. A researcher might compare the data from cohorts organized by age, race, sex, and region in two sources and calculate estimates of the differences for each cohort. The corrected cohorts were then reaggregated to generate an overall estimate of the accuracy of the count.

Demographic analysis as a technique has the advantage of being relatively easy to undertake. The researcher may have to make a very large number of individual cohort analyses. A matrix based upon, for example, two sex categories, fifteen five-year age cohorts, and two racial groups (White and non-White) in two data systems generates 120 individual cohort estimates. Price's selective service/1940 census comparison generated 98 cohort estimates of undercount—that is, for the two race categories in the forty-eight states plus the District of Columbia. Nevertheless, once the appropriate data are available, the analysis is relatively straightforward. The disadvantage of demographic analysis is its inability to pinpoint exactly why the undercount (or overcount) exists. As an aggregate methodology, it cannot identify which particular individuals were missed, nor can it provide more specific information on the sources of undercount beyond the information available from the original cohort variables.

To overcome these disadvantages, the Census Bureau developed new techniques, particularly the postenumeration survey (PES). After the 1950 census, the bureau undertook a sample reenumeration of the country to try to identify households missed by the enumerators, household members who were not reported within households, and other classification and categorization errors in the original enumeration. The survey used trained interviewers to improve the quality of the information reported. The bureau then matched the information from the sample survey to the original census forms and developed estimates of the quality of the original count. Analysis of the results again indicated an undercount and poorer coverage of the nonwhite population (see table 4.1). The PES results also showed an interesting pattern: the PES uncovered only 40 percent of the "net underenumeration" expected from demographic analysis. As bureau officials later explained, the PES "was very successful in finding space that the original census enumerator had missed but was much less effective in uncovering missed persons—those residing in previously enumerated space who were unreported and those without any recognizable place of residence" (Pritzker and Rothwell 1968, 61, 63).

By the time of the 1960 census, census officials and the community of professional demographers were well on their way to understanding census undercounts. They built evaluations procedures in the form of a postenumeration survey and demographic analysis into the 1960 census design. Professional discussions continued quietly on the best means to estimate undercounts for particular groups in the population, as well as to develop new census methodologies to count more accurately in the first place. These methodological discussions are evident in the Census Bureau technical reports and in the general social science literature of the late 1950s and early 1960s.

What was still missing from the undercount discussion was any sense that there were any larger political or social implications of the discovery of the undercount. From the 1940s through the mid-1960s, the literature was totally "methodological"—of interest to demographers, statisticians, and survey researchers but not to members of Congress, policy makers, or the undercounted communities. This situation was to change dramatically in the mid-1960s.

The Politicization of the Undercount

Three separate trends merged to propel the census undercount onto the political stage in the mid-1960s. First, since the turn of the century, Congress had built the grant-in-aid system as a mechanism for allocating revenue to state and local governments. By the 1960s, Congress had used the grant-in-aid system to allocate federal funds for initiatives in vocational education, highway construction, agricultural extension, and public health programs. The extensive programs of the postwar era, for example, urban renewal, the interstate highway system, and hospital construction subsidies had used the grant-in-aid system. In 1960, 15 percent of state and local funding came from federal aid. Census data underpinned many of the formulas Congress used to allocate the funds to particular jurisdictions.

Second, in 1962, the Supreme Court ruled that malapportioned state legislatures were unconstitutional and opened the way for the decade of lawsuits that led to the "reapportionment revolution" of the 1960s. For forty years the federal courts, and particularly the Supreme Court, had refused to rule on apportionment cases. The courts had argued that legislative apportionment was strictly a legislative matter. In 1962, the Supreme Court reversed itself and ruled in *Baker v. Carr* (1962) that the Tennessee legislature had to be reapportioned. A series of cases that followed overthrew apportionments in other legislatures and in Congress. By 1964, the phrase "one man, one vote" had entered the nation's political vocabulary to define the new principle of legislative apportionment. Suddenly, accurate census data for small geographic areas came to be of added importance. Not only were the grants-in-aid of the Great Society programs of the mid-1960s prompting increased use of census data. The apportionment cases also suggested that the Census Bureau had a strict constitutional duty, under the equal protection clause of the Fourteenth Amendment, to count everyone.

Third, the civil rights movement of the 1950s and 1960s framed many of its arguments about discrimination in the labor force, in public participation in the community, and in access to housing in terms of underrepresentation of minorities in these areas of American life. Attorneys and activists used census data to make the case. If, for example, 30 percent of a local labor market was Black, then, activists argued, true nondiscrimination would require that Blacks hold roughly 30 percent of the jobs up and down the occupational scale. After a decade of lobbying and political action, Congress responded and passed several major pieces of civil rights legislation in the late 1950s and early 1960s, which also relied on high-quality census data for administration and implementation. For example, the Voting Rights Act of 1965 enforced the Fifteenth Amendment to the Constitution, which stated that the "right . . . to vote shall not be denied or abridged by the United States or by any State on account of race, color, or previous condition of servitude." Congress created clear numerical tests of compliance with the constitutional goals of voting rights. As written in the original 1965 provision, if a state used a literacy test for voter registration, and if voter registration or turnout was less than 50 percent of the voting-age population of a jurisdiction, then the law presumed a violation of the Fifteenth Amendment. In such a case, the literacy tests were suspended, and the Justice Department could send federal registrars and election observers to monitor elections. Such jurisdictions also had to "preclear" any new voting qualifications with the attorney general of the United States. Six southern states came under these rules; counties in several other states were also affected. Again, census data would have a direct impact on a highly charged political issue.

During the planning phase for the 1970 census, all of these issues came into sharp focus. The differential census undercount of hard-to-count populations, especially minorities and the urban poor, took on new meaning. Once the Supreme Court had invalidated the massive legislative malapportionments of the past, the statisticians and politicians realized that the census undercount also could have the effect of denying representation to the uncounted. The undercount ceased to be a technical problem of census field procedures; it became an explosive political issue. A 1967 conference on social statistics and the city marked the change (Heer 1967). At that conference, census officials and prominent social scientists met in Washington to discuss the extent and cause of the undercounts. They articulated the constitutional principle that made elimination of the differential undercount imperative. "Where a group defined by racial or ethnic terms, and concentrated in special political jurisdictions," wrote David Heer, in the conference report, "is significantly undercounted in relation to other groups, then individual members of that group are thereby deprived of the constitutional right to equal representation in the House of Representatives and, by inference, in other legislative bodies." They are also "deprived of their entitlement to partake in federal and other programs designed for areas and populations with their characteristics" (Heer 1967, 11). In other words, miscounting the population could unconstitutionally deny minorities the political representation or protection guaranteed by the Voting Rights Act. It could also deny local jurisdictions grant funds from federal programs. Suddenly, Congress, demographers and statisticians, the Census Bureau, and state and local government officials recognized that they not only had to estimate the differential undercount, but they would also have to correct for it. Only slowly, however, did they realize just how hard it would be to develop the administrative and statistical innovations necessary to do so.

Chapter 3

The Undercount and the 1970 and 1980 Censuses

B y the time census officials, policy makers, and Congress began to understand the political implications of the census undercount, planning for the 1970 census was well under way. These plans included ambitious technical improvements in the 1970 count that would allow the bureau to provide more data more quickly and at the same or lesser cost than in previous censuses. Officials could envision such an agenda because they could point to an impressive list of technical improvements in census taking over the previous generation. They had extended the sampling innovations begun in 1940 in the 1950 and 1960 counts. They had raised the professional standards of the agency by hiring and developing the talents of a whole new generation of sampling statisticians, survey researchers, and technicians. They had conceived and contracted for the first nondefense electronic computer, UNIVAC, to process the 1950 census. In 1960, the bureau instituted FOSDIC, the Film Optical Sensing Device for Input to Computers, to read electronically the respondents' answers on the census schedule. This device eliminated the phase of census processing that required the transfer and keypunching of all the pen-and-pencil answers on the census form to punch cards for tabulation.

The chief innovation the bureau planned for 1970 was the mail census. It would involve a major new departure in procedures. Heartened by tests done in 1960, officials planned to count the majority of the population with a mail census. Since most Americans lived in metropolitan areas with standard postal addresses, the bureau hoped to use commercial mailing lists to reach these households. This innovation would eliminate the expensive and logistically complex process of hiring, training, and dispatching local enumerators to count the approximately 60 percent of the population that resided in metropolitan areas. For the previous thirty years, all these innovations had produced dramatic cost savings without a loss in quality. These savings, in turn, fueled a much more elaborate tabulation and publication program of census results, research and evaluation studies on census methods, and seed money for new innovations. Thus, from the bureau perspective, remedying the undercount was an emerging research-and-development problem to be attacked systematically and solved just as the bureau had attacked the other extraordinarily complex statistical, logistical, and operational tasks involved in taking a high-quality census of a country of 200 million people.

Planning and Administering the 1970 Census

By the 1960s, decennial census planning was carried on throughout the decade. As early as 1961 and 1962, when the Census Bureau's main tasks were still confined to processing and publishing the results of the most recent count, officials began a series of small field tests of address registers and other mail census instruments in hopes of perfecting procedures for the 1970 census. In 1963, the Census Bureau created the 1970 Census Planning Committee, made up of division chiefs within the agency. In 1965, on the basis of the experiments conducted to that point, the bureau determined to develop the mail census for 1970. As the bureau completed the evaluations of the 1960 census in the mid-1960s, the basic outline of methods for the 1970 count had already begun to emerge. By 1967, the pace of planning had picked up. The bureau decided on the final content of the questionnaire, determined the mix of enumeration strategies (mail, personal, or phone) for 1970, and planned the spring 1968 "dress rehearsals" (U.S. Bureau of the Census 1976, 1–2).

In the context of this ongoing work flow for 1970, census officials developed procedures for dealing with the undercount. In 1966, the bureau established a "Committee on Difficult-to-Enumerate Groups . . . with two task forces, one on methods and the other on evaluation" (ibid.). At the 1967 Social Statistics and the City conference, Assistant Director Conrad Taeuber reported that the Census Bureau intended to give "special attention to the groups that may not be reached through the regular efforts" (Heer 1967, 80). Two types of difficult-to-enumerate areas required different enumeration strategies: For the "congested areas of our large cities," which were part of the 60 percent of the country to be covered by the mail census, Taeuber emphasized that the preparation and checking of the address list required for the mail census would itself insure that all housing units were identified. But good lists were not sufficient. The bureau already knew that response rates to a mail census were some 20 percent lower in urban "poverty areas." To deal with the problem of nonresponse, Taeuber noted, the bureau intended to use "general publicity" of the census to enlist "the help of community leaders" in its promotion and "intensive" efforts at completing the count in "congested areas." The other difficult-to-enumerate areas were "rural poverty areas," which were to be covered by traditional enumeration methods. For these areas, enumerators would have to make intense efforts to identify and count people. Taeuber made it clear that these intensive enumeration efforts would require additional funding. The "tentative price tag" was between $10 million and $12 million (ibid., 81, 85, 87).

In 1968 and 1969, as the actual census day drew closer, scholars, political leaders, and the general public began to take a keener interest in the 1970 count. As in the past, bureau officials explained their plans for the 1970 count, testified before Congress, and pressed for the funds they needed to fulfill their plans. Questions about the undercount came to be fairly routine as public discussions developed. But the undercount was not the only challenge raised. Between 1967 and the late fall of 1969, conservative representative Jackson Betts (Rep.-Ohio) conducted a campaign challenging the census as an invasion of privacy. Betts introduced legislation making the responses to all questions, beyond a basic seven, voluntary. Through 1968 and 1969, high-level bureau officials spent a good deal of time and energy defending the integrity of the census and developing arguments opposing a "voluntary" census. A broad coalition of data users, officials from other federal agencies, and key members of Congress raised enough objections to the bill that it was amended before House passage. It died without Senate action when Congress adjourned in the late fall of 1969 (Eckler 1972).

The Betts bill created uncertainty at a crucial stage in the planning of the 1970 count, because if passed, the legislation would probably have required a completely new schedule. The thrust of the proposed legislation—the implication that bureau officials were meddling unnecessarily in people's lives—was deeply antithetical to the professional ethos of the Census Bureau. The agency saw itself as performing a public service, quietly collecting confidential data while making summary results available for the benefit of policy makers and the general public.

In contrast, the growing public pressure to attend to the differential undercount did not initially offend the sensibilities of the bureau itself, because comments expressing concern about the undercount did not initially attack the agency for malfeasance. For example, in early 1969, the bureau reached out to the professional community "for advice on ways to improve the completeness and accuracy of information collected in the decennial censuses of population and in intercensal household surveys" (Advisory Committee 1971, v). In May 1969, the National Academy of Sciences (NAS) created the Advisory Committee on Problems of Census Enumeration to assist the bureau in reviewing the current state of knowledge on the undercount and eventually recommending methods to reduce or mitigate it. The panel became the first of a series of NAS panels to address the question of the undercount over the quarter century. It prepared an interim report in the fall of 1969 encouraging research on the expected undercount in the 1970 count. In 1971, the panel submitted a final report, which was published in 1972, in revised form, as *America's Uncounted People*.

At the same time, civil rights leaders began to notice and comment on the undercount. In January 1969, for example, *Ebony* published an editorial pressing "for an accurate Black count." *Ebony* informed its readers of the importance of census numbers to governments and private industry for political apportionment, program planning, and analysis. "And the figures they use are a lie," *Ebony* claimed, because "roughly 10 percent" of "non-Whites (primarily Blacks)" are "missed." "Why the error [exists in Black neighborhoods] is easily understood by anyone who understands the ghetto," they continued: most enumerators are Whites who "are afraid to go into dimly-lit tenements to count Black heads." Blacks living in overcrowded housing, for example, might be unwilling to give information about their situation, and some young Black men "do not want to be counted." *Ebony* was less enthusiastic than bureau officials about the possibility that the mail census might improve the count. Although it might work in "middle-class areas, it is doubtful that it will be of much use in slum ghetto areas." *Ebony* suggested that the Black community get involved in the census and that "only Black census interviewers" take the census in "ghetto areas" (Editorial 1969). That same year, the National Urban League scrutinized the 1970 census plans, met with presidential advisers Patrick Moynihan and John Ehrlichman and Census Bureau Director Dr. George Brown in the fall of 1969 to discuss its concerns about the "shortcomings" in the 1970 census plans. Meetings continued with census staff. In February 1970, the Urban League organized a Coalition for a Black Count to monitor the enumeration and encourage participation "to assure a full and accurate minority count in the 1970 census" (U.S. House 1970, 108–10). The bureau expressed guarded optimism that the new mail census, and the special efforts to count the "hard to count," would bear fruit in lowering the differential undercount in 1970. Professional statisticians and members of the NAS panel urged the bureau to go further—not only to improve the original count but also to expand their evaluation studies to determine just how good the count was.

Since the 1940s, the bureau had conducted an impressive series of evaluation studies of the decennial enumeration. They agreed to step up their coverage evaluation studies and planned an elaborate program to test the effectiveness of all their methods and to monitor their ability to improve the count. A series of coverage evaluation projects were aimed at measuring undercounts, overcounts, and erroneous enumerations. They utilized a variety of techniques. Demographic analysis, as developed since the 1940s, was the chief tool for evaluating coverage. The bureau conducted several additional coverage evaluations of portions of the population to develop estimates of coverage of particular subgroups of the population. These included a comparison between the census and the records of eight thousand Medicare recipients to evaluate coverage of people over sixty-five. Another test compared census records of children with a sample of children born from 1964 to 1968 as identified in the Current Population Survey (CPS), the Health Interview Survey, and vital records. The bureau also conducted a study matching the records in the March CPS to the census. In further projects, trained enumerators resurveyed twenty thousand addresses from the address registers in the mail census areas. They canvased eight thousand city blocks to make sure that each address was listed in the address registers. Finally, the bureau targeted a number of coverage-evaluation projects specifically for difficult-to-enumerate areas. These included checks on people who moved, efforts to evaluate the effectiveness of local community-action groups in improving the count, a postenumeration post office check (PEPOC) of addresses in sixteen southern states, and a vacancy recheck of fifteen thousand local addresses initially identified by enumerators as vacant. Armed with their new procedures and evaluation projects, the 1970 census went into the field in the spring of 1970 (U.S. Bureau of the Census 1976).

Every decennial census creates a flurry of public attention, local and national press coverage, and a barrage of cartoons, human-interest stories, and commentary by local boosters. A good deal of the publicity is generated by the Census Bureau itself, to heighten public interest in the census and encourage cooperation and a speedy field count. And since the snags encountered along the way make better press than do the more routine processes, the bureau could also expect to see all the problems it encountered held up to the bright light of public scrutiny. The scale of a modern American census is truly impressive. In 1970, as the national population topped 200 million, a field staff of 193,000, including 158,000 enumerators, in 393 temporary district offices over-saw the count. The offices opened in January and February 1970 for training and preparation. By April 1, forty-five million mail question-naires had been distributed by the postal service. Enumerators carried another quarter-million questionnaires on their house-to-house canvas in the first two weeks of April. By May, between 85 and 90 percent of the questionnaires were in. The lion's share of the district offices closed in June.

Nevertheless, there were problems. In May, in a number of large cities, district offices were still hiring enumerators to go out to ad-dresses that had not returned their questionnaires. Thirteen district offices in large cities were still open in July. Local officials around the country complained that their populations had not been counted properly. By November, the number that registered formal complaints with the bureau had reached nineteen hundred. A number of local officials and community groups sued the bureau to enjoin the census and change procedures. In September 1970, the House Subcommittee on Census and Statistics held a series of hearings on the "accuracy of 1970 enumeration and related matters" and focused the congressional spotlight on the problems of the 1970 count. Dozens of local officials, civil rights leaders, academics, and members of Congress documented problems in administering the count in their local areas. In response, Census Director George Brown explained bureau procedures and noted that the complaints were often about figures from the prelimi-nary count. He also noted that the bureau had prevailed against any challenges in court. He admitted that people were still being added to the count from the vacancy check, PEPOC, and the Were You Count-ed? programs. But, he cautioned, these additions should not be seen as evidence of a failure of bureau procedures. Rather, he emphasized, speaking in particular of the fifty-four hundred people (seven per ten thousand enumerated people) added during the Were You Counted? program in 185 local areas, "we believe most, if not all, of these missed persons would have been located in our vacancy checks, post office checks, and central office review of local work." The Subcommittee chair, Representative Charles Wilson (Dem.-Calif.), proposed draft legislation permitting recounts of local areas that expected undercounts. The legislation did not emerge from committee and effectively became moot as the Census Bureau reported the final counts for apportionment on November 30, 1970 (U.S. House 1970, 8).

By late 1970, the bureau had shifted gears to the tabulation phase of the census, and as it did so, the undercount complaints faded from public view. Nevertheless, the 1970 census left its detractors with the sense that not enough had been done to remedy the undercount. Disgruntled big-city mayors facing population declines, newly mobilized minority political leaders, and a good number of social scientists knew that the 1970 procedures had not solved the problem of the undercount. Thus, everyone awaited the publication of the evaluation reports, which would document just how well the bureau had done and where improvements for 1980 might be made.

The Evaluation of the 1970 Census and Planning for 1980

For the rest of 1970, 1971, and 1972, public attention shifted to the results of the census as the Census Bureau reported the massive volume of census figures. The total population topped 200 million, though the decennial growth rate was only 13.3 percent, the second smallest in U.S. history.[1] Eleven seats in the House of Representatives were reapportioned. California's population topped New York's, and California became the nation's most populous state. In general, the South and West gained proportionate shares of population. So did the suburbs and "coastal areas." Half of the Black population was concentrated in fifty cities, though the Black migration to the North "had tailed off sharply" (*New York Times*, Dec. 1, 1970; Mar. 4, 1971; May 19, 1971). Metropolitan areas grew faster than central cities. Older Americans were moving south, chiefly to Florida; rural areas lost population.

Along with these results were less prominent reports on the undercount. Whitney Young of the Urban League reminded the nation of the problems with the Black count as the national census results were released (*New York Times*, Dec. 1, 1970). On December 26, 1971, the *New York Times* presented data on the probable 1970 undercount.

Census Bureau Director George Brown responded that he was "confident" the 1970 census was "the most accurate ever taken." The report of the National Academy of Sciences panel, *America's Uncounted People*, summarized the state of social science knowledge on the undercount within the scholarly community in 1971, as the report was issued, and in 1972, as it was published. The report conceded there was an undercount in 1970 and laid out a research approach for understanding the undercount, but could not identify statistical, operational, or political solutions to the problem. The report was concerned about drawing attention to what the panel members called "the social psychology of anonymity." Conceptually, they pointed out, "'missing' people are not inherently missing, or invisible, or anonymous, until they are made so by a lack of fit between the assumptions and procedures that guide the counting operation that attempts to locate them and the subjective, experiential categories, or characteristic behaviors, in which they define their own life situations." "Social data," the report continued, "are not simply out there for the asking but rather are structured in terms of purposes, assumptions, instruments, and interactions among people, which to varying degrees perturb, focus, and depend on the customary ambits of everyday life."[2] Research into the undercount and how to fix it had to be designed with this conception in mind, and the report defined a host of questions to be asked about the census schedules, the enumeration process, advertising, scheduling, and so on.

Finally, in April 1973, the Census Bureau reported the results of its analysis of the undercount in 1970 (*New York Times*, Apr. 25, 1973). The census, officials conceded, had missed 5.3 million people, about 2.5 percent of the population. The undercount was smaller than it had been in 1960, but the differential between the undercounts of Whites and Blacks remained. In 1970, 1.9 percent of White Americans were missed in the census, and 7.7 percent of Blacks were missed. In July, the Urban League's research director, Robert Hill, presented a widely reported analysis of the sources of the missed people. Roughly one-half million people were missed in both California and New York. He estimated that 171,515 Blacks in California and 186,352 in New York had been missed. The cities of New York and Chicago had the largest number of Blacks missed. In 1974, further evidence on the minority undercount emerged from the U.S. Commission on Civil Rights. In a report titled *Counting the Forgotten: The 1970 Census Count of Persons of Spanish-Speaking Background in the United States*, the commission called the bureau's efforts to provide a precise and accurate count of Hispanics in 1970 "disastrous" (*New York Times*, July 24, 1973; U.S. Civil Rights Commission 1974).

By the middle of the decade, criticism of the 1970 census results had mounted sufficiently to prompt new research interest on the undercount and political efforts to defuse the growing criticism of the bureau. Critics conceded it was too late to do anything about the deficiencies of the 1970 count and turned their attention to improving the next census. They pressed the bureau to improve the census technically and to identify which political actors should make the decisions on innovations. In the process, two major themes came to characterize both the technical discussions and the political efforts to improve the census in 1980. On the one hand, bureau officials and census critics wanted the bureau to do a better job of counting the population at the April enumeration. On the other, officials and critics conceded that it was probably impossible to count everyone in a nation as diverse and mobile as the United States. This latter line of argument led to discussion of whether it was possible or prudent to "adjust" or "correct" the traditional enumeration for the known undercount for apportionment and policy purposes. For the rest of the 1970s, in a rather confused discussion, both approaches shaped the procedures for 1980. In the mid-1970s, federal officials within the bureau and other agencies began to attend to the political problems created by dissatisfied minority communities and their champions. Between 1974 and 1976, the bureau created three advisory committees on the Black, "Spanish-origin," and "Asian and Pacific American" populations. They planned to expand coverage improvement efforts over 1970; to expand the mail census in 1980 to 95 percent of the country; and to introduce a number of procedures to improve address lists before the census. The Census Bureau also planned a "local review" process in 1979, by means of which local officials could check counts of addresses before the final mailing lists for the enumeration were prepared. Congressional hearings on 1980 census plans scrutinized all these changes in detail (Panel on Decennial Census Plans 1978, 32; U.S. Bureau of the Census 1986a, ch. 1, 6; 1986b, 1986c, 1989a, 1989b).

Outside the agency, scholars also contributed to the growing understanding of the undercount and its impact. Economists began to investigate the impact of census undercoverage on revenue-sharing allocations. Demographers compared the United States census undercoverage with the experience in other nations. Congress commissioned legal analyses of the constitutional implications of census undercoverage. By the late 1970s, a growing body of information and analysis existed on the national character and implications of census undercounts (U.S. Bureau of the Census 1980, 257–92).

What did not exist was any consensus that the Census Bureau was capable of "fixing" the undercount, either through better counting procedures or methods of "correcting" the local population figures needed for policy. In fact, the more Congress, local public officials, and the scholarly community examined the issue, the more intractable it became. Bureau officials were, of course, well aware of the logistical difficulties of counting a diverse and mobile population of more than 200 million. They had, after all, pioneered in the statistical estimation of the undercount and were unwilling to admit that they could ever conduct a "perfect" count. But as they explained the logistical details of developing address registers, sampling frames, and FOSDIC or their difficulties in hiring enumerators, census critics reacted skeptically. What, after all, was so difficult about going house to house to count? Why didn't the bureau just get on with it? The very ordinariness of the census as a public process initially impeded the discussion of the technical difficulties the agency faced in the field. Bureau officials continued to talk about the need for public cooperation, and critics exhorted the agency to "reach out" to the public and count. Slowly, census officials and their critics focused on the intractable fact that it would be possible to improve the actual enumeration, but it was probably impossible to eliminate the differential undercount through traditional methods of enumeration, either by mail or by a house-to-house count. This conclusion raised the second major thrust of the discussions: whether it was possible to develop an accurate "adjustment" or "correction" of the undercount and, if it was possible, whether it would be legal, or prudent, to do so.

As the 1980 census drew closer, a series of events symbolized the shift. First, in 1977, the secretary of commerce requested that the Committee on National Statistics of the National Research Council establish a panel to perform "an independent evaluation of the technical and procedural designs for the 1980 census." The fourteen-member Panel on Decennial Census Plans, chaired by Nathan Keyfitz, was formed in December 1977; it met three times in early 1978 before publishing its report, *Counting the People in 1980: An Appraisal of Census Plans*. The panel reviewed the findings of the 1972 National Academy of Sciences panel report, *America's Uncounted People* (Advisory Committee 1971), commented broadly on the increased public pressure on the census, and evaluated the plans for 1980. It pointedly praised the Census Bureau for expanding its advisory committee networks of local officials and community groups concerned about the undercount and for moving to improve coverage in 1980. But it also criticized the bureau for instituting procedures, particularly local review, without adequate coordination with local officials. And the panel urged the bureau to move much more aggressively into the research and controversies surrounding adjustment. The panel reviewed the three major technical methods, "synthetic, demographic, and matching," that showed some promise as adjustment strategies. It detailed the advantages and problems with each and recommended that the bureau adjust the 1980 census results for allocation purposes but not for apportionments. The panel did not recommend a particular method of adjustment but rather advised that the secretary of commerce was the appropriate official to make the decision on whether to adjust and that the bureau was the appropriate location for the technical decision on the feasibility and method of adjustment (Panel on Decennial Census Plans 1978, 86–90, 96, 132–33).

The panel report increased the pressure on the Census Bureau to take the lead on adjustment methodologies and gave significant ammunition to bureau critics who charged the agency with dragging its feet on plans for a possible adjustment. In January 1979, rumors began to circulate that Manuel Plotkin, Jimmy Carter's census director, was not successfully handling the delicate process of preparing for the 1980 census and was under pressure to resign; in early February, he did so. In April 1979, the Carter administration turned to former Nixon administration census director Vincent Barabba to return to the agency and carry the bureau through the 1980 count. In late April, Barabba accepted the position.

Barabba quickly moved to restore confidence in the census and in the bureau's ability to count the population in 1980. In the summer of 1979, Barabba announced that the bureau would host a conference in February 1980 "to assess the feasibility of measuring and adjusting for census undercounts at different levels of geography and for selected characteristics, and to discuss possible techniques and approaches for both measuring and adjusting for the undercounts" (U.S. Bureau of the Census 1980, 229). The Conference on Census Undercount brought together key congressional observers of the census, such as Representative Robert Garcia (Dem.-Calif.), Senator Daniel Patrick Moynihan (Dem.-N.Y.), high-level federal officials, and leading statisticians and survey researchers. In his opening remarks to the conference, Barabba acknowledged that the political and technical landscape for the bureau had changed since 1970. The undercount had taken

center stage in bureau planning, and he would have to consider seriously adjusting the 1980 census. He expressed guarded support for
the NAS panel's position encouraging adjustment. But he and other
bureau officials also conveyed real reservations about both the technical capacity of the bureau to develop a defensible adjustment methodology and the political feasibility of doing so. To emphasize the latter
point, he proposed a hypothetical:

> A very senior congressional delegation from State A will accept with-
> out contest the apportionment of the 435th member of the House of
> Representatives to State B rather than their own State on the basis of
> fewer than 300 people. They will do so even when the final count
> for the apportionment was adjusted by the Census Bureau, using a
> projection from a revisit to a national sample of vacant dwelling units
> so that State B had 300 more people added to its "count" than did
> State A. (U.S. Bureau of the Census 1980)

Barabba opened the conference to full discussion. As the meeting
proceeded, all parties agreed that the undercount damaged the census
and impaired its use for apportionment and funding allocations. There
was little consensus, however, about the feasibility or the legitimacy
of adjusting the 1980 count.

There were serious reservations among the technical experts about
the feasibility of the extant methods for accurately estimating undercount—even at the national level. Census officials, Jacob Siegel and
Charles Jones, explained that the "present plans of the Census Bureau
rely primarily on the use of demographic analysis for deriving preferred estimates of underenumeration at the national level." But, they
warned, "great uncertainty remains about the accuracy of specific
components necessary for demographic analysis, particularly emigration and net illegal immigration." "By its very nature," they continued,
"a census undercount can be elusive to estimate exactly, but demographic analysis seems to give reasonable and reliable results." Critics
of the use of demographic analysis for measuring undercount pointed
out that the national estimates would have to be allocated to much
smaller levels of geography if they were to be used for adjustment and
that no reliable method existed to do so. Siegel and Jones agreed (ibid.,
18–19).

The bureau also reported on the second major method for measuring undercount: the postenumeration program (PEP) planned for
1980. Officials intended to match the April and August Current Population Survey (CPS) responses to the April census enumeration. They

also proposed to draw a sample of households from the April census enumeration and match the households to the April and August surveys. They would then calculate a dual-systems estimate of the total population based upon the two samples. The PEP would avoid some of the difficulties of demographic analysis because it did not require the estimation of demographic patterns (for example, of illegal immigrants) that affect demographic analysis. Nevertheless, the PEP was also not without its detractors. Siegel and Jones pointed out that undercount estimates from postenumeration surveys in earlier censuses "were seriously biased downward." The problem was caused by "correlation bias." "Persons enumerated in the census tend to be enumerated in the survey at a greater relative rate than persons missed in the census; that is, persons missed in the census tend not to be reported in the survey for the same reasons that they were missed in the census" (ibid., 19).

Other statisticians and bureau officials also raised questions about the ability of the Census Bureau to accurately match the roughly one-half million records that would be generated by the project. Were the computer algorithms good enough to match people correctly? Would the August CPS represent a sufficiently similar population, given the mobility of Americans, to actually match to April data? The bureau could give no assurances that the PEP had solved these problems. These difficult questions were compounded even further as the participants began to discuss the second question about a census adjustment: even if one could develop reliable, accurate national estimates of undercount, how did one go about adjusting the local census figures for the roughly thirty-nine thousand jurisdictions for which the bureau reported data? Again, there was disagreement over method. Eugene Ericksen, of the University of Pennsylvania, discussing the possibilities of using regression models or synthetic estimates, found advantages and disadvantages to each. Robert Fay, of the Census Bureau, added further methodological considerations by proposing what he called "empirical Bayes refinements" to a method using aspects of both regression and synthetic estimation. These ideas would ultimately find their way into formal Census Bureau procedures for undercount adjustment (ibid., 55–61, 98).

For two days the conferees debated these complex statistical issues and their impact on the actual use of census data. When conference chairman Conrad Taeuber sat down to summarize the conclusions to be drawn, he reported splits of opinion on almost all issues. The majority of the conferees supported "some form of adjustment," though "there was one strong statement arguing that no adjustment should be made." Congressman Garcia supported adjustment for all uses of census data; Senator Moynihan opposed adjustment for House apportionment. Everyone realized that the current state of statistical knowledge was inadequate to answer the questions framed at the conference and that "more and intensive research" was called for (ibid., 3, 4).

Taking the 1980 Census

Less than two months after the Conference on Census Undercount, the 1980 census went into the field. Relative to what had been done in the 1970 census, the Census Bureau substantially increased the efforts to reach hard-to-count populations (U.S. Bureau of the Census, 1976, ch.1; 1986a, ch.1; Edmonston and Schultze 1995). As in previous years, the bureau initiated a barrage of public service announcements and promotional efforts to make the public aware of the census and to encourage cooperation. And, as in previous years, the mass media covered the field enumeration phase in great detail, focusing on both the complexity and logistical issues involved in taking a census and the mistakes, confusions, and problems in the field work. The bureau made sure that their advertising described the 65,000 cardboard desks and 10,000 cardboard tables, the 52,000 folding chairs, the 4 million pencils, the 750,000 pencil sharpeners, and the 265,000 plastic portfolios required for the field staff of 460,000 in 409 temporary district offices (U.S. Bureau of the Census 1986a, ch. 1, 12; 1986b, ch. 5, 10). But the bureau also found that the press reported the fire in the Brooklyn district office, the cancellation of the first phase of the local review process, and the complaints that mail questionnaires had not been delivered. By the summer, the bureau began to face a new challenge: lawsuits. The Federation for American Immigration Reform (FAIR) had filed suit in December 1979 to force the bureau to exclude undocumented aliens from the census count. In the spring of 1980, Detroit filed suit asking the courts to mandate an adjustment of what they claimed would be the "inevitable undercount" of minorities and hence of Detroit's population (Choldin 1994, 104; Anderson 1988). These cases began to wend their way through the courts. As of the beginning of August 1980, these legal challenges, though time consuming for staff, did not seem much more troublesome than challenges of other kinds in 1970 and earlier. But as the press reports of the difficulties with the actual count emerged, a host of new lawsuits appeared, demanding adjustment of the census count on new grounds: namely, that bureau procedures themselves were partly responsible for the differential undercount. The Detroit case, *Young v. Klutznick*, went to trial in August, and prominent social scientists, including the University of Chicago sociologist and former acting director of the Census Bureau Philip Hauser, testified in favor of Detroit's position. At the same time, eight new suits were filed by states and localities, including what would become the most significant case, *Carey v. Klutznick*, later *Cuomo v. Baldrige*, filed by New York City and the State of New York.

By the fall, when preliminary counts were released to local officials for checking (the second phase of local review), suspicious local officials in areas facing population declines were armed with complaints about the conduct of the count. In August and September of 1980, the bureau faced a firestorm of bad publicity as big-city mayors complained about the preliminary numbers. In Detroit, District Court Judge Horace Gilmore ruled in favor of Detroit and ordered the bureau to adjust the population counts to correct for undercount. The bureau appealed. Eleven more suits were filed from September to November 1980, challenging bureau procedures or seeking adjustment (U.S. Bureau of the Census 1989b, ch. 10, 12–15).

In December, the bureau announced the 1980 population of 226.5 million, 4 million more than they had expected. Census Director Vincent Barabba also announced that the bureau would not adjust the April count for the known undercount. He did so for two reasons. First, he argued, the enumeration, because the bureau had exceeded its own estimates of the population, was clearly better than those of the past. Second, because the bureau could not estimate "the number and distribution of the illegal aliens in the country," officials could not make accurate national demographic estimates of undercount. Hence, there was no "statistically defensible" method of defining an undercount and then allocating it to states and other political jurisdictions (U.S. Bureau of the Census 1986a, ch. 1, 24). Barabba pledged that the bureau would continue to pursue research for such a method.

Ultimately, fifty-two lawsuits challenging the procedures used in 1980 were filed against the Census Bureau (Mitroff, Mason, and Barabba 1983). Most were filed by state and local governments challenging the bureau to correct for the known undercount of minorities and hard-to-count populations. With Barabba's announcement, local officials went back to court to enjoin the bureau from proceeding further on processing the data and to stop the announcement of the numbers for reapportionment. In New York, District Court Judge Henry Werker ruled against the bureau and ordered an adjustment. The higher federal courts were not sympathetic to such claims and decisions. The Supreme Court stayed all lower-court decisions in late December so that the bureau could release the 1980 count to the president. The two suits filed in Detroit and New York City had received more favorable treatment from district court judges and would generate further legal challenges to the bureau, but clearly the bureau had the legal upper hand at the end of 1980. The bureau could point to an improved census count and to the fact that the experts could not agree on a defensible method of estimating national undercount or a defensible method of allocating the national undercount to smaller local areas. But the bureau was also vulnerable: officials had clearly admitted that the differential undercount was a problem and one that, theoretically at least, was correctible. Local officials had also begun to charge, and to find statistical experts willing to agree, that census methods themselves led to undercounts of minority and other hard-to-count populations and that the bureau itself was preventing the development of the procedures needed to adjust. As the 1980 census reports were issued, the shape of the debates about the undercount for 1990 had already begun to appear.

Evaluating the Undercount in the 1980 Census

In 1980, a presidential election year as well as a census year, the fate of the American hostages in Iran and the fall presidential campaign between Jimmy Carter and Ronald Reagan were, for most Americans, much more newsworthy events than the arcane questions of census underenumeration. So it was only in hindsight that most census officials and other observers recognized that the election of Ronald Reagan and a Republican Senate in November 1980 would also have an impact on the publication and interpretation of the results of the 1980 census. The first indication was the normal changing of the guard of presidentially appointed officials. Director Vincent Barabba resigned in January 1981, and President Reagan nominated Bruce K. Chapman, former secretary of state of the State of Washington, to replace him. By late 1981, the budget cuts from the beginning of what would come to be called the Reagan revolution had begun to delay the publication of census results; no planning money had been appropriated for the new middecade census; and a number of senior officials had announced their retirements without any sign of their replacements (*New York Times,* July 13, 1981; Nov. 25, 1981). By 1982, Chapman was announcing layoffs, "RIFs" (reductions-in-force), and furloughs of employees because of "economy moves" and budget cuts (*New York Times,* Jan. 31, 1982). The planned publication dates for the detailed results from the 1980 count were delayed further, into 1983.

It was in this environment that the legal challenges to the 1980 count worked their way through the courts. In June 1981 and 1982, federal appeals courts and the Supreme Court ruled that the Census Bureau did not have to turn its address lists over to the court, questioned whether the plaintiffs had standing to sue in the first place, and agreed that there was no technically feasible method by which to adjust the 1980 count. By early 1982, it appeared that the bureau had prevailed decisively in the raft of suits. At the same time, detailed evaluation results from the census, from both the demographic analysis and the PEP, indicated that although the estimate of the absolute size of the undercount had declined from 2.6 percent to 1.2 percent of the population from the 1970 census to the 1980 census, the differential undercount by race had remained. The difference in net undercount between Blacks and Whites was still around 5 percent.[3] Hence, even though the courts had ruled in favor of the bureau, both urban officials and their legal advisers still thought they had grounds to pursue their claims further. As the Supreme Court denied certiorari to the New York case in the spring of 1982, attorney Robert Rifkind, whose firm, Cravath, Swain, and Moore, had been litigating the case pro bono for the city, told the *New York Times* (Mar. 9, 1982), "We think we can win notwithstanding the Supreme Court decision." New York's attorneys went back to court, claiming a need for further trial proceedings. A second district court trial in the New York challenge to the 1980 count began in January 1984 before Judge John Sprizzo.

Almost four years after the census, the terms of the arguments about adjustment had shifted somewhat. Vincent Barabba's responses to his critics in late 1980 that the census results should stand as taken rang somewhat less true than they had initially. Yes, it was true that the Census Bureau had counted about four million people more than anticipated. And yes, it was true that demographic-analysis methodologies did not permit accurate estimation of the illegal alien population and hence an accurate measure of the national undercount. But almost four years later, proponents of adjustment claimed, census officials had done serious work in estimating the size of the undocumented alien population, and moreover, the results of the PEP indicated undercount patterns similar to those evidenced in the demographic analysis; and the PEP could provide estimates of undercount at lower levels of geography and for more subgroups of the population. So perhaps the census results could be adjusted after all, even if it was too late to reapportion and redistrict Congress and other legislative districts. Moreover, statistical improvements in adjustment methodology had also proceeded apace. In particular, Eugene Ericksen, of the University of Pennsylvania, and Joseph Kadane, of Carnegie Mellon University, had analyzed the data from the 1980 PEP and claimed, using regression analysis, that it was possible to project from the sample to the rest of the population and thus to adjust local census counts for the known undercount (see, for example, Ericksen and Kadane 1985).

The Census Bureau and its lawyers, for their part, disagreed. The PEP was fraught with matching problems, testified bureau officials Barbara Bailar and Charles Cowan. Theoretically, they suggested, a dual-systems estimator of the undercount would provide a method for measuring the undercount and allocating it to local levels of geography. But in practice, the ambiguities in matching the census and the survey data made it impossible to do so. The bureau created more than a dozen different methods of estimating the undercount from the PEP, but the ambiguities in them swamped the error in the undercount estimates. The bureau solicited the testimony of a mathematical statistician, David Freedman, from the University of California, Berkeley, to buttress its claims that the assumptions underlying Ericksen and Kadane's methods were highly questionable (Freedman and Navidi 1986 provides the details of this testimony).

These arcane methodological arguments were presented to Judge Sprizzo in trial testimony, hearings, memorandums, documents, and a raft of court filings. The judge took in the testimony and materials but did not issue a timely ruling. In fact, he did not rule until late 1987, much too late to influence the publication of 1980 census results and too late, it seemed, to affect the planning for 1990 (*Cuomo v. Baldrige* 1987). He ultimately decided that the original 1980 census results should stand, because it could not be shown that the bureau's decision not to adjust was arbitrary and capricious. There was no showing of bad faith or improper procedures by the bureau. Because experts disagreed on the feasibility of adjustment, Sprizzo argued, the bureau had the authority to make the decision. In so ruling, the court subtly shifted the grounds of the argument once again. Judge Sprizzo's ruling implicitly increased the burden on the bureau to make sure its methods could not be challenged as arbitrary and capricious. Once again, the bureau faced new pressures to solve the undercount problem.

Legal Stalemate, Technical Challenge

By the mid-1980s, census officials could look back at a whirlwind of challenges to their methods since 1980. Going into the census in the beginning of 1980, they had faced disgruntled state and local officials and some scholars who wanted them to adjust for the differential undercount. Five years later, despite having prevailed in court, they faced the same disgruntled state and local officials and an increasingly expert group of survey statisticians who pressured for adjustment of the undercount. In the early 1980s, a group appointed by the American Statistical Association recommended that the Census Bureau again request expert advice on census methodology—and undercount measurement, in particular—from the National Academic of Sciences. The bureau did so. In 1983, the Committee on National Statistics of the National Research Council established the Panel on Decennial Census Methodology. The panel was to provide advice to the bureau on adjustment, sampling in the census, and the use of administrative records. At the same time, the bureau set up an Undercount Research Staff and the Undercount Steering Committee to focus efforts to improve the methodology of the postenumeration survey program. All these groups began to work on planning and tests for 1990. It would remain to be seen whether the bureau could solve the matching problems that had faced the 1980 PEP.

Chapter 4

Dual-Systems Estimation and Other Methods for Undercount Correction

Probably every human society that ever existed has had at least one methodology of counting. Counting a set of organisms, objects, people, or things is a deceptively simple project. Children learn their numbers and count their fingers and toes, arms and legs, eyes and ears, and modern societies have a penchant for counting almost everything—from votes to people to widgets. At least since the eighteenth century, Americans have been, as Pat Cline Cohen has noted, a "calculating people" (Cohen 1982). Summing, reckoning, and averaging are time-honored techniques for understanding and managing physical and social phenomena.

But when there are many units to be counted, when the definition of the unit is ambiguous, or when the phenomenon changes during the counting process, counting becomes a complex process. Children also learn the frustrations of trying to count stars in the sky, or blades of grass on the lawn, or leaves on a tree. And counting phenomena that are changing while they are being counted—for example, wildlife—invites us to throw up our hands and give up (see figure 4.1) even when well-known statistical methods exist to help do the job.

American census takers have, of course, confronted these counting problems since 1790 and have succeeded in producing a count of the population each decade despite wars, local catastrophes, shipwrecked schedules, and the confusion of respondents. Their dogged pursuit of each decennial population count is testimony to the importance of the census to American life and to the ingenuity of the officials who devel-

Figure 4.1

oped many of the modern techniques of counting. They have done so, we may suggest, by adhering to one fundamental principle: devise a procedure to find all the people in the country at their "usual place of abode" and then count them. The decennial census process produces what is commonly referred to as a complete count. And it is a process done just once each decade.

Census officials break down the process of counting into manageable portions by devising hierarchical administrative systems that run from the national census office to the individual household. In 1990, for example, the Census Bureau national office in Suitland, Maryland, created 13 regional offices and 487 district offices to collect and process the forms. The district offices were responsible for counting between 175,000 and 200,000 housing units each. For the 94.4 percent of households slated to get a form delivered either by mail or a bureau enumerator (U.S. Bureau of the Census 1995b, ch. 1, 1–7), the bureau prepared one census form for each address in the country, based on its master address file. All addresses were coded by state, county, other local geography, district office, census tract, "address register area," census block, and "walking sequence," in case a follow-up enumerator had to reach a housing unit.

The final link in this chain of counting occurs at the household. One person reports the number of people in the household on the mail census form or to the enumerator. The forms are then collected, edited, and tallied to successively higher levels of geography (Choldin 1994, 170–93). The success of the system depends upon the capacity of the procedures to deliver a census form or send an enumerator to each household and then to retrieve the information on the completed form from the household.

Needless to say, many things can go wrong, from lost forms to bad or missing addresses to confused or suspicious respondents. The Census Bureau has historically dealt with such counting problems by building many follow-up and checking procedures into the census process to catch errors and make sure that targeted households are counted. Nevertheless, the controversies surrounding the undercount have made the flaws in the counting system painfully clear and thus have led critics to propose fundamentally new ways to count, derived from different traditions of counting.

These new methods all involve, as we discussed in chapters 2 and 3, some form of systematic double-counting, not just checking to make sure that the count that one has is accurate. The most promising method also involves using sampling methods to count households. Thus, the new methods are very different from the time-honored methods of the once-a-decade population count, and they rely on different guarantees for their efficacy. The traditional methods rely for their validity on careful bureaucratic procedures, the administrative chain of command, legal sanctions for nonresponse, and public cooperation of respondents. The new methods rely on the principles of statistical theory and probability for validity.

Errors and Uncertainty

Statisticians have a specialized vocabulary, and many of the terms they use have both everyday and technical meanings. For example, the words *significant, power, random, unbiased*, and *independent*, when used in a statistical context, all have precise technical meanings that differ from the interpretations put on them in everyday conversation. The word *error* presents us with one such case. No matter how carefully any scientific investigation is carried out, no measurement process is perfect, and the statistician usually uses the term *error* to denote the difference between what we observe and what we were trying to measure. In common parlance, *error* is used to denote a mistake and to impute blame or even censure. Nothing could be further from our use of the term in the context of the work of the Census Bureau on the decennial census.

Errors in measurement contribute to the uncertainty we have about the quantities we attempt to measure. Some measurement errors that occur in the implementation of a particular stage of the census process are corrected by efforts in subsequent stages; others are carried through to the data and retained as official census records. Thus, the error that occurs when a house is left off the master list of addresses can be corrected at many subsequent stages, during which the location can be added back into the address file. On the other hand, the error of omission that results when a household respondent deliberately fails to include one of the occupants on the census form may never be detected and corrected.

When the measurement process is complex and measurements are aggregated, as they are in the decennial census, some of these recorded errors fortuitously cancel one another out; others are compounded to induce systematic differences or biases in the estimates of the quantities of ultimate interest. Thus, the Census Bureau might fail to enumerate every one of the twenty-nine occupants of an apartment building in Pittsburgh and thus distort substantially the count for the census block in which the building is situated, but that error alone will have little impact on the population totals for Pennsylvania. The omission of these twenty-nine apartment dwellers in Pittsburgh might be balanced against the inadvertent duplication of census records for twenty-nine individuals in twenty-nine different blocks in nearby Wilkinsburg, Pennsylvania, yielding a net census error of zero for the Pittsburgh metropolitan area. But even if this canceling out of omissions and duplicates happens, there is nevertheless an increase in the overall level of uncertainty about the total for the state of Pennsylvania and even about the total for the nation as a whole.

As we already noted in the opening chapters, considerable evidence, accumulated over decades, supports the existence of a systematic undercount in the decennial census, one that differentially affects different population groups. What is often overlooked in discussions of census undercount is the array of errors in the census itself and how they contribute not only to the undercount estimates but also to our uncertainty regarding the overall quality of the decennial census at disaggregated levels.

As a precursor to the discussion of methods for undercount correction, it is useful to review a few of the sources of census error and to indicate their possible implications for the accuracy of the census counts. In appendix A, we list specific examples of sources of census error and summarize the nature of the error and its possible impact on undercounts or overcounts for 1990.

The impact of each of the sources of error listed needs to be understood when one talks about assessing the accuracy of data from the census counts. The census process moves from housing-unit addresses (that is, labels for physical structures) to housing units to housing units that are enumerated, either through the mail or through some other process, to actual individuals. At each stage the cumulative impact of errors leads to units or people not counted or miscounted in terms of information recorded about that unit or individual in the census files. Errors in the classification of housing units inevitably propagate errors in enumerating housing units, and errors in enumerating housing units propagate errors in the enumeration of individuals. At some levels of aggregation, the "miscounts" do not show up as errors, for example, in determining the population total; but when we discuss who makes up the population total and where they reside at the state or local level, the miscount category may be very important.

For the 1980 census, the Census Bureau determined that there were at least 6 million erroneous enumerations in the census, of which as many as 1 million were fabrications and as many as 2.5 million were people erroneously included twice at the same location. Given the bureau's report of a net undercount of 1.4 percent, or 3.2 million people, in 1980, we have an estimate of 9.2 million omissions (people who were missed) from the 1980 census count. By adding omissions to erroneous enumerations we get a total of 15.2 million gross errors in counting individuals, which corresponds to almost 7 percent of the official 1980 census total. For 1990, the estimates of gross error ran even higher than in 1980, with a widely cited value being in excess of 8 percent.[1]

Measuring the Undercount

Two Approaches

There are basically two quantitative techniques that have been used to estimate the undercount at a national level: demographic analysis and the dual-systems, or capture-recapture, technique. Demographic analysis combines aggregate birth, death, immigration, and emigration records with other administrative records, such as enrollment in Medicare, to carry forward the population count from one census to the next, deriving an estimate of the overall population size and thus the overcount or undercount. The methodology can provide population and undercount (or overcount) figures by age, race (typically restricted to Black and non-Black, at least through 1980), and sex, but only at a national level. The approach was introduced by Ansley Coale (1955) as a check on the results of the 1950 census and then refined in successive censuses by bureau demographers.

Demographers at the Census Bureau used this methodology to calculate the numbers in table 4.1. The accuracy of the demographic analysis depends on the accuracy of the inputs. Several of the statistical inputs are incomplete. For example, all births are not registered in vital statistics sources, and emigration data are generally poor. Furthermore, the growth of illegal immigration through the 1970s and 1980s posed special problems that led demographers to develop special estimates for this component of the population:

> The exact number of undocumented immigrants in the United States is a demographic mystery that has been puzzling demographers for years. . . . When the preliminary results from demographic analysis were released in 1981 and 1982, little was known about the number who were counted in the 1980 census. These initial coverage estimates made no allowance in the demographic estimate of the resident population for undocumented immigrants in the United States. (Fay et al. 1988, 13)

The official Census Bureau report on the demographic estimates for 1980, prepared by Robert Fay, Jeffrey Passel, Gregory Robinson, and Charles Cowan, gives three million as its preferred estimate of the number of undocumented aliens, and this estimate is reflected in the figures in table 4.1. Thus, although bureau officials initially declared a

Table 4.1   Estimated Net Census Undercount from 1940 to 1980, as Measured by Demographic Analysis (Percentage)

Year	Black	Non-Black	Difference	Overall Net Undercount
1940	10.3	5.1	5.2	5.6
1950	9.6	3.8	5.8	4.4
1960	8.3	2.7	5.6	3.3
1970	8.0	2.2	5.8	2.9
1980[a]	5.9	0.7	5.2	1.4

Source: Fay et al. 1988.

[a]The figures for 1980 are based on the assumption that three million undocumented aliens were living in the United States at the time of the census.

slight overcount in 1980 based on the initial demographic analysis estimates, the bureau ultimately accepted the estimate of an overall net undercount of 1.4 percent.

The major strengths of the demographic analysis estimates are their use of largely independent data sources and their basic consistency from one census to the next. The weaknesses are that racial data are available in a reasonable form mainly for Black versus non-Black comparisons and only at the national level. Furthermore, the errors and uncertainties associated with counting undocumented immigrants and shifting racial identification combined with increasing intermarriage make the numbers increasingly problematic, except as a broad coverage-evaluation tool. This is, of course, what demographic analysis was created to be.

The second technique for estimating the net national undercount, dual-systems estimation, was the method of choice adopted by the methodologists at the Census Bureau for 1990 and was the source of the ongoing controversy about methodology for a statistical adjustment. Its defining characteristic is the use of two sources of information to arrive at a better estimate of the population than could be obtained from one source alone. The procedure is an old one, widely accepted among statisticians, and it has been used for a host of different practical population-estimation problems. It is most familiar in the context of estimating the size of wildlife populations, where it is known as the capture-recapture technique. We illustrate the technique with a hypothetical example to show how it can be applied to a counting problem associated with a question of public policy.

The Wildlife Policy Problem

The wildlife management specialists in state X propose developing a policy for stocking fish in the lakes in the state. There are only two types of fish in the state lakes, red fish and blue fish,[2] but our wildlife management specialists already know that they will need separate stocking policies for each type of fish, since the problems of breeding the fish are different.

They begin by going to one lake and determining how many fish are in it. They do this by twice attempting to catch and count each fish in the lake. In order to keep track of which fish were counted the first time, they use the simple expedient of marking each fish caught before releasing it. As the fish are caught the second time, they can then determine whether each fish was counted in the first attempt. The important feature here is that our wildlife management specialists can use information from these two counts to derive a more accurate estimate of the size of the fish population than the estimates made from either of the two counts alone. As it happens, the first count was done on a sunny day, and the fish were somewhat difficult to catch. As a result, the wildlife specialists counted only 150 fish. The day of the second count was cloudy, and the fish were easier to catch; as a result, they were able to catch 200 fish. Suppose, further, that of the 200 fish counted the second time, 125 bore marks indicating that they had been among the 150 fish counted the first time. There are thus three distinct classes of fish that have been counted: fish caught both the first time and the second time (which in this example number 125), fish caught the first time but not the second (25 in this example, or the total number of fish caught the first time minus the number of marked fish recaught the second time), and fish caught the second time but not caught the first time (75 here, equaling the total number caught the second time minus the number of marked fish caught the second time). The total number of fish in the three classes is 225. Note that all 225 have been directly observed by the wildlife management specialists and that this number exceeds the number of fish observed in either of the two counts.

We can display the data in the form of a 2×2 table with rows corresponding to presence and absence in the first attempt and columns corresponding to presence and absence in the second attempt (table 4.2).

The task at hand is to proceed from this information to an estimate

Table 4.2

		Day 2: Cloudy		
		In	Out	Total
Day 1:	In	125	25	150
Sunny	Out	75	?	?
	Total	200	?	??

of the total number of fish in the population, including an estimate of a fourth class of fish, those that were not caught either time. This can be done as long as the two counts are independent random samples. A random sample by its nature permits us to estimate the incidence of any observable characteristic in the larger population from which the sample is drawn. In this case, the characteristic we are interested in is that of having been captured in the first count. The examination of our random sample—the second count—shows that 125 out of 200 fish, or five-eighths of the sample, were captured in the first count. Generalizing from the sample, we can conclude that five-eighths of the total fish population in the lake was captured in the first count.

Having learned that five-eighths of the total population was captured by the first count, we are in a position to estimate the true fish population on the basis of the available information. The total number of fish counted the first time, 150, is five-eighths of the total population, that is,

$$150 = \frac{5}{8}\hat{N},$$

where $\hat{N}$ is the estimate of true population size, N. To arrive at our estimate, a little high school algebra suffices:

$$\hat{N} = \frac{8}{5} \times 150 = 240.$$

Of this estimated 240 total population, 225 have been observed in one or the other or both of the two counts. Thus, we infer that there are 15 fish in the population that were not counted either time.

We present our test results from our one lake to the wildlife management specialists, who in turn ask what the proportions of red fish and blue fish are in the lake. We report that 30 red fish were counted the first day, and 40 the second day; conversely 120 blue fish were counted the first day and 160 counted the second day. As we return to our original data, we notice not only that are there fewer red fish than blue fish, but also that the rates of "catchability" for the two kinds of fish differ. That is, the two types of fish do not quite show up proportionately in the lake in the two attempts to catch all of the fish. We realize that we have to recalculate our estimates of the fish in the lake by making separate calculations for red fish and blue fish. We discover that 20 red fish were caught on both the first and second days, which means that 105 blue fish were caught on both days.

As we reexamine the data, we now have two tables, one for red fish and one for blue fish (table 4.3). By looking at the two tables we see that

- red fish appear to be less numerous than blue fish (there are only 50 red fish but there are 175 blue fish observed).
- more fish, both red and blue, are caught on the cloudy second day than on the sunny first day (40 red fish on day two versus 30 on day one; 160 blue fish on day two versus 120 on day one).
- on the sunny first day, the catchability rate for the red fish is less than that for the blue fish ($20/40 = 50$ percent for red versus $105/160 = 65.6$ percent for blue fish).
- on the cloudy second day, the catchability rate for the red fish is also less than that for the blue fish ($20/30 = 66.7$ percent for red versus $105/120 = 87.5$ percent for blue).
- the catchability rates for the cloudy day exceed those for the sunny day, for both red and blue fish.

If we now apply the same logic as above to the red and blue fish separately, we get

$$\hat{N}_r = \frac{40}{20} \times 30 = 60, \quad \text{and}$$

$$\hat{N}_b = \frac{160}{105} \times 120 = 182.85.$$

Because our estimate for blue fish involves a fraction, we count only whole fish, and so we use $\hat{N}_b = 182$. We now have as our estimate of the total number of fish in the lake $\hat{N} = \hat{N}_r + \hat{N}_b = 242$. By taking into account the types of fish and the different patterns of "catching" fish,

Table 4.3

		Red Fish					Blue Fish		
		Day 2: Cloudy					Day 2: Cloudy		
		In	Out	Total			In	Out	Total
Day 1:	In	20	10	30	Day 1:	In	105	15	120
Sunny	Out	20	?	?	Sunny	Out	55	?	?
	Total	40	?	??		Total	160	?	??

we learn that our original estimate of the total number of fish, 240, should be raised to 242.

When we report back to the wildlife management specialists, they are pleased, but they then ask what will happen for a different lake where the proportions of red and blue fish are different. We explain that the same approach works no matter what the composition of the lake, but if catchability rates for red fish and blue fish vary according to the location of the lake (for example, in the northern as opposed to the southern part of the state), then we will need to gather separate data. Finally, the wildlife management specialists ask whether they will really need to count all the fish in all the lakes twice to get an estimate of the total numbers of red and blue fish. We then suggest that if we carry out one count for all the lakes on the same day but then do a second count (on a second day) using only a sample of the lakes for the north and a sample for the south, we can apply the catchability rates from the second day's sample to the remaining lakes, separately for the two parts of the state and separately for red and blue fish in each of the lakes. The wildlife management specialists express relief, as they have been able to mount an appropriate force of fishermen for one day only, and they are pleased that they can then use the best trained ones to follow up in the counting for the sample on day two.

Dual Systems and the Census-Counting Problem

This method, which works for counting fish, can also be used to measure the size of a human population. In our case, the first attempt to measure the population size is the census, and the second is a special sample.

For example, suppose we are trying to estimate the number of people living on a block in the Bedford-Stuyvesant neighborhood of Brooklyn. The first count of the population could be a list of the names and addresses of people counted in the census. Assume that 300 people were counted by the census on this particular block. For the second count of the population, let us imagine that a specially commissioned, independent count, carried out with even greater care than the census, yields 400 people. In the hypothetical Bedford-Stuyvesant block, the second count surely includes many of the same 300 people counted by the census. We determine how many people were counted both times by comparing the list of names and addresses in the first count with the list of names and addresses in the second count. Suppose that, through matching these two lists, we find that 250 of the 400 people counted in the second count on this block were also included in the census. The three observed categories of the population are thus the 250 counted both times, the 50 counted the first time but not the second, and the 150 counted the second time but not the first. Thus, we have observed a total count of 450. If the second count is a random sample of the population of the block as a whole, then 250 out of 400, or five-eighths of the whole population of the block, were counted in the census. The fraction of members of the second count included in the census is an estimate of the fraction of the total population of the block counted in the census. Finally, we can estimate that the total population is the number of people counted in the census, or 300, divided by five-eighths. This yields an estimate of the total population of 480 people. Thus, the estimated census undercount in this hypothetical block is 180 out of 480 people, or three-eighths of the population.

The numbers here are hypothetical, and the astute reader will recognize that the counts are exactly double the numbers used in the example of fish in the lake. And just as there were red fish and blue fish in the lake, so there are people from different population groups in our block in Bedford-Stuyvesant—that is, Blacks and others—and we will need separate estimates for the the numbers of Blacks and non-Blacks in this block. The breakdown this time might be quite different, as table 4.4 suggests.

The vast majority of people in the block are Black, and the estimates for the total numbers of Blacks and non-Blacks in the block are:

$$\hat{N}_{Black} = \frac{360}{214} \times 262 = 440.74, \quad \text{and} \quad \hat{N}_{non\text{-}Black} = \frac{40}{36} \times 38 = 42.2.$$

Again, counting only the whole numbers of people, we get a total of 482 (440 + 42). The result is slightly higher than our earlier

Table 4.4

		Black					Non-Black		
		Recount					Recount		
		In	Out	Total			In	Out	Total
Census	In	214	48	262	Census	In	36	2	38
	Out	146	?	?		Out	4	?	?
	Total	360	?	??		Total	40	?	??

estimate of 480 from the two groups combined, and this is because the catchabilities are so different and the numbers so disproportionate. There is a serious differential undercount in this hypothetical block, however, with 40.5 percent $(100[1 - 262/440])$ of the Blacks being missed compared with only 9.5 percent $(100[1 - 38/42])$ of the non-Blacks being missed.

Because the undercount rate varies among different kinds of blocks, we must estimate separate undercount rates for each of a sample of blocks. We would not, for example, expect our dual-systems estimate of the undercount rate of a block in Bedford-Stuyvesant to tell us much about the undercount in an upscale suburb. Accordingly, in selecting the sample, we start with a list of all the blocks or equivalent-size rural units in the United States and group the blocks into categories, or "strata," according to their demographic characteristics. Such characteristics might include racial composition, proportion of home owners to renters, and average household size. Rates of undercount are determined for each stratum by measuring the undercount of a sample of blocks within the stratum by dual-systems estimation. The undercount rate of these blocks is then applied to the other blocks in the stratum throughout the country. The actual correction of census counts consists of adjusting the raw census count for each stratum to compensate for the estimated undercount in that stratum.

This is the basic idea and methology underlying the dual-systems approach employed by the Census Bureau in the 1980s and 1990s. Before we explain the added complications associated with the full Census Bureau methodology, we need to be a bit more formal in our description of the dual-systems estimation ideas.

The Dual-Systems Model: More Formal Details

Suppose there are n_1 individuals counted in the census and the second source of population count contains n_2 individuals, a of whom match with individuals in the census. Then there are $b = n_1 - a$ individuals who are in the census but not in the sample, and $c = n_2 - a$ individuals who are in the sample but not in the census. The traditional capture-recapture estimate for the overall population size, N, is

$$\hat{N} = \frac{n_1 n_2}{a} = \frac{(a+b)(a+c)}{a} = a + b + c + \frac{bc}{a}. \qquad (4.1)$$

A closely related way to think of the estimation process is in terms of a 2×2 table of counts (see table 4.5). The rows of the table correspond to being included (or not) in the census and the columns correspond to being included in the second source.

By matching the two counts—n_1 from the census and n_2 from the second source—we find a, and, by subtraction, we also get b and c. Finally, d (and thus $N - n_1$, $N - n_2$, and N) is unknown, and we must estimate it. If being counted in the census is independent of being counted in the second source, then we expect

$$\frac{a}{b} = \frac{c}{d},$$

and thus we use as our estimate of the unobserved d:

$$\hat{d} = \frac{bc}{a}.$$

Finally, we add this estimate for the missing cell to the three observed counts to get our estimate of the population size N:

$$\hat{N} = a + b + c + \hat{d} = n_1 + c + \frac{bc}{a}, \qquad (4.2)$$

which is identical to the estimate we gave initially in equation (4.1). The final version of the estimate of N in expression (4.2) has three components:

Table 4.5

		Sample		
		In	Out	Total
Census	In	a	b	n_1
	Out	c	d	$N - n_1$
	Total	n_2	$N - n_2$	N

1. the basic count from the first source, n_1.
2. the count of those included in the second source but not in the census, $n_2 - a = c$.
3. the projection from the model of the projected number of those missed in both, bc/a.

Provided that the matching of records from the second source with those from the census is done without error, the second of these components represents actual individuals who were not included in the census but should have been.

This same basic methodological approach has long been linked to the analysis of census data (see, for example, Tracy 1941; Shapiro 1949, 1954), although the details in these early references are sparse and the necessary theoretical work is absent. C. Chandra Sekar and W. Edwards Deming (1949) applied the method to estimate the number of births and deaths in several Indian villages and suggested the label, "dual systems." Karol Krótki (1978) provides more details on the use of dual-systems approaches for vital records in various countries. The research on capture-recapture methodology in the wildlife literature and on dual systems in the study of human populations has progressed substantially over the years, sometimes with direct links between fields but for the most part independently. Stephen Fienberg (1992b) provides an annotated bibliography with special attention to the literature of direct relevance to human populations and census taking. Among the most important empirical developments was the actual use of the method to adjust the count in the Australian census (see Choi, Steel, and Skinner 1988).

As we noted in chapter 3, the Census Bureau itself was an early user of the technique, matching the results from a sample to the census records for coverage evaluation in connection with the 1950 decennial census. This dual-systems approach has evolved and is currently used in the United States to measure the census undercount nationwide by taking an independent count of the populations of each of a large number of blocks nationwide and then matching the results of these counts to the results of the census for the same blocks. This second count is known as a postenumeration survey, or PES. The census and the PES are the two counts used to estimate the population of each of the blocks.

Dual-Systems Model Assumptions and Their Empirical Base

As with the demographic analysis method, the dual-systems estimation method is based on a set of assumptions linked to an explicit statistical model. The three assumptions most widely discussed are

1. perfect matching: the individuals in the first list can be matched with those in the second list, without error.
2. independence of lists: the probability of an individual being included in the census does not depend on whether the individual was included in the second list.
3. homogeneity: the probabilities of inclusion do not vary from individual to individual.

Perhaps the greatest problem with the dual-systems approach as it was used in conjunction with the 1980 census was the rate of matching errors—that is, the failure of assumption (1). There are two kinds of matching errors: false matches and false nonmatches. If two different individuals are erroneously matched, then a (the number of people captured by both counts) is erroneously increased and b (the number of people included in the census count but not in the sample) and c (the number of people included in the sample but not in the census) decreased. The net effect of false matches is to decrease the second and third components in the estimate of the population size from equation (4.2) and thus to underestimate the population size. If individuals in the sample cannot be matched with their records in the census, then a is erroneously decreased and b and c increased, leading to overestimation of the population size.

The matching problem as it emerged in the context of the 1980 census coverage evaluation program was discussed at length in the analyses reported by Fay et al. (1988) and was the focus of a major research program in the 1980s, which included the development of new computer-based matching algorithms. Matthew Jaro (1989) reports on the new methods and their accuracy. Approximately 75 percent of the 1990 PES records were matched using these algorithms, and special features of the redesigned PES reduced other difficulties associated with the matching process. Yet there was still a residual group of nonmatches, some of which were real matches, and thus the bureau statisticians set about finding a suitable statistical approach to allocating the residual group to the match and nonmatch categories. The method they ultimately settled on treated the match status of the problematic cases as "missing" and then employed an imputation to assign them a match status. Nathaniel Schenker (1988) describes the imputation methodology used to allocate the residual unmatchable records in 1990.

The failure of assumption (2) is known as correlation bias. In the presence of positive correlation bias (being missed in the census is positively correlated with being missed in the second list), the traditional estimator of expressions (4.1) and (4.2) tends to underestimate the actual population size but yields an improvement over the unadjusted value (see Hogan and Wolter 1988). Although it is widely believed that there was positive correlation bias in the 1980 PES estimates (see, for example, Freedman and Navidi 1986 and Hogan and Wolter 1988), there is little solid empirical evidence on the issue. The only direct statistical method available to measure the extent of correlation bias involves a generalization of the dual-systems approach to multiple lists and the estimation techniques developed for multiple-capture problems (see, for example, Bishop, Fienberg, and Holland 1975; and Fienberg 1972). This alternative is complex and has only been used in an indirect test-census context (see Zalavsky and Wolfgang 1990), and not as part of the full-scale census process. Thus, we have a major assumption associated with our model that most believe to be false, and we have insufficient empirical evidence to replace it with a more reasonable one. As part of the 1990 census correction process, the Census Bureau produced several indirect estimates of correlation bias (Bell 1993) using techniques such as those suggested in Wolter 1990, all of which reaffirm what has been widely assumed that correlation bias appears to be positive. Thus the PES-based procedure used in 1990 could only partially correct for the differential undercount.

Heterogeneity of capture probabilities for both the census and the sample is clearly an issue in any real population setting. The issue is not so much whether assumption (3) is violated but rather to what

extent and with what implications for the results of dual-systems estimation. Following the 1980 census, many statisticians and others argued that such heterogeneity was endemic and contributed to correlation bias as well. What is quite clear is that the correlation between
census and sample catchabilities and the effects of heterogeneity are
confounded in the simple dual-systems estimation model, since in a
2×2 contingency table with a missing cell (the d cell in table 4.5)
there are no degrees of freedom left over to separate the two. Nonetheless, careful methodological research on this topic was lacking, and it
was only later, after the 1990 census and postenumeration survey were
complete, that statisticians began to address the precise nature of the
effects of heterogeneity.

Statisticians now understand that the problem of heterogeneity can
be handled in at least two different ways. One can model the effects
of heterogeneity, or one can attempt to reduce it directly by stratification, or grouping the data into small relatively homogeneous groups.
The latter strategy, stratification, was built into the design for the 1990
PES, and this reduced but did not eliminate the concern at the Census
Bureau about heterogeneity. The tricky thing here is that there is a
trade-off between making the strata smaller and thus more homogeneous, on the one hand, and making sure that the counts in the 2×2
table used for dual-systems estimation are large enough to make the
assumptions of the estimation statistically valid, on the other hand. As
part of the follow-up to the PES, the Census Bureau examined several
indirect measures of the impact of residual heterogeneity. A statistical-
modeling approach that actually attempts to account for individual-
level heterogeneity is possible, but it requires matching three or more
sources rather than just the two in the traditional census approach.
John Daroch, Stephen Fienberg, Gary Glonek, and Brian Junker
(1993) and a number of subsequent authors have proposed an alternative approach to the estimation of heterogeneity, based on multiple
lists, which may be of value in the future. These methods emerged too
late to affect the 1990 adjustment approach, and they still have not
worked their way into the methodological planning of the bureau for
2000 and beyond.

Modifying Dual-Systems Methods for Use in the Decennial Census

The dual-systems method takes as a starting point the assumption that
individuals observed are "real," and it then attempts to deal with the

problem of omissions. But as we observed at the outset in this chapter, there are two kinds of census errors—omissions and erroneous enumerations. Moving to the full-census use of the dual-systems approach involves two major changes from the structure we just described. First, we need to deal with the issue of erroneous enumerations. Then we need to address how to deal with the use of a sample from the census results rather than the census itself. The Census Bureau developed the methods in the late 1970s and early 1980s, and Kirk Wolter (1986) and Charles Cowan and Donald Malec (1986) subsequently described them.

To address the problem of erroneous enumerations, let us consider first a single census block. For the "sample," we redo the census in that block and, in the process, identify the count of erroneous enumerations, EE. In essence, we replace equation (4.1) with

$$\hat{N}^* = \frac{n_1^* n_2}{a^*}, \tag{4.3}$$

where $n_1^* = n_1 - EE$, and a^* is the number of people counted in both the census and the sample (clearly corrected for EE).

The main difference between expressions (4.1) and (4.3) is the correction for EE. The resulting corrections to the original census counts, $\hat{N}^* - n_1$, can be negative. Notice that if all the original census count is erroneous, then $n_1^* = n_1 - EE = 0$, and the estimate for the block total given by (4.3) is also 0, as it should be. Furthermore, if none of those we observe in both the census and the recount are erroneous, the only way we will get a decrease in $\hat{N}^* - n_1$ for the block is if the recount is smaller than the original census count *and* the original count contains a large proportion of erroneous enumerations. Let us illustrate this phenomenon by taking our earlier hypothetical example from a block in Bedford-Stuyvesant and exchanging the results for the census and the recount for non-Blacks only (see table 4.6). Now suppose that three non-Black people in the census count are there erroneously, reducing the census total from forty to thirty-seven. Applying the dual-systems estimator from equation (4.3) yields an estimate of

$$\hat{N}^* = \frac{37 \times 38}{36} = 39,$$

which is less than the original census count before we corrected for the erroneous enumerations.

Table 4.6

		Black					Non-Black		
		Recount					Recount		
		In	Out	Total			In	Out	Total
Census	In	214	48	262	Census	In	36	4	40
	Out	146	?	?		Out	2	?	?
	Total	360	?	??		Total	38	?	??

One of the consequences of the differences between an estimate that takes the census count at face value and one that corrects for erroneous enumerations is that the standard statistical theory of capture-recapture methods needs to be altered. The practical way of dealing with this and other empirical issues related to the small size of a census block is to aggregate data across blocks. For these aggregates, or "poststrata," the wild fluctuations that might result in negative estimates would essentially go away, because the rate of erroneous enumerations is relatively small. This was effectively the case in the uses of the methodology for the 1980 census, but the experience there did not fully prepare Census Bureau statisticians for the more careful measurement of erroneous enumerations that would come in 1990, linked to the revised methodology.

We began this discussion by focusing on a single census block, and we attempted a repeat enumeration for that block, which we called a sample. If we break the block-level data down by racial and ethnic groups, the counts in the 2×2 table become very small; consequently, we need to aggregate data across selected blocks according to some type of stratification scheme. To estimate the missing people for the nation as a whole, we employ a complex stratified sample of blocks; thus, we need to weight the counts from different blocks according to the sample design when we combine them. As a consequence, we need to adapt equation (4.2) somewhat further by replacing actual-count versions with weighted versions. Thus, for stratum s, we have as our estimate for the population total

$$\hat{N}_s^* = \frac{n_{s1}^* n_{s2}^*}{a_s^*}, \tag{4.4}$$

where $n^*_{s1} = n_{s1} - EE_s$ is simply the census count for stratum s corrected for erroneous enumerations, n^*_{s2} is the weighted sample count for stratum s, and a^*_s is the weighted number of people in both the census and the sample in stratum s (clearly corrected for EE).

Generalizing from a Sample to the Nation and Smoothing

The census modification of this technique can be used directly at the national level as well as at state and substate levels. This modified dual-systems estimation approach was used in conjunction with both the 1980 and 1990 censuses as part of the PEP and the PES in 1980. In the 1980 PEP, the Census Bureau took a sample of 110,000 households from the census, selected in clusters of approximately ten housing units per enumeration district, and matched it to the households in the April and August Current Population Survey (CPS), which each contained approximately eighty-four thousand households. The bureau produced estimates of the undercount for the United States as a whole, as well as for all fifty states and for several large local areas (for further details, see Fay et al. 1988). Substantial controversy surrounded the subnational undercount estimates that emanated from the 1980 PES (see, for example, the extended debate between Ericksen and Kadane [1985] and Freedman and Navidi [1986] and its continuation in Ericksen, Kadane, and Tukey [1989] and Freedman and Navidi [1992]). What was this fuss all about?

First, we have described how to estimate the population totals only for individual strata based on blocks where we have actually gone out and taken a second count. Because we take only a sample of such blocks, we need to be able to generalize from the sample, appropriately aggregated, to all of the other blocks in the nation. This is a simple task in principle but quite tricky in practice. The method of choice has turned out to be a version of traditional sampling regression estimation. This not only solves the generalization problem, but also helps address the issue of how much to aggregate the data to form the strata for estimation purposes. Earlier, we pointed out the need to aggregate data across multiple census blocks to get stable counts that help ensure the validity of the dual-systems estimation approach. Empirically, we are left with the issue of just how much to aggregate and what to do if the resulting estimates fluctuate too much. One simple notion is to dampen the magnitude of the adjustment allowed and thus control these fluctuations. The usual way to accomplish this is through some form of regression-like model, in which characteristics of the aggregations of blocks or strata are used as the predictors. The use of regression-like approaches can effectively deal with both the generalization and the excess fluctuation problems.

A special feature of the procedure proposed by Ericksen and Kadane (1985) in connection with adjustment of census counts for 1980 was the smoothing of the PES-based dual-systems estimates for each of sixty-six areas, using a multiple regression model. Much of the critique by Freedman and Navidi (1986) focused on this model, the choice of predictor variables for inclusion in it, and the appropriateness of the standard regression assumptions. In planning for the 1990 PES, the Census Bureau did extensive analysis of possible predictor variables, which would be available as part of the census enumeration data, for use in a new "smoothing" multiple regression model. This research included simulation studies using 1980 data (see Isaki et al. 1988), and the Census Bureau statisticians ultimately decided upon a partially prespecified set of multiple regression models. There were separate regression models for each of several regions of the country, with one group of variables being included with certainty in all models and other variables selected from a second group based on their predictive power for each model (region) separately.

Overview of Census-Based Dual-Systems Methods

In this chapter, we have attempted to provide an elementary and intuitive description of the statistical ideas underlying the proposed methods for correcting the census enumeration for the differential undercount. We began where the methods were first developed, with an example of estimating the number of fish in a lake, and we showed how, even in that setting, many complexities arise that require more elaborate methodology. We then reviewed how these ideas can be adapted to human populations, especially in a census context, and we discussed some of the key assumptions associated with the methodology.

To some extent we have simplified the description of some of the basic ideas of the dual-systems estimation technique, but we do not wish to disguise the difficulties that some statisticians have claimed are inherent in the methodology. The controversy over this approach to correcting the enumeration counts needs to be understood in the context of the details of the methodology actually used in the 1990 census. Thus, we will return to these technical details at end of the next chapter, following our narrative of the political and other developments of the 1980s that prepared the ground for the 1990 decennial census.

Chapter 5

New for 1990:
Implementing the New Methods
in a Census Context

From the perspective of the general public, ten years is an awfully long time between population counts. During the decade, census officials—it would seem—would have time to perform other surveys and statistical work, as they of course do. Practically, though, the modern Census Bureau is always working on at least two censuses at once, the most recent one and the one coming up. What changes over the decade is the bureau's emphasis on the different parts of the process—planning, implementation, evaluation, and publication. Hence, as in previous censuses, planning for the 1990 census began in the early 1980s at the same time as the 1980 publications were being issued and the controversies surrounding the 1980 count still swirled.

In 1982, for example, the American Statistical Association's Technical Panel on the Census Undercount recommended that the bureau "sponsor an outside advisory group on undercount estimation and related problems" (quoted in Citro and Cohen 1985, xii). In response, in 1983 the Committee on National Statistics (CNSTAT) recommended the creation of another CNSTAT panel at the National Academy of Sciences/National Research Council, the Panel on Decennial Census Methodology. The panel began its work in January 1984, issued an interim report later that year, and published a hefty report on census improvements in 1985 (ibid.). In fiscal year 1984, the Census Bureau received its first planning funds for 1990. Field tests of proposed 1990 methodological improvements were scheduled for 1984, 1985, 1986, and 1987. The census dress rehearsal was scheduled for

1988. Over these five years of planning and tests, the bureau had to address a wide variety of interconnected and complex counting problems. Officials had to develop an efficient, practical, and politically acceptable method for counting the hard-to-count population and adjusting the census for the known undercount, if called upon to do so.

On the technological side, the plans for 1990 included automation of the address registers and creation of a complete national digitized address register and mapping system. What became the TIGER (Topologically Integrated Geographic Encoding and Referencing) system identifies and codes addresses on both a map and a list. The world of computing was shifting toward small but powerful networked machines, such as the mini Vax from Digital, and the bureau's computing specialists had to revamp the procedures for processing the raw census forms, carrying out edit checks, and transmitting the coded information to central computers. During the decade, the personal computer (PC) came on the scene, and additional efforts were expended to bring the census publications and information delivery processes into the emerging desktop computer age.

As in past census planning, in the mid-1980s the shape of the issues and controversies for 1990 was discernible but yet not completely clear. The pressures to do something about the differential undercount were strong, and for the first time in decades, as noted in their statements in court, Census Bureau officials were cautiously optimistic about developing a feasible adjustment method for 1990. But what other issues would emerge, in Congress or from the general public, as usual were not apparent. The bureau thus applied itself to what it could control: the technical developments in delivering a census form to an identifiable address and adjustment methodology to guarantee a more complete count. One group of census officials in the Geography Division focused on the development of the TIGER system and a national master address file. Another group, in the Statistical Research Division, came together to form the Undercount Research Staff in charge of developing a feasible adjustment methodology and applying the principles of dual-systems estimation to a census context. In the middle of the decade, these separate operations proceeded at their own pace, seeking funding, defining problems, and taking up the small incremental tasks that would lead to systematic change by the end of the decade.

The problems the two groups had to solve were somewhat different. For the geographers, the task itself was deceptively clear: map every address in the country. Their main challenge was funding and creating efficient procedures for accurately mapping 100 million addresses. Throughout the 1980s, the bureau moved forward on the project and gained so much support that the process that was originally to take two decades was collapsed to one. The TIGER system was on the innovation fast track, picking up support from local government officials as the census approached.

For the Undercount Research Staff, exactly what to do was far less clear. At the beginning of the 1980s, a variety of proposals for matching census responses to other data sources existed. Officials considered whether it made sense to match census data to Internal Revenue Service returns, to vital or other administrative records, or to the CPS, as the bureau had done in 1980. By the mid-1980s, with input from the CNSTAT Panel on Decennial Census Methodology and other advisory groups, they had rejected all of these proposals and focused their efforts on the development of a large PES designed specifically for matching with the decennial census. All the other variants on these methods that had been tried, as in the 1980 census PEP, had foundered on the problems of matching the census records to the other survey or administrative records.

The Development of Postenumeration Methodology in the 1980s

The first thing the Census Bureau statisticians needed to do was to address some of the widespead criticisms of the PES and dual-systems estimation. For example, critics repeatedly pointed out that the method relied heavily on the success of the matching process, equivalent to the "tagging" step used in the first count of fish or other wildlife. People cannot be "tagged" so that they can be identified in the second count. Hence, bureau officials searched for a method to determine that a household or individual identified in the PES but not "matched" to the census had really not been counted in the census or the survey and was not simply a mismatch. Until the officials could determine successfully that a PES nonmatch was really an individual or household undercounted in the census, they could not guarantee that their measurement of the undercount improved the original census count.

Critics of the PES also complained that counting people is fundamentally different from counting fish, in that people "cluster" geographically and socially on known demographic dimensions. Hence, the same conditions that contribute to the differential undercount in the first place will also plague the PES methodology: namely, an individual or household missed in the census will also most likely be missed in the survey. Because of the mechanics of the dual-systems estimation process (see chapter 4), the resulting estimate of the missed people in the census would be biased downward by the same counting problems that affect the census.

Input to the process of revamping the PES for 1990 came in multiple forms. The bureau's Undercount Research Staff set to work to update the methods used in connection with the 1980 PEP program that matched the census records with data from the CPS for evaluation purposes only. Second, ideas for actually implementing dual-systems estimation for the nation arose in the litigation brought by New York City against the bureau; Ericksen and Kadane (1985) published their proposal for smoothing dual-systems estimates, and Freedman and William Navidi (1986) published an extensive critique. Finally, the CNSTAT panel reviewed a number of alternative methodological proposals and interacted extensively with the Census Bureau statisticians, as did the bureau's own external advisory committees.

Armed with this input, the Undercount Research Staff tested several innovations in PES methodology designed to deal with these matching issues in a 1985 test in Tampa, Florida. Instead of relying upon a survey designed for a totally different purpose (the CPS), the Census Bureau designed a separate PES using a sample design based on blocks and directly linked to census geography. Once the bureau had identified a block for the sample, interviewers collected household and population data from all the households living on the block. Such a sample design would make it easier to search the census records for the matching household or person. Second, officials improved and computerized the matching procedures to cut down the time it took to match the sample data with the census data. And they redesigned the questionnaire to make sure that the interviewers captured the extra information needed for the statistical parts of the matching process (Choldin 1994, 123) for those cases where information in the PES and census would not be identical (Jaro 1989).

We recall from chapter 4 that the application of the dual-systems estimation at the block level often yields considerable uncertainty because of small counts. Thus, there is the need to aggregate data across blocks. Aggregation, however, is likely to induce heterogeneity in the data, owing to varying capture probabilities, and so research at the Census Bureau focused on the best way to achieve this aggregation.

Ultimately, bureau officials proposed to "poststratify" the matched dual-systems data into more than one thousand strata, using geographic and demographic information. Specifically, they proposed calculating undercount rates for each "poststratum" based on a cross-classification of age, sex, race, region, and tenancy cohort and then aggregating these individual undercount measurements back up to produce an adjusted national total. Even this level of aggregation was expected to yield estimates with nonnegligible uncertainty, and thus the Census Bureau statisticians began to explore in earnest the use of regression models for smoothing the adjusted values for the poststrata.

The Tampa test proved successful and encouraged the Undercount Research Staff to continue to perfect the procedures they were developing. The next step in the process was a larger test of an integrated census and PES in what the census undercount staff called a "true census context," building the new survey process into the operational steps of the actual census. Bureau officials scheduled the Test of Adjustment-Related Operations (TARO) as part of the 1996 census test in Mississippi and Los Angeles, California. Their goal was to see if the theoretical and statistical innovations of the previous smaller tests could be transferred to the larger and more difficult counting environments of East Los Angeles and rural Mississippi. They also hoped that the TARO could demonstrate the bureau's ability to implement a successful PES, perform the matching and adjustment operations, and produce adjusted data in the short time frame needed if the method were to be used to adjust the census in 1990.

Census day for the 1986 test was March 16, 1986. Officials chose the sites to be able to test the adjustment procedures in hard-to-count areas plagued in 1980 by such problems as a low mail-return rate, difficulty in recruiting census workers, or nonstandard addresses. They built numerous tests of operational innovations into the census, including tests of phone follow-up, reminder cards, and motivational training. The Census Bureau had expected low mail-response rates, though the actual rates were even lower than expected: 34 percent for Los Angeles and 56.7 percent for Mississippi. In this difficult counting environment, the bureau mounted the PES and tested the procedures for matching the census and the PES and providing a dual-systems estimator for adjustment. By early 1987, the Undercount Research Staff had declared the test a success (U.S. Bureau of the Census, 1995a, ch. 2, 37–41). They produced adjusted data in February 1987 and began to think ahead to larger implementation for 1990. Despite the low mail-response rate, the officials concluded that they had successfully implemented the census and postenumeration survey, matched them, and produced adjusted data in a timely fashion. The bureau's technical evaluation of the Los Angeles TARO was extensive, and bureau officials presented the results at professional meetings and in print (see Diffendal 1988; Hogan and Wolter 1988; and Mulry and Spencer 1988).

The next task facing the officials was to determine the decision-making process for considering the possibility of adjustment in 1990. Two years earlier, they had mapped out a set of decision dates they felt they would need to meet in order to be able to announce that they could adjust the census in 1990 if called upon to do so. In 1986, Director John Keane and Barbara Bailar, associate director for statistical standards and methodology, had reported to Congress that the first deadline would be in the spring of 1987. "In early 1987," Bailar told the Subcommittee on Census and Population of the House Committee on Post Office and Civil Service, "we will decide on the statistical and operational feasibility of adjustment. This is not a decision about whether the adjusted numbers will be the official 1990 census counts. What appears feasible in 1987 may not be feasible in 1990" (quoted in Choldin 1994, 125). If officials decided in 1987 that adjustment was feasible, they would build procedures for adjustment into the overall 1990 census design. But they proposed that any decision to implement an adjustment would be made in December 1990, after the enumeration was complete. This was another indication of the cautious approach adopted by the Census Bureau throughout the considerations of major changes in procedures for census taking.

During the spring of 1987, therefore, the Census Bureau planned a major review of the results and implications of the TARO, both inside the bureau and with their external advisory committees and statistical experts interested in census issues. Inside the bureau, officials discussed how to integrate the PES into other census processes. The questions were many: How soon after the April 1, 1990, census day would the PES begin? From where would the bureau recruit interviewers for the PES? How would the new PES operations impinge on the budget and priorities of the traditional enumeration? As usual, bureau statisticians painstakingly worked through each question, producing detailed memorandums evaluating the results of the tests and planning procedures of 1990 (Bureau of the Census 1995a, ch. 2, 1–19).

In April and May, Census Bureau officials made major presentations to the professional community. On April 9 and 10, 1987, the

Census Advisory Committee of the American Statistical Association and the Census Advisory Committee on Population Statistics met to discuss the results of the tests of the new coverage improvement and adjustment procedures. No one underestimated the logistical and technical difficulties still facing the bureau on adjustment. And a good many statistical experts inside and outside the bureau still expressed serious reservations about the feasibility of actually adjusting the census enumeration. Nevertheless, after the meetings, both committees endorsed the direction of the research in the Census Bureau and also endorsed the plans for implementing the new PES in 1990. One month later, on May 7 and 8, 1987, the CNSTAT Panel on Decennial Census Methodology also met to discuss the plans for 1990 and the results of the TARO. The panel concurred in the judgment of the bureau staff that the TARO had been a success and that the adjustment methods were operationally feasible. It also endorsed the plans for a PES of three hundred thousand households as an integral part of the coverage improvement plan for 1990, and, in a special letter report to Bureau Director John Keane, recommended that "adequate funds be provided for the large-scale post-enumeration survey (PES) and other activities necessary to prepare for an adjustment of the 1990 census."[1] In a preview of another debate to come three years later, the panel also signaled

> the need for the Census Bureau to establish in advance guidelines and procedures to be used for evaluating the quality of the 1990 census enumeration and PES results in order that objective, informed decisions on adjustment can be made. We believe, however, that it is neither advisable nor feasible to set explicit quantitative thresholds that an adjustment procedure must achieve. Rather, the evaluation should involve the highest levels of statistical and demographic judgment, taking into consideration the entirety of available information.

In July, the House Subcommittee on Census and Population held yet another hearing on the statistical and operational feasibility of adjusting the 1990 census counts, and at that time the testimony was strongly supportive of the new methods and endorsed their successful implementation.

It appeared, therefore, by mid-1987 that the new methodology had passed several major tests. The new adjustment methods had stood up to the stringent methodological research standards inside the Census Bureau. And they had met with approval ranging from guarded support to outright enthusiasm from the statistical community and key demographers and census users. As the bureau looked forward to 1990, it appeared that for the first time since the undercount controversies had erupted in the late 1960s, officials could be cautiously optimistic about their technical capacity to correct for the differential undercount if called upon to do so. The lynchpins of the new procedures were the newly designed postenumeration survey and the dual-systems estimation process for carrying down adjustment to the local level.

Cancellation of the Postenumeration Survey

Four months later, on October 30, 1987, Robert Ortner, under secretary of commerce for economic affairs, issued a press release announcing that he was canceling the Postenumeration Survey phase of the 1990 census process because "the department does not intend to adjust the 1990 decennial population count for purported undercount and overcount of population subgroups." The decision sent shock waves through the Census Bureau and the statistical community, though some of the warning signs of the decision had been on the horizon for some months. The announcement had a far-reaching impact on the 1990 count and signaled a fundamental politicization of the 1990 census and the bureau.

In hindsight, it is easy to see the array of decisions that led to the announcement: they were revealed in painful detail in the congressional hearings, legal proceedings, and public statements of the actors in subsequent years. Rarely, in fact, do later observers and historians get such voluminous and detailed information about the mundane inner workings of the federal bureaucracy, if for no other reason that such day-to-day activities are usually fairly dull stuff. But from mid-1987 onward, the Census Bureau and the office of the under secretary of commerce for economic affairs in the Department of Commerce became venues for intensive bureaucratic intrigue and conflict. Many aspects of this intrigue and conflict were captured on paper in a form that emerged as part of the later litigation over the 1990 census results. As the Department of Commerce came to wield increasing control over the plans for the 1990 census and its personnel, critics, particularly Democratic members of Congress and big-city mayors, charged that a Republican Commerce Department was politicizing the Census Bureau.

Key officials in the bureau who had developed the new methods, including Barbara Bailar and Kirk Wolter, were aware in May and June of 1987 that something was amiss in the plans for the announcement of the new PES and attendant plans for possible adjustment. As they recalled in congressional testimony and court depositions in later years, they were called downtown in the spring to the Commerce Department meetings to explain the new methods to department officials. Commerce officials raised questions about the political implications of a possible adjustment, and the Republican National Committee raised objections to adjustment. When Commerce officials received the same endorsements of the new methods from most Census Bureau officials that the advisory committees had produced, they began to probe further for "problems" with the new methods.

On May 19, 1987, for example, Harry Scarr, then executive assistant for statistical affairs in the office of the under secretary for economic affairs in the Commerce Department and later deputy director and acting director of the Census Bureau, reported in a memorandum to Robert Ortner on the problems with adjusting census numbers.[2] "You asked," Scarr noted, "for problems with adjustment. Here are some. I am continuing to look for others. This set was prepared with the help of a very knowledgeable Census employee." Scarr summarized the problems under headings of apportionment, redistricting, public relations, and technical. He concluded by identifying "groups that are likely to be pro adjustment," naming "politicians from those cities or places with large minority populations: for example, New York, Detroit, and presumably the others who sued after 1980." "Groups that are likely to be against adjustment" included "voting and redistricting experts who believe that adjusted figures will paralyze the electoral system until the matter is adjudicated in the courts," "politicians representing those areas which might be expected to lose shares of fixed pies (seats in the House, and many state revenue programs), i.e., those areas with small minority populations," and "some statisticians who have serious questions about either the Bureau's ability to do the required procedures or the ultimate advisability of adjustment."

Publicly, from May to October 1987, the Census Bureau had moved forward with plans for the PES and continued the development work for the adjustment methodology. Director Keane testified before Congress in August and did not mention the objections of Commerce officials to the PES or the intense pressure the bureau was facing. By late summer, high-level officials clearly recognized that the Commerce Department intended to stop the PES, though they were not allowed to speak to their staffs or to census stakeholders about the issue. In early August, Commerce officials noted in budget memorandums that they had not approved the bureau's budget requests for the PES. And they continued to question the feasibility of the PES and the adjustment procedures, ignoring the endorsements of them by the various advisory committees and outside groups.

The October 30 announcement brought the behind-the-scenes conflict out into the open. Commerce officials presumed that the general public would accept the cancellation of the PES as a minor budgetary decision of a cost-conscious Republican administration. Reagan administration officials had, in the previous six years, challenged and cut budgets for many government programs they considered expendable and were committed to continuing to reduce the size of government. Ortner claimed that the "purported undercount and overcount of population subgroups" was a problem not amenable to technical solution. He claimed a PES and adjustment methodology would divert resources from and undermine public confidence in the traditional enumeration. He pledged a high-quality count in 1990, and he detailed innovations to make it the best ever. The proposed PES, in other words, was unnecessary, technically suspect, and not worth the cost.

Ortner expected that Democratic supporters of adjustment in Congress would attack his decision. Predictably, then, as the *New York Times* (Oct. 31, 1987) reported, Representative Charles E. Schumer (Dem.-N.Y.) charged that the decision was "politically motivated because most people missed lived in areas that voted Democratic." The week before the announcement, Representative Mervyn Dymally (Dem.-Calif.) introduced a bill in Congress to require the Census Bureau to adjust for undercounts. Yet Ortner and the Commerce Department also expected the furor to die down in a few days. The *Washington Post*, for example, had editorialized against adjustment on August 22, 1987, and again on November 5. And there were much bigger news stories in the headlines: the stock market had crashed on October 19, and the controversies surrounding the nominations of Robert Bork and Douglas Ginsburg for seats on the Supreme Court and the ongoing Iran-Contra investigations merited much more extensive news coverage.

Hence, only slowly did it become obvious to Commerce officials and the general public that the Ortner announcement would have a profound impact inside the Census Bureau and within the professional statistical community. Statisticians and survey researchers inside and outside the bureau clearly still expressed many professional doubts about the feasibility of an adjustment in 1990. Particularly for those responsible for the operational side of the field enumeration of the census, the new PES was a logistical headache that might require earlier truncation of the field portion of the count and hence interfere with existing methods (Choldin 1994, 134 ff.). But Ortner's announcement sent another message to the statistical community: namely, that the Census Bureau was not master of its own fate. Ortner's decision generated shock at the interference of a political official from the Commerce Department in the scientific work of the bureau. Hence, even statisticians and officials who still harbored doubts about the feasibility of the PES found themselves forced to consider the issue of census underenumeration from a different perspective: namely, shouldn't the scientific agency have the autonomy to make these kinds of decisions? Wasn't the credibility of the agency as a whole threatened if it could not follow the best advice of the professional statistical community?

The decision to cancel the PES prompted these questions because it recalled other controversies about statistical policy that had been brewing in the Reagan administration. Since the early 1980s, officials in the Reagan administration had challenged the federal statistical practice in many ways. By 1987, for example, old statistical hands in Washington told the story of the elimination of the Office of Statistical Policy and Standards in 1981 and the attendant downsizing of the central coordinating statistical staff (Anderson 1988, 234–35). Previous congressional hearings by the House Subcommittee on Census and Population had documented other effects that reduced budgets had had on all the federal statistical agencies (U.S. House 1982). During the summer of 1987, the Office of Management and Budget (OMB) challenged the questionnaire for the census dress rehearsal (Choldin 1994, 137–44). This latter controversy, resolved in the fall of 1987 to the satisfaction of Census Bureau officials, nevertheless consumed precious time and energy as bureau officials explained their decisions and testified before Congress. Data users—from members of the Council of Professional Associations on Federal Statistics (COPAFS) to the Association of Public Data Users (APDU) to the American Planning Association, the American Library Association, the state data centers, and many others—lobbied the OMB successfully to restore the majority of the questions on the form as developed and, as they did so, worried at possible further threats to federal statistics.

The Controversy Deepens

Two months later, in December 1987, the fallout from Ortner's decision became public. In mid-December, Barbara Bailar, associate director for statistical standards and methodology, abruptly resigned from the Census Bureau. On January 15, 1988, the *Washington Post* reported that "she quit her post as a high ranking Census Bureau official . . . because she believes Republicans in the Commerce Department had political motives in killing a plan to compensate for an expected severe undercount of Blacks and Hispanics in the 1990 census." Bailar stated that Ortner's decision "was dressed up like a technical decision when everyone knew it was a political decision. That kind of hypocrisy I just can't live with." Ortner responded that Bailar's charge was "unfounded and irresponsible . . . She ought to know better than that." There were "no calls from the White House," according to Ortner: "You can't say there was an absolute, airtight case in favor of adjustment." Deputy Director Louis Kincannon agreed with Ortner that there was "substantial opposition" to adjustment "from some Bureau officials." But he also added that Bailar is "a person of unimpeachable integrity" and "a brilliant mind." Kincannon carefully concluded his remarks, saying, "I don't have any concrete reason . . . on which to base a conclusion that the department's decision about proceeding with an adjustment was based upon politics, by which I mean a biased partisan decision to favor one party or the other."

There the controversy might have ended, but for the impact of the another December 1987 action, the decision of Judge John Sprizzo to dismiss the 1980 census undercount case, *Cuomo v. Baldrige* (1987). As we noted in chapter 3, New York City brought its case against the Census Bureau back to court in the mid-1980s to try to show that recent innovations in statistical methodology made it possible to adjust the 1980 census for undercount at the local level. The technical and legal discussions in the court turned upon differing interpretations of the technical success of the 1980 PES and its usefulness for adjusting the 1980 census. In that case, Barbara Bailar had been one of the chief witnesses for the Census Bureau. She testified to the severe problems matching the responses on the PES to those of the original census and indicated that a dual-systems estimator based upon such a poorly matched set of responses would not improve census accuracy. She and other Census Bureau officials pledged their good faith efforts to improve their methods, pointing to the ongoing research efforts in the bureau for 1990. Judge Sprizzo accepted the bureau's arguments and ruled that the appropriate standard for review of whether New York City had sustained their burden of proof was whether the "Bureau's decision not to adjust . . . was 'arbitrary' or 'capricious' pursuant to the Administrative Procedure Act" (ibid., 1104). He rejected New York's claim that its experts disagreed with the bureau's technical evaluation and therefore that the court could challenge the bureau's authority: "Certainly the Bureau, which has the necessary experience, expertise, and resources to collect and analyze the complex statistical data, is better equipped than the courts to decide whether, in view of this dispute among the experts, the census should be adjusted." And, he continued, "The Bureau has and should have substantial discretion to accept one body of expert opinion over another, especially in light of the concession by plaintiffs' own experts that reasonable experts could disagree with their conclusion that an adjustment was feasible" (ibid., 1106). In other words, as long as the bureau decisions and actions were competent, and not arbitrary and capricious, they should stand.

Although Sprizzo's decision brought the 1980 census lawsuit to an end, it also opened up a new set of legal arguments about census adjustment and the Ortner decision. In particular, Sprizzo noted that according to Title 13 of the U.S. Code, Congress "entrusted to the Secretary of Commerce the discretion to conduct the census 'in such form and content as he may determine'" (ibid., 1105). Traditionally, the secretary of the Commerce Department had delegated the authority to conduct the census to the director of the Census Bureau. The emerging controversy between the bureau and the department raised the question of who had the ultimate decision-making authority.

For the remainder of the election year of 1988, that issue grew in importance. In early March, Ortner and Bailar both testified before the House Subcommittee on Census and Population on the adjustment decision (House 1988) (John Keane, census director, and Albert Madansky, a member of the CNSTAT census Methodology Panel, also testified). Their testimony dramatically exposed the different interpretations between the research staff of the Census Bureau and the Commerce Department on the feasibility and advisability of the PES and a dual-systems adjustment for 1990. The formal subject of the hearing was the Dymally bill to require the 1990 census be adjusted for undercount. The thrust of the questions from the committee members addressed the Ortner announcement and questioned its support by the experts in the Census Bureau. Robert Garcia (Dem.-Calif.), Dymally, and Charles Schumer charged that Ortner was interfering in a decision rightfully made in the bureau. Under sometimes relentless questioning, they pressed Ortner and Census Director John Keane on the decision-making process during the summer of 1987. Ortner defended the Commerce Department's decision by noting that the bureau still planned a 150,000-household PES for evaluation purposes. He reminded the committee that bureau staff was divided on the operational feasibility of integrating the PES into the mail enumeration process and producing adjusted data in a timely fashion. Schumer brushed aside this explanation and pressed his questions.

Mr. Schumer: Excuse me, I would like to say, yes, they [the Census Bureau technical staff] were in favor of planning for adjustment and proceeding along technically to see how well, how proficient they could be in deriving a methodology at gaining an adjustment.

Dr. Ortner: Now, my understanding is that you are misrepresenting—or let me say it the other way. You are misrepresenting the situation at the Census Bureau. There are a lot of technical people at the Census Bureau, and the opinion at the Census Bureau was very divided on this issue, on whether an adjustment could be done and how we should proceed to plan for the 1990 census.

Mr. Schumer: Did the Steering Committee recommend to go ahead, the Steering Committee which is a group of the experts? Are you aware that they did?

. . .

Dr. Ortner: They were divided on it.

Mr. Schumer: Did they recommend to go ahead, Dr. Keane? Did they?

Dr. Ortner: I think Dr. Keane should answer that because I can repeat to you what Dr. Keane said to me: that the technical people at the Census Bureau were divided on it.

Mr. Schumer: Dr. Keane, did the Steering Committee recommend that the Bureau should move forward?

Dr. Keane: On balance, more people were for going ahead than not. It was controversial.

Mr. Schumer: No one is denying the controversy here. It has been a controversy that has been flaring for a long time.
What is under my skin, and I think a good number of people's skin, is that while there was a methodology to resolve the controversy in a nonpolitical way, Commerce people, like the Secretary, who had far less expertise than the technical experts, came in and said,

	"No, we are not doing it," before it came to a head. Now, is that fair to say?
Dr. Keane:	No.
Mr. Schumer:	Dr. Keane?
Dr. Keane:	No.
Mr. Schumer:	I do not mean to put you on the hot seat, Dr. Keane, but we have a very, very serious issue here, a very serious issue.
Dr. Ortner:	Yes it is. It is a serious issue because—
Mr. Schumer:	I would like to ask just Dr. Keane to answer the question. I am sorry, but I must ask you to. Would you like for me to restate it?
Dr. Keane:	Yes, I would, please.
Mr. Schumer:	Okay. The question is: While there was no consensus among the technical experts in the Census Bureau on operational feasibility, that the Steering Committee had recommended that plans continue to go ahead to see what kind of statistical methodology could be determined for an adjustment; and that the Commerce Department said, "Stop. We are not going to do it." What is inaccurate about that statement?
Dr. Keane:	I find nothing essentially inaccurate about it.
Mr. Schumer:	Thank you.

(U.S. House 1988, 48–49)

Barbara Bailar testified after Ortner and Keane. In a prepared statement, she detailed the technical developments of dual-systems estimation and the PES methodologies in the 1980s, her expertise as a twenty-nine-year veteran of the Census Bureau, and her evaluation of the state of opinion on adjustment within the bureau. "My overall professional assessment," she stated, "is that, first, adjustment is a correction operation that will make the census counts more accurate, and two, adjustment is technically feasible" (ibid., 79). She again charged that the decision to cancel the 300,000 household PES was a political decision. She analyzed Ortner's decision and rationale in the bluntest possible terms: "Dr. Ortner's arguments against adjustment are so seriously flawed and so inconsistent as to suggest utter indifference whether they are even believed" (ibid., 123). And she reminded the

committee that the department's proposal for a 150,000-household
PES for "evaluation purposes"" would not "get the priority needed to
make it as accurate and timely as it must be." She urged support of the
Dymally bill, noting that the "integrity of the census will be irreparably
damaged if the official census numbers are uncorrected, and known to
be inferior to those that could be produced with an adjustment. . . .
Only by this means or by court action will we see a 1990 census that
is as fair to all Americans as we can make it" (ibid., 125).

During questioning by the committee, Schumer acknowledged the
power of Bailar's testimony, noting, "I would like again to praise your
courage, Ms. Bailar, for coming forward. I think if you had not come
forward, there would be a hearing like this and we would be exchanging nice pleasantries, and nobody would know what is going on. So it
really is all because of you, in a sense, in a very real sense. The testimony of Dr. Ortner and Dr. Keane has been your vindication because
they proved many of the things that you had asserted in your testimony" (ibid., 128).

Although the March hearing laid open the bureaucratic controversies surrounding the Ortner decision, it did not resolve the conflict.
The Dymally bill languished in Congress. Commerce Department officials continued to assume that the controversy would die down and
1990 planning would proceed according to the wishes of the department. In midyear, Kirk Wolter, chief of the Statistical Research Division and a second key official involved in developing the PES and
adjustment methodologies for 1990, quit the Census Bureau and made
it known that he also disagreed with the Commerce Department's decision. At the same time, Democrats in Congress watched the presidential campaign between George Bush and Michael Dukakis and considered whether a Dukakis victory in November would change the
leadership in the Commerce Department and encourage a new look at
census planning and the reinstatement of the PES. But by fall, the polls
were not encouraging. Nor was there much time before the April 1990
census date to restructure plans.

Advocates for a census adjustment methodology using the PES and
a dual-systems estimator recognized that time was running out, as
Bailar had noted in her March testimony. Neither the authority of the
technical experts in the Statistical Research Division nor Congress was
about to change the department's position. Thus, on November 3,
1988, five days before the presidential election, New York City, the
State of New York, and a coalition of local governments and citizen
groups filed suit in federal court in New York and charged that Ort-

ner's October 1987 ban on adjustment and cancellation of the PES were arbitrary and capricious decisions. They asked that the court reinstate the 300,000-household PES and prepare for an adjustment. On November 8, Vice President George Bush won the presidential election and vowed to continue the "Republican revolution" started in the Reagan administration.

The New York Adjustment Suit, the New Administration, and the 1990 Count

The year before a decennial census is conducted typically involves finalizing the methods to be used, ordering materials, setting up offices, and building the temporary staff. The dress rehearsal and tests are complete. The operational phase of census taking goes into high gear, and the timely completion of tasks and the maintenance of planned schedules is a high priority. Superficially, this was the case in 1989; however, two additional processes threatened to overshadow the smooth implementation of the decennial census count. First, although the Republicans had retained the presidency in the 1988 elections, there was a change in presidents. The attendant change of administration led to shifts in political appointees in both the Census Bureau and the Commerce Department. In early 1989, Census Director John Keane resigned. Robert Ortner left after eight years at Commerce. Filling these positions, falling as it did to the normal process of presidential appointments at the start of the new administration, might take some time. Second, the New York suit began to move through the courts. On behalf of the Census Bureau and Commerce Department, the Justice Department filed motions to dismiss the suit "for want of subject matter jurisdiction" and lack of "standing" among other issues. On April 27, 1989, Judge Joseph M. McLaughlin denied the Justice Department motion and ended any hopes the bureau had that they could avoid costly litigation before the count. McLaughlin's decision set in motion the discovery phase of the lawsuit, which would lead rapidly to a trial.

Two days earlier, on April 25, 1989, the *Los Angeles Times* had reported that Alan Heslop was in line for the position of census director. The next day, the *Washington Post* reported that Heslop, "a California redistricting specialist closely associated over the years with Republican political planning" and director of the Rose Institute, was running into opposition from Democrats. Willie Brown, speaker of the

California Assembly, called Heslop "a political hit man." Senate Democrats said they would "try to determine if he is too partisan for the job." Two months later, on June 23, Heslop withdrew his name from consideration (*Washington Post,* June 22, 1989). Less than one year before the census, the bureau was leaderless. It also faced a lawsuit that opened all its actions to detailed scrutiny, and it had lost the first round in court.

By mid-July, the Commerce Department took several steps to defuse the charge that it was politicizing the upcoming census. Behind the scenes, as soon as the news of Heslop's withdrawal became public, Commerce officials approached Barbara Everitt Bryant to determine whether she was available for the position of census director. Bryant was a close associate of Robert Teeter, George Bush's polling expert and political adviser. As vice president at Market Opinion Research, Teeter's firm, she had been contacted earlier in the spring for the position (Bryant and Dunn 1995, 49 ff., and oral interview, Oct. 20, 1995, with Margo Anderson). The proposed nomination of Bryant had not generated a visceral reaction from Democrats. Bryant expressed interest and began the long process of FBI investigation and culminating in confirmation. Over the summer, she came to Washington as a consultant but was not permitted to speak for the Census Bureau "or act like the presidential nominee I was about to become" (quoted in Bryant and Dunn 1995, 54). On July 17, on the morning the adjustment lawsuit trial was scheduled to begin, New York and the federal government announced a partial settlement of the suit and issued a stipulation vacating Ortner's October 1987 decision barring adjustment. The stipulation and order (see appendix B) reinstated the PES "in a manner calculated to ensure the possibility of using the PES, not solely for evaluation purposes, but to produce corrected counts usable for congressional and legislative reapportionment, redistricting, and all other purposes for which the Bureau of the Census publishes data." As part of the negotiations over the stipulation, at the insistence of the government, the size of the PES was reduced from 300,000 households to 150,000. The agreement also called for an eight-member panel of experts to be appointed, to provide advice on adjustment-related activities, and stipulated that the decision on whether to adjust would be made by July 15, 1991.

After two years of controversy, the decision reset the course for adjusting census counts originally set by the statisticians in the Census Bureau, albeit with a PES of reduced size. It would remain to be seen whether the 1990 count could now proceed smoothly.

Polishing Up the Postenumeration Survey Methodology for the 1990 Census

In chapter 4, we described the general statistical approach for combining data from two sources to estimate a population total, and we explained how it could be adapted to the census context in the form of dual-systems estimation. Once the 1989 stipulation and order became official, the Census Bureau statisticians dusted off their original plans for the PES, which had been in the works back in 1987, and scaled it down in size. They also went back to attend to the myriad technical details they had been focusing on when Under Secretary Ortner issued his 1987 order to abandon the PES for adjustment purposes.

Following the "completion" of the original enumeration, roughly in July 1990, the bureau planned to implement a PES to gather information from the inhabitants of approximately 5,290 block clusters across the nation, matching the information collected with the results of the original census enumeration for these blocks. In all, the final design for the PES involved checking on the occupants of 165,000 households nationwide (slightly larger than the size specified in the stipulation and order).

In effect, the same sample of blocks produces two samples: the *P*-sample, consisting of all people living in the sample blocks at the time of the PES interview, and the *E*-sample, consisting of all census enumerations coded to the sample blocks. These two samples were to exclude people living in institutions, the military living in barracks or on ships, and the homeless. The key step for the dual-systems estimation approach was to be the matching of persons between the two samples and the placement of people into the three observable cells of the 2 × 2 table cross-classifying census enumeration status with PES status (see table 4.5). Exact matching of names, addresses, and so on was not to be a requirement. Persons enumerated in a sample block were to be treated as correctly enumerated if they had been counted anywhere in the block containing the address or in a ring of adjacent blocks, known as a search area.

The design of the PES allows for the use of information from the *E*-sample to measure the proportion of erroneous census enumerations. Erroneous enumerations consist of duplications, fictitious enumerations, people who were born after census day or who died before census day, people counted in the wrong location, and census enumerations with insufficient information to allow both matching and follow-up reinterviews. Movers pose special problems for this determination. People who move from outside the search area into the sample block after census day and are nonetheless counted there as part of the enumeration are deemed to be erroneous enumerations. If they move from one address in the search area to another, the matching process deems them to be correctly enumerated as long as they are counted only once. The details of this process of matching, evaluation of status, and field follow-up are inevitably complex, and their implementation would become an essential part of the evaluation of the success of the PES adjustment process. As one of the processing steps, individuals with unresolved status in the enumeration are imputed a status using a form of statistical modeling (Howard Hogan [1993] provides many further details.)

With information on erroneous enumerations, matches, and imputations in hand, the Census Bureau statisticians would be able to apply the dual-systems estimation approach to each of the 1,392 poststrata. This involves just a minor reinterpretation of formula (4.4) from chapter 4. Thus for stratum s, we again write the dual-systems estimate for the population total as

$$\hat{N}_s^* = \frac{n_{s1}^* n_{s2}^*}{a_s^*}, \tag{5.1}$$

where n_{s2}^* is the weighted P-sample total for stratum s and a_s^* is the number of P-sample matches for stratum s. But now n_{s1}^* is the census count for stratum s corrected for both imputation and erroneous enumerations, that is,

$$n_{s1}^* = (n_{s1} - II_s)\left[1 - \frac{\widehat{EE}_s}{\hat{N}_{es}}\right], \tag{5.2}$$

where II_s is the number of whole people imputed to match status for stratum s, $\widehat{EE}_s$ is the weighted estimate of E-sample erroneous enumerations for stratum s, and $\hat{N}_{es}$ is the weighted E-sample total for stratum s.

This estimation process yields "adjustment factors" for each stratum that are the ratio of the estimated true population for that stratum divided by the actual census count for that stratum, that is,

$$Y_s = \frac{\hat{N}_s^*}{n_{s1}}. \tag{5.3}$$

As we noted in the previous chapter, when the sample count is less than the census count and when a large proportion of those in the census and not in the sample is due to erroneous enumerations, it is possible for the adjustment factor to be less than one, that is, for the overall count after correction to be less than the original census count. But the full extent of the corrections for erroneous enumerations in equation (5.2) yields an even more anomolous result, that

$$n_{s1}^* - a_s^* < 0. \tag{5.4}$$

The quantity in equation (5.4) is the estimate of the number of individuals in the census but not in the sample, and, because of sampling error and other errors associated with the correction for erroneous enumerations, it can take on a negative value. In the 1980 postenumeration program (PEP) coverage evaluation program, about 25 percent of the male age-race-state 2×2 tables yielded cells corresponding to equation (5.4) with negative values (see Fay et al. 1988, ch. 7). Before 1990, there was some sense among statisticians that this type of downward correction of the original counts would not happen all that often. The way the Census Bureau proposed to cope with such negative cell values was to treat them as if they were zeroes (see Bell 1993). In this case, the adjustment factor will be less than one if the weighted sample size for the stratum, n_{s2}^*, is less than the original census count n_{s1}.

Finally, the bureau planned to use "smoothed" dual-systems estimates combined with the original dual-systems estimates using an empirical Bayes procedure, which generated final estimates that were a weighted average of the two. In essence, the idea was to pull each "raw" dual-systems estimate toward its predicted value from the multiple regression model, with the degree of shrinkage being weighted by factors depending on their variances. The regression model was to take the following form:

$$Y = X\beta + w + e, \tag{5.5}$$

where **Y** are the adjustment factors ({Y_s} for the 1,392 poststrata), **X** contains values for smoothing variables, **w** represents model errors, and e represents sampling errors. Hogan (1993) again provides more details.

This smoothing and shrinkage is a modification of the statistical approach proposed by Ericksen and Kadane (1985) for use with the 1980 PES during the litigation that followed that census. (For contrasting views about the appropriateness of the assumptions of this methodology in the context of the census, we refer the interested reader to a pair of 1991 articles in *Science* by David Freedman [1991] and Kirk Wolter [1991], and then subsequent critiques and evaluations that appeared as a special section of the *Journal of the American Statistical Association* in 1993 after the methodology had actually been implemented.)

The following is a step-by-step summary description of this 1990 census adjustment procedure using the modified dual-systems approach that we have just outlined.

STEP 1
Select an area probability sample of about 5,290 blocks. The sampling unit, the "block," is essentially a city block, in urban and suburban areas, and a well-defined piece of geography, in rural areas.

STEP 2
The 5,290 sample blocks generate two probability samples of people: the population, or *P*-sample, and the enumeration, or *E*-sample. The *E*-sample consists of all persons in the 1990 official enumeration (OE) in those blocks and is to be used to estimate erroneous enumerations. The *P*-sample consists of all persons counted in an independent enumeration of the blocks to be conducted some time following the OE. Together, the two samples make up the PES.

STEP 3
Match the *P*-sample persons to lists of persons counted in the OE, using name, address, and various other characteristics. The objective here is to determine which *P*-sample people were counted in the OE and which were not. Perform the initial phase of matching by an automated computer matching program (expected to match about 75 percent of the *P*-sample to their corresponding OE).

STEP 4
Each *E*-sample enumeration will either match or not match to a *P*-sample enumeration. Ultimately designate *E*-sample enumerations as correct or erroneous.

STEP 5

Screen the data for any incomplete, missing, or faulty items. Estimate values for all the missing data by statistical imputation techniques.

STEP 6

Calculate estimates of the total population within each of 1,392 poststrata, based in part on the characteristics of the P- and E-sample people. The poststrata, based on demographic (age, racial or ethnic group, gender, owner or renter) and geographic variables, are mutually exclusive and span the entire U.S. population. We can write the modified dual-systems estimator of total population within a poststratum from equation (5.1) above to take the form

$$\widehat{N} = \frac{X - \widehat{E}}{\widehat{p}},$$

where X denotes the actual population count achieved in the OE, $\widehat{E}$ denotes an E-sample-based estimator of the total erroneous enumerations in the OE, and $\widehat{p}$ denotes a P-sample-based estimator of the proportion of the total population enumerated in the OE.

STEP 7

Smooth the 1,392 ratios, or "raw" adjustment factors, $\widehat{N}/C$, where C is the count from the OE, in order to reduce the sampling variability. Obtain the smoothed adjustment factors by shrinking the raw adjustment factors toward a predicted value from a multiple regression model, with the degree of shrinkage determined by the variance of the predicted value and the inherent sampling variability in the raw factor.

STEP 8

Apply the smoothed adjustment factors to the OE, block by block, for each of the approximately seven million blocks in the country. Because the application of these adjustments does not necessarily result in values corresponding to whole numbers of people in each block, reallocate the "excess" fractions of people, using the method of "controlled rounding," so that the count for each block is an integer and the block totals add up to some prespecified totals.

Chapter 6

Counting the Population in 1990

pril 1, 1990, was the official date for taking the 1990 census, the day all American households theoretically would fill out and return their census forms for the decade. To guarantee that Americans would be able to fill out their forms as planned, census officials had to guarantee that more than ninety million American households received a census form or a visit from an enumerator on April 1—or as close to that date as possible. And they had to plan to retrieve all the forms; check and correct them for mistakes, omissions, and duplications; tabulate the responses on the forms; and prepare a report to the president for apportionment by the end of 1990.

Those general procedures were fundamentally similar to those in previous censuses. But the integration of the postenumeration survey (PES) for a possible adjustment of the raw census counts added an elaborate new process to the overall census design. In the summer of 1990, the PES was slated to go into the field. And the stipulation agreement with the New York litigants also created a new reporting deadline of July 15, 1991. On that date, the secretary of commerce had to report whether the 1990 census would be adjusted for undercount as a result of the dual-systems estimation of the population derived from the census and the PES.

In short, the American public saw a 1990 census taken on April 1 and reported in December—as in the past. On the heels of the stipulation agreement, however, census officials and the New York litigants saw a complex counting process that stretched from the summer of 1989 to the July 1991 adjustment decision. This community of census officials, statisticians, and politicians was acutely aware of the bureaucratic, political, and logistical hurdles they would face along the way (figure 6.1).

Aftermath of the Stipulation Agreement

On the morning of July 17, 1989, the drama in the courtroom of District Court Judge Joseph M. McLaughlin was palpable. The settlement relieved the tension arising from the anticipated confrontation between

Figure 6.1

Source: Illustration for "The Census in One Not-So-Easy Lasso," by Felicity Barringer. *New York Times,* "Week in Review," 1990, 1, 4. Drawing by Nicolae Asciu. Copyright 1990 by the *New York Times.* Reprinted by permission.

the federal government and the New York plaintiffs and redirected everyone's attention to the details of the stipulation agreement. Was it a good agreement? Could a postenumeration survey be reinstated into the census process so soon before the count? Would the Commerce Department really permit a census adjustment, or was the decision to agree to a PES merely a face-saving stalling device?

Certainly, had the trial actually taken place, it would have been a major statistical event, replete with statistical witnesses and technical presentations on both sides. Plaintiffs had planned to present a series of expert witnesses at the trial to support their contention that the announced decision by the Commerce Department was arbitrary and not based on technically justifiable grounds. The principal witnesses were expected to be Barbara A. Bailar, Eugene P. Ericksen, Stephen E. Fienberg, and Kirk M. Wolter. Other expected witnesses included William Baumol, Franklin M. Fisher, and Donald B. Rubin. The defendants had announced plans to call as witnesses several senior Census Bureau officials, including Peter A. Bounpane, William B. Butz, Charles Jones, Susan Miskura, and John H. Thompson, to support the technical claims made as part of the 1987 Commerce Department decision. The only non-Census Bureau witness slated to testify at trial on behalf of the defendants was David A. Freedman, statistician from the University California, Berkeley.

Several of these statistical experts had testified earlier in the decade in the lawsuits over adjustment of the 1980 census. This time, however, Barbara Bailar and Kirk Wolter were expected to support plans for adjustment rather than oppose them. Moreover, unlike the 1980 litigation, there were fewer outside experts willing to defend the technical basis for the Commerce Department decision not to adjust. The settlement agreement and Judge McLaughlin's decision (see appendix B) contained the following components:

1. The decision on whether or not to carry out a statistical adjustment of the 1990 results would be reconsidered.

2. The Commerce Department and the Census Bureau agreed to carry out a PES of at least 150,000 households and other tests to ensure the possibility of using the PES for adjustment.

3. The Commerce Department and the Census Bureau would develop, produce, and publish standards for adjustment by December 10, 1989.

4. If the decision was made to adjust the counts, the adjustment would be made no later than July 15, 1991.

5. All census data released or published before an adjustment decision had been made would carry a disclaimer saying that the results were subject to possible correction.

6. The secretary of commerce would appoint an independent eight-member panel of experts by September 30, 1989, to provide advice on adjustment-related activities.

In many ways, the settlement appeared to be a major step in the direction advocated by the proponents of adjustment. Advocates of adjustment recognized that if the census counts were adjusted, their impact would extend over the domain of all federally supported household surveys. Even if the decision in 1990 was ultimately one not to adjust, the stipulation agreement made it possible for the Census Bureau to continue its work on dual-systems estimation and to be prepared for an adjustment in 2000. More important, however, was the restoration of technical decision making to the professional staff of the Census Bureau. Although the settlement stipulated that the secretary of commerce retained authority over the Census Bureau and "the decision whether or not to adjust the 1990 decennial census," the terms of the settlement made clear that responsibility for technical statistical decisions resided with the bureau. The settlement strengthened the authority of the professional statisticians and career staff in the federal statistical system.

At the same time, it was clear that the settlement represented a serious compromise relative to the plan that the bureau would have implemented had its original plans been allowed to go forward. In pressing for a PES of reduced size, that is, 150,000 households rather than 300,000, Commerce Department officials forced the bureau to implement new smoothing methodology that would compensate for the increased uncertainty in the adjusted counts. Both the increased uncertainty and the new methodology would turn out to be flashpoints for the criticisms of the adjusted data after the results were in hand. Furthermore, the development of the official standards for evaluation of PES-based adjusted data was really left in the hands of the Commerce Department, which could attempt to place insurmountable obstacles in the path of the implementation of adjusted counts. Clearly, the specter of political intervention had not been eliminated from the technical statistical decision-making process.

Moving Toward the 1990 Count

A key aspect of the July settlement was the appointment of the special eight-member panel of experts by the secretary of commerce to provide advice on adjustment-related activities. The members of the panel were announced on September 30, 1990: Eugene Ericksen, of Temple University; Leo Estrada, of the University of California, Los Angeles; William Kruskal, of the University of Chicago; Michael McGehee, of McGehee and Associates; Lance Tarrance, of Tarrance and Associates; John Tukey, of Princeton University; Kenneth Wachter, of the University of California, Berkeley; and Kirk Wolter, of A. C. Nielsen. The panel was split ideologically, with four of the eight members aligned with each side of the lawsuit. Ericksen, Estrada, Tukey, and Wolter had been selected from a list of experts recommended to serve by the New York litigants; Kruskal, McGehee, Tarrance, and Wachter were drawn from Commerce Department solicitations. The two cochairs, Ericksen and Tarrance, could also be seen to reflect the two sides of the lawsuit. It would remain to be seen if the entire panel could function as a unified group.

The panel held its first meeting on October 30 and 31, 1989, in Washington, D.C., and a second meeting in Chicago on November 18. At these two meetings, the panel prepared a report on the proposed adjustment guidelines, scheduled for publication in the *Federal Register* by December 10. The preliminary version of the guidelines (see appendix C) set out standards by which the quality of the postenumeration survey was to be assessed as a means for adjusting the 1990 decennial census population counts. The guidelines left considerable discretion to the Commerce Department in judging the PES results as a basis for a possible adjustment. A final version of the guidelines was scheduled to be published in the *Federal Register* by March 10, 1990, following a ninety-day period for comments.

In October 1989, at the same time that the special panel was beginning its work, President George Bush officially nominated Barbara Bryant, senior vice president of Market Opinion Research, as the next director of the Census Bureau. The position of director had been vacant since John Keane resigned in December 1988, although Bryant had been serving as a consultant to the bureau since late summer, and her proposed nomination had been well received. Nevertheless, with the census only months away, Senate confirmation hearings on Bryant's appointment still had not yet been held.

At the same time, the Census Bureau moved ahead with plans for the census and the PES. Howard Hogan, head of the Undercount Research Staff, and his staff were transferred from the Statistical Research Division to report to Associate Director Charles Jones, the official responsible for the decennial count. The Undercount Research Staff released preliminary results from the census dress rehearsal in St. Louis, Missouri, and the state of Washington that suggested the possibility of a larger overall undercount and a larger differential undercount in 1990 than had occurred in 1980. The other notable results of the dress rehearsal were the high response rate for the PES, 96 percent with another 3 percent or more from proxy interviews, and the relatively low error rates of the matching procedures, which linked records from the PES with records from the census.

In a second major development in the plans for the PES, the Census Bureau decided to drop the vacant/delete check procedure from the census process. In 1970, this check was done on a sample basis, but in 1980 the bureau had decided to do a 100 percent check. The problem with the check was that it produced a large number of duplications in the overall counts. Some experts argued that the vacant/delete check should be done on a sample basis in 1990 as part of the PES, but the bureau rejected that suggestion. What the net impact of this change would be on the census results was not completely clear, although some experts believed that it might increase the undercount. But this decision was to have a major impact on the timing of the PES, which could now go into the field in June 1990, approximately four to six weeks ahead of the original schedule. This change would allow more time to evaluate the quality of PES-adjusted counts before a decision had to be made on whether to adjust.

The work of the special panel, the imminent appointment of a Census Bureau director, and the operational changes in the census process boded well for the census and the new PES process. But the controversies surrounding the upcoming count still swirled behind the scenes. At the October 1989 meeting of the Committee on National Statistics (CNSTAT), Mark Plant, deputy under secretary for economic affairs at the Commerce Department, announced that the department was relying on its recently appointed panel to provide advice on adjustment and that it would not provide support to any other panel to review these issues. The event was described in *Numbers News* as follows: "You could have heard a pin drop . . . as . . . Mark Plant told the group that the department appreciated its interest in the 1990 census, and would be pleased to hear any recommendations its panel might have for improving the 2000 census. However, Plant said, 'It would be inappropriate for the department to continue to fund the panel's consideration of the adjustment issue'" (*Numbers News* 1989, 5). The CNSTAT panel included several members, notably Stephen Fienberg, who had been deposed and slated as possible witnesses to testify for the New York litigants on the feasibility of adjustment. The Commerce Department, already required to receive the advice of one advisory panel, was not about to complicate the decision-making process by supporting another.

CNSTAT statisticians, however, did not see the matter that way. The announcement was met with considerable concern among statisticians present, because it had the effect of cutting off CNSTAT's own Panel on Decennial Census Methodology, which had been studying the issue of adjustment since early in 1984. The panel had expected to resume activities where it had left off just before the filing of the New York City lawsuit. In the panel's view, the decision of the Commerce Department to withhold funding for these activities led to the disbanding of one of the most visible and independent sources of advice on census adjustment and coverage evaluation. There remained, they told Plant, no other major channel of input into census decision making, and they urged the department not to lose the many years of accumulated knowledge regarding census procedures. The department action, they warned, threatened to undermine the openness of the adjustment process to input from the professional statistical community.

At the October 17, 1989, oversight hearing of the House Subcommittee on Population and Census, the prognosis was still guarded on whether the 1990 census would avoid further controversy. Mark Plant, attorneys representing the plaintiffs in the lawsuit, and Daniel Melnick, of the Congressional Research Service, testified. There were few surprises in the testimony, but observers came away with the impression that New York City and the other plaintiffs would continue to observe the implementation of the settlement agreement very closely and would not hesitate to return to court if the Commerce Department did not adhere to the settlement terms. The subcommittee planned further hearings on the lawsuit agreement and on the guidelines for adjustment.

As the year ended and Congress went home on recess without holding confirmation hearings, President Bush made a recess appointment of Barbara Bryant as census director. Bryant recalled the events with some humor, noting that while waiting for confirmation that fall, she "fretted" that, with "the clock ticking" and "census troops getting mighty anxious," the bureau would "start the census without me." She also noted the date of the appointment: December 7, 1989, was the "48th anniversary of the Japanese attack on Pearl Harbor" (Bryant and Dunn 1995, 55).

The Census Process Goes into High Gear

The opening months of 1990 marked the full-scale mobilization of the field portion of the census. District offices opened in 1989 and began hiring the hundreds of thousands of workers who would take the census. Public service advertising campaigns went into high gear. Final address checking went on with local government review, special place prelisting, and a final post office check of addresses.

Meanwhile, comment poured in to the Commerce Department on the preliminary version of the adjustment guidelines. The preliminary guidelines had engendered considerable public discussion and were not well received by the statistical community or the New York litigants. Typical of the comments submitted by statisticians was that of Morris H. Hansen of Westat, Inc., a former associate director of the Census Bureau:

> I am especially concerned over the fact that the proposed guidelines appear to reflect a pre-determination by the Department of Commerce that an adjustment will be disadvantageous and will not be made. . . .
>
> [The explanation to one of the proposed guidelines ignores] the fact that the methodology of the decennial census has been constantly improved over the past two hundred years, through experience and research. Presumably it can be further improved, perhaps by an adjustment. This statement reminds me of the statements of a former patent commissioner (. . . close to a century ago) that all useful inventions had been made and no additional worthwhile inventions can be expected. (Quoted in Fienberg 1990b, 32).

The plaintiffs in the New York City adjustment lawsuit also openly expressed concern about the implementation of the stipulation and order at a January 30 hearing before the House Subcommittee on Census and Population on the adjustment guidelines. Speaking on their behalf, Robert Rifkind, from the New York City law firm of Cravath Swaine and Moore, noted,

> Mr. Chairman, no good can come from these Guidelines. Any decision that was based upon them would clearly be invalid and, indeed,

unconstitutional. If the Department of Commerce presses this crown of thorns down upon the brow of the Bureau, it will do grave injury to the reputation and character [of] what has been a highly respected, non-partisan technical agency. And it will, I fear, shake the confidence of the public in the census, which has served for 200 years as the fundamental mechanism for the allocation of the political power in this nation. (Ibid., 33).

On March 15, 1990, the Commerce Department issued the final guidelines that the secretary would use for his decision on possible adjustment for undercount (see appendix D). The plaintiffs' concerns remained that the guidelines were biased against a full consideration of adjustment. The final guidelines, in turn, triggered a return to court by the plaintiffs to ask the court to set them aside and order their redrafting.

On March 20, the first major newsworthy event of the decennial season caught the eye of the media: Street and Shelter Night, or S-Night, the new procedure that dispatched almost twenty-three thousand enumerators to count the homeless. It was perhaps unfortunate that S-Night preceded the April 1 mail enumeration: by definition, a census is based on a count of people at their "usual place of abode," "at home," and the S-Night search highlighted the emergence in the 1980s of the troubling new problem of homelessness. Television news crews followed census enumerators trying to "find" the homeless in shelters or places where they might be sleeping. In Pittsburgh, for example, TV crews attempted to follow specially trained enumerators as they set out for areas under bridges and other selected locations. The S-Night program met open resistance from homeless groups in some cities; in others, there was considerable cooperation. In Los Angeles, officials claimed that nineteen known shelters were missed in the one-night blitz. The procedure was protested by a number of vocal advocates of the homeless, including Mitch Snyder, who dumped sand in front of the headquarters of the Commerce Department in Washington and placed signs in the sand proclaiming, "Counting the homeless is like counting grains of sand" (quoted in Bryant and Dunn 1995, 99). Snyder claimed a national homeless population of three million. S-Night counted slightly less than a quarter of a million people and was the subject of severe congressional scrutiny for the next year or more as well as commentary and editorial cartoons in the press (see figure 6.2).

Figure 6.2

Source: Rob Rogers, reprinted by permission of United Features Syndicate, Inc.

Early Returns Are Lower Than Expected

By late March, the full-scale mail-back enumeration process, which would cover 94.4 percent of the housing units in the country (U.S. Bureau of the Census, 1995b, 1–7), was under way. On approximately March 23, households all over the nation received 1990 census forms. Approximately 84 percent of the questionnaires were delivered by the U.S. Postal Service. For the 10 percent of the housing units where addresses were unavailable, enumerators delivered the form. All of these households were expected to return their forms by mail. The remaining 5.6 percent of households, primarily in sparsely settled remote or rural areas, were canvassed by enumerators who visited the housing unit. Households receiving mail forms were to complete and return them to the bureau by mail. As of April 13, only 57 percent of these forms had been returned, a substantial shortfall relative to the 70 percent return rate for which the bureau had been budgeting. Newspapers across the nation carried reports of various snafus in the mail-out/mail-back enterprise, including reports from areas that had received essentially no forms at all. Not only was the 13 percent shortfall in returned forms of considerable concern, but it is worth noting that the 70 percent target for 1990 was already much below the actual return rate of 78 percent for mail returns in 1980.

The *New York Times* reported on April 12 that, in New York City, "the return rate was 46.2 percent as of yesterday and the rate from a low of about 34 percent in north-central Brooklyn to a high of 55 percent in Staten Island." In Boston, "officials say they know the census will be inaccurate because the city records show more than 20,000 housing units that do not appear on the census's list" (*New York Times*, Apr. 12, 1990).

Observers in the media attributed a substantial part of the problem to the U.S. Postal Service. By early April, many households were still waiting for the delivery of their forms. Officials in Pittsburgh, for example, discovered a small pocket of the city for which as many as six thousand forms had not been delivered, and they had difficulty getting the Census Bureau to deal directly with the problem. Meanwhile, on the West Coast, the *New York Times* reported, "the Post Office in Los Angeles reports that more than 70,000 census forms could not be delivered because of incorrect addresses. . . . The return rate ranged from a low of 43 percent in the inner-city neighborhoods of south-central Los Angeles, to a high of 60 percent in the affluent West San Fernando Valley." The most notable case of nondelivery occurred in Ross, California, just north of San Francisco. "All 900 residents of the wealthy enclave use post office boxes. To date none of them have received census forms" (ibid.).

But the U.S. Postal Service could not be blamed for all the problems with the mailing of the census forms. The decade-long attempt to update computerized address lists did not work as efficiently as Census Bureau officials had expected. In mid-April, no one was prepared to apportion the blame.

At the time, it was difficult to know what the low mail-return rates meant for the overall accuracy of the census counts, but one thing was clear: poor return rates could make the undercount problem worse. And given the areas in which the mail-delivery problems tended to occur nationwide, the differential undercount, reflecting the larger undercount for various minority groups, was likely to be larger than in 1980. As the daily reports of returns came in, Census Bureau officials realized that the shortfall would be costly, as well. Officials knew that each percentage point of mail nonresponse cost the bureau $10 million for follow-up by enumerators.

On April 26, as the door-to-door phase of the census began, only 63 percent of the forms mailed out in March had been completed and returned. This was far below the expected rate of return of 70 percent that the Census Bureau had budgeted for, and the bureau found it necessary to request $190 million of additional funding from Congress to attempt to solve the problems caused by this shortfall (U.S. Bureau of the Census 1996a, ch. 11, 19). Extra enumerators were hired, and the deadline for the completion of the door-to-door canvas was extended from June 7 to June 30.

As the schedules came in, it became clear that the rate of return of the mail-out questionnaires was not uniform across the nation, with Boston logging in 48 percent, New York City 53.7 percent, Los Angeles 62.6 percent, and San Diego 66.2 percent. Because of differing availability of enumerators in different parts of the country, the Census Bureau made a decision to allow enumerators' salaries to reflect the local differences in prevailing wage rates. In New York City, where the eight-dollars-an-hour rate was already the highest in the nation, the rate was raised to ten dollars an hour in early June to help address the shortage of enumerators and the massive effort required to complete the New York enumeration on schedule. Early reports from the bureau indicated that the door-to-door count was also progressing more slowly than had been expected, but in late June the bureau was still counting according to the existing plans.

Newspapers reported on a variety of unusual census-taking events throughout the spring. For example, the New York Times (Apr. 11, 1990) ran a special story on the enumeration of the employees of the Ringling Brothers and Barnum and Bailey Circus, and the Pittsburgh Press (Apr. 29, 1990) carried a brief account of a census worker in Alton, Illinois, who was attacked and bitten on the shoulder by a woman who mistook her for a fund-raiser. Even Judge McLaughlin got into the act, as he noted in his ruling on the adjustment lawsuit that "shots rang out as census takers recently approached one building in Brooklyn, thereby aborting further attempts to count that building's occupants." It was also not clear whether the difficulties the bureau encountered would affect the quality of the data returned. Congressional budget cuts had led to cutbacks in some quality-control procedures. A careful and systematic check on completed forms is required to catch errors and erroneous enumerations. Would there be many examples like those reported in the New York Times (Apr. 15, 1990) of one returned form that "listed a family member's name as Puss E. Cat and his race as Siamese"?

New York Litigants Return to Court

It was in the context of the Census Bureau's troubles in the enumeration phase of the census that the New York litigants returned to court to challenge the March 15 Commerce Department guidelines and to ask for a declaratory judgment in the suit. Their objections to the guidelines were several:

1. The guidelines had no technical content and provided no rules for decision on the question of correction.

2. The guidelines were biased against correction.

3. In the guidelines, the Commerce Department took the outer limit for timeliness for a decision on adjustment, July 15, 1991, and took the position that it would publish adjusted data either on July 15, 1991, or not at all.

New York also alleged improper treatment of the eight-member Special Advisory Panel appointed by the secretary of commerce as part of the stipulation and order. In particular, the plaintiffs argued that some panel members claimed that the Commerce Department

1. had repeatedly delayed giving panel members access to information on the plans, schedules, and progress on adjustment and in some cases had denied access altogether;

2. had wrongfully diminished the panel's $500,000 fund by using it to pay for various expenses it had incurred; and

3. had made panel members sign an oath of confidentiality regarding any information they might acquire while serving as panel members.

On April 11, the New York plaintiffs filed a Notice of Motion in federal district court to rectify the claimed violations of the stipulation and order. The notice stated that the plaintiffs would move on or before April 26, 1990, for a declaratory judgment and a court order providing the following relief:

1. declaring the guidelines promulgated by the Commerce Department on March 15, 1990, null and void;

2. holding that statistical adjustment of the census to correct for the differential undercount did not violate the Constitution, nor sec-

tion 195 of Title 13 of the U.S. Code, and was required by the Constitution if necessary to increase the accuracy of the census;

3. ordering defendants to adjust the census, unless they set forth by June 1, 1990, a set of guidelines establishing standards and procedures for evaluating accuracy and demonstrating to the court, pursuant to those guidelines, that the original enumeration was more accurate, or that there was some other compelling reason not to adjust;

4. ordering defendants to restore to the budget of the Special Advisory Panel funds improperly withheld or purportedly expended and to cooperate fully and fairly with the panel, including responding within forty-eight hours to any request by a panel member or their staff for any existing document; and

5. declaring null and void the confidentiality oath imposed by defendants on panel members in so far as it exceeded the scope of section 9 of Title 13 of the U.S. Code.

This dispute over wording of the guidelines was far more than legal hairsplitting. The entire framing of the guidelines was the antithesis of that which the Census Bureau would have used for its evaluation in the absence of the Commerce Department's intervention in its activities. The bureau had made plans for special studies of eight sources of error in the PES, and a listing of these actually appeared deep down in the discussion of the technical grounds supporting guideline (1). The role of these evaluation studies, however, was distorted by the requirement that "the Census shall be considered the most accurate count of the population of the United States, at the national, state, and local level, unless an adjusted count is shown to be more accurate." Such language raised troubling questions in the minds of those who had followed the development of the PES-based methodology and understood how a statistical agency would normally have proceeded with the implementation and evaluation of a change in methodology. How could the bureau realistically respond to the presumption that the raw census enumeration counts were error free and were to be taken as a standard, coupled with the requirement that the proposed adjustment be shown to improve "convincingly" upon them at all levels of geography? Would the bureau or the Commerce Department formulate the "statistical tests" to determine if the adjusted counts met these requirements? Given past evidence of extensive error in the census, one could rationally argue that the choice between the two sets of counts should be based on a more even-handed technical assessment.

The Judge Rules, and Counting Continues

In May, a hearing was held in federal district court for the presentation of arguments on a motion filed by the City of New York and the other plaintiffs. Lawyers for the defendants (the Commerce Department and various administration officials) argued that all the claims of the plaintiffs were without merit, that the claims for a declaratory judgment and for a supplemental order were "not ripe for review," and that it was not proper for the court to entertain "such imagined grievances at this juncture." On June 7, Judge McLaughlin issued his ruling on the motion, supporting some of the plaintiffs' requests and denying others. On the matter of the guidelines published by the Commerce Department, which were to serve as the basis for the decision whether or not to make a statistical adjustment to the census enumeration results, he noted that they were the "bare minimum" required under the original stipulation and order and thus he denied the plaintiffs' request to have them set aside. He also observed that "because defendants have chosen to contribute adequate but minimal performance to satisfy their obligations at this stage, defendants clearly incur a heavier burden to explain why no adjustment was made in the event the Secretary [of Commerce] elects to proceed with an actual enumeration [without adjustment]." Furthermore, he warned the defendants that "intentional inaction will not be tolerated. Defendants are expected, and indeed required, to honor their solemn commitments embodied in the Stipulation. . . . [Defendants] are on notice, if it is not already clear, that backdoor attempts to evade their commitment will not be countenanced" (Fienberg 1990c).

On the matter of the constitutionality of adjustment, the judge held that the U.S. Constitution "is not a bar to statistical adjustment" and that "the concept of statistical adjustment is wholly valid, and may very well be long overdue. . . . That said, it does not follow that any and all forms of statistical adjustments will be sanctioned. . . . Whether it has been done legally and constitutionally can only be determined after the Secretary has decided how he wishes to adjust, if at all."

In another part of the thirty-one-page opinion, the judge found that the defendants had improperly depleted a fund of $500,000, which had been created as part of the court's order for the use of the

Special Advisory Panel of experts advising the secretary on undercount correction. Judge McLaughlin noted: "Even by the government's own estimates rendered in February of this year, more than $340,000 has been siphoned from the fund." Finally, the judge's opinion did not comment on the confidentiality oath that the panel members had been required to take.

Between late April and early May 1990, for the households that had received questionnaires in the mail, the field portion of the census shifted gears to a house-to-house enumeration to retrieve information on the households that had not responded (as in figure 6.3). This phase of the counting process, termed nonresponse follow-up, or NRFU, encompassed all the addresses from which, by April 22, questionnaires had not been returned. The district offices dispatched enumerators to all the housing units that had not returned questionnaires to that point, instructing them to get population information from the household or find out if the housing unit was vacant. Enumerators were to make up to six contacts by personal visit or phone contact to confirm information. Ultimately, two hundred thousand people worked on the NRFU operation to count more than thirty-four

Figure 6.3

Source: Tony Auth, copyright 1990, *The Philadelphia Inquirer.* Reprinted with permission from the Universal Press Syndicate. All rights reserved.

million housing units by the end of July 1990 (U.S. Bureau of the Census 1993a, 6–36).

The remaining field portion of the traditional census included "field follow-up" procedures designed to check questionnaires with inconsistent or missing data and a series of special procedures designed to count hard-to-count groups. These included people who lived in "special places," such as institutions, military bases and vessels, and transient housing. And they conducted a Were You Counted? advertising campaign over the summer of 1990 to encourage individuals who believed they had been missed to contact a census office. This provision added 200,000 people to the final 1990 count. Finally, probably the most controversial counting procedure in 1990 was in response to lobbying from its minority advisory committees. The bureau instituted a program to solicit lists of parolees and probationers from state officials; enumerators then used these administrative records to obtain population and address information from local departments of correction and probation and parole officers. The information was recorded on a special form and matched against existing census questionnaires. The 1.4 million forms processed added 400,000 people to the census count (ibid., 6–55; Choldin 1994, 200–202).

The PES Begins

By the summer of 1990, as the enumeration phase of the U.S. 1990 decennial census was approaching completion, the PES began. Starting on June 25, 1990, enumerators contacted "nearly 172,000 housing units in 5,290 sample block clusters, or 7,500 blocks" to capture population information about the household as of April 1, 1990 (U.S. Bureau of the Census 1996a, 11–19). The responses to the enumerators became the cases of the P-sample, which would then be matched with the results of the decennial census for the same blocks (the E-sample). As we discussed in chapter 4, analysis of the two data sources together would permit the construction of a set of dual-systems estimators of the proportion of people missed in the April count.

Although the PES was the largest single survey distinct from the census itself in the history of the bureau, the seventy-five hundred blocks recanvassed were still, of course, a small fraction of the seven million blocks in the nation. Hence, the technical details of the execution of the survey, including the sample design and the field procedures, were subject to detailed scrutiny within the bureau, by the special panel appointed after the stipulation agreement, and by statisticians and survey researchers outside the bureau. Any slip in the PES procedures could jeopardize the quality of the dual-systems estimates and their potential use for adjustment. The original bureau plans for the 1990 PES recognized the level of precision required for the survey and had, in 1987, proposed a sample size of 300,000 housing units. That sample design was halved by the 1989 stipulation agreement, and the reduction put even greater pressure on the precision built into other phases of the survey. Even as the survey began, some observers expected the level of nonresponse in the PES to be a major factor in evaluating its usefulness for census adjustment. If the high levels of nonresponse that appeared to have plagued the census itself over the previous months carried over into the PES, then the validity of the PES as the instrument for adjustment would be in question.

Officials in the bureau had drawn the P-sample in the months before the count. The sample was designed to be representative of the national population and to provide enough cases to effectively measure undercount for each of 116 poststrata groups, or smaller samples, which officials thought would display different patterns of undercount. As we noted in chapters 3 and 4, because census officials already knew that undercount rates differed for groups of people by region, size of place, housing tenure, racial background, age, and sex, they intended to calculate separate dual-systems estimates for each subgroup and then aggregate these separate estimates back to a national estimate. They began with four census regions, nine census divisions, seven categories for the size of place (central city, metro area, rural area, and so on), four race categories (Black, non-Black Hispanic, Asian and Pacific Islander, non-Hispanic White and other), and two housing tenure categories (owner and nonowner). Many of these subgroups would not have individuals fitting the classification—that is, they would have empty cells—so the officials collapsed the number of poststrata groups to 116. Officials intended to calculate undercount rates for six age cohorts for males and females for each of the 116 poststrata groups, or for 1,392 undercount estimates in all. If response was good and the survey performed properly, the overall sample would provide the data to model the undercount successfully.

The field portion of the P-sample was basically completed by the end of July. The last cases came in early in September. Computer matching to the E-sample census records took place in August and September, with "about 80 percent of the P-sample persons" matched "to their corresponding original enumeration" (Ericksen, quoted in Choldin 1994, 212). The remaining cases had to be checked again to see if they could be matched to the E-sample or whether they represented individuals who had not been counted in the April enumeration. Furthermore, individuals in the April E-sample who were not matched in the P-sample had to be checked to see if they were missed in the P-sample or had been erroneously enumerated in April. Before the dual-systems estimators could be calculated, the officials had to assign a "matched," "not matched," or "match status unknown" to every person whose match status was ambiguous. Clarifying these cases took until December 1990. Bureau officials and outside observers were generally pleased with the performance of the survey up to this point and were especially encouraged that they had successfully avoided the matching problems that had plagued the 1980 PES.

As the PES was completed in the field and matching proceeded, the bureau reported the preliminary population counts from the April enumeration to state and local governments. As part of the second phase of the local review process, the thirty-nine thousand local jurisdictions had several weeks to challenge the counts and attempt to resolve the problems. The preliminary figures showed an April 1990 count of 243.2 million, substantially below the estimates the bureau had anticipated (see table 6.1).[1] New York City's preliminary count, for example, was 7,033,179, or 4.3 percent below the predicted count. Not surprisingly, local government officials used the counts to challenge the quality of the April enumeration and question whether the low mail-return rates were at fault.

Counting and data processing of the April enumeration continued through the fall, as the coverage improvement and checking procedures added people to the preliminary counts. On December 26, 1990, the day after Christmas, Census Director Barbara Bryant reported the official 1990 census count of 249,632,692 (official residential count of 248,709,873 for fifty states and the District of Columbia, plus 922,819 federal employees overseas), up 9.8 percent from 1980. Commerce Secretary Mosbacher reported the figure to President Bush, who formally transmitted the tabulations by state and the proposed congressional reapportionment to Congress on January 3, 1991 (New York Times, Dec. 27, 1990; Choldin 1994, 203; Bryant and Dunn 1995, 142–43). The 1990 census led to the reapportionment of nineteen seats in the House of Representatives (see appendix G for full details). Arizona, Georgia, North Carolina, Virginia, and Washington each gained a seat. Texas gained three, Florida four, California seven, Iowa,

Kansas, Kentucky, Louisiana, Massachusetts, Montana, New Jersey, and West Virginia each lost one seat; Illinois, Michigan, Ohio, and Pennsylvania lost two seats each, and New York lost three. Eight states gained from the 1990 reapportionment; thirteen states lost. The average size of a congressional district rose to 574,000 people as a result of the 1990 census. The smallest district in the nation was in Wyoming, where one congressional district encompassed 454,000 people. The lone representative in nearby Montana, which would lose one of its two congressional districts after reapportionment, represented a population of 800,000.

The Census Bureau reported block-level data for apportionment for the seven million census blocks in the nation, as required by PL 94-171, between January and March 1991. All these data carried the qualifying statement from the 1989 stipulation agreement that the "population counts set forth herein are subject to possible correction for undercount or overcount. The United States Department of Commerce is considering whether to correct these counts and will publish corrected counts, if any, not later than July 15, 1991."

Producing and Evaluating the Dual-Systems Estimates

For the first four months of 1991, Census Bureau statisticians worked on the measurement of the undercount. Results from the demographic analysis of the 1990 population were available first. They showed an undercount of 1.8 percent, up from 1.2 percent in 1980, and a continuation of the national differential undercount by race. The bureau documented its estimates of the extent of the undercount by age, race, and sex. As we saw in chapter 4, from 1940 through 1980 these estimates showed improved overall accuracy of the census in terms of its national coverage, but the difference in the rate of undercount for Blacks and non-Blacks had remained roughly constant, somewhere between 5 and 6 percent. The top panel of table 6.2 gives the figures from table 4.1 updated to include the 1990 results.

There are various versions of the demographic analysis estimates. The estimates at the top of table 6.2 are the "traditional" ones, based on the demographic analysis methods in use through 1980. But in 1990, Census Bureau demographers implemented a key change. As Robinson et al. (1993) note, the consistency in classification of births by race is of critical importance in making comparisons between the demographic analysis estimates and the census results. In 1990, the

Table 6.1   Preliminary Census Counts by State
(Including the District of Columbia and Puerto Rico)

State	Preliminary 1990 Count	1990 Estimate	Percentage Difference
Alabama	3,984,000	4,174,000	−4.6
Alaska	546,000	525,000	+4.0
Arizona	3,619,000	3,673,000	−1.5
Arkansas	2,337,395	2,427,000	−3.7
California	29,279,000	29,313,000	−0.1
Colorado	3,272,000	3,350,000	−2.3
Connecticut	3,226,929	3,271,000	−1.3
Delaware	658,031	679,000	−3.2
District of Columbia	575,000	605,000	−5.0
Florida	12,775,000	12,878,000	−0.8
Georgia	6,387,000	6,594,000	−3.1
Hawaii	1,095,000	1,132,000	−3.3
Idaho	1,003,558	1,012,000	−0.8
Illinois	11,325,000	11,650,000	−2.8
Indiana	5,499,000	5,613,000	−2.0
Iowa	2,766,658	2,808,000	−1.5
Kansas	2,467,000	2,521,000	−2.1
Kentucky	3,665,220	3,745,000	−2.1
Louisiana	4,180,831	4,379,000	−4.5
Maine	1,218,053	1,234,000	−1.3
Maryland	4,733,000	4,760,000	−0.6
Massachusetts	5,928,000	5,903,000	+0.4
Michigan	9,179,661	9,328,000	−1.6
Minnesota	4,358,864	4,371,000	−0.3
Mississippi	2,534,814	2,652,000	−4.4
Missouri	5,079,285	5,159,000	−1.6
Montana	794,329	796,000	−0.2
Nebraska	1,572,503	1,601,000	−1.8
Nevada	1,193,000	1,122,000	+6.3
New Hampshire	1,103,163	1,143,000	−3.5
New Jersey	7,617,418	7,820,000	−2.6
New Mexico	1,490,381	1,545,000	−3.5
New York	17,626,586	17,950,000	−1.8
North Carolina	6,553,000	6,670,000	−1.8
North Dakota	634,223	657,000	−3.5
Ohio	10,778,000	10,909,000	−1.2

Table 6.1 *Continued*

State	Preliminary 1990 Count	1990 Estimate	Percentage Difference
Oklahoma	3,124,000	3,025,000	+0.2
Oregon	2,828,214	2,822,000	+0.2
Pennsylvania	11,764,000	12,040,000	−2.3
Puerto Rico	3,599,258	3,291,000	+9.3
Rhode Island	988,609	1,003,000	−1.4
South Carolina	3,407,000	3,558,000	−4.2
South Dakota	693,294	715,000	−3.0
Tennessee	4,822,134	5,012,000	−3.8
Texas	16,825,000	17,565,000	−4.2
Utah	1,711,117	1,736,000	−1.4
Vermont	560,029	569,000	−1.6
Virginia	6,128,000	6,214,000	−1.4
Washington	4,827,000	4,796,000	+0.6
West Virginia	1,782,958	1,847,000	−3.5
Wisconsin	4,869,640	4,886,000	−0.3
Wyoming	449,905	468,000	−3.9

Source: Data from Fienberg 1990c, 34, from the *New York Times* and the U.S. Bureau of the Census.

National Center for Health Statistics altered its practice of assigning race to newborns whose parents were of mixed race in a way that used the race of the father unless the father was White and moved implicitly to a "mother" rule by not making any such assignments and, instead, simply tabulating statistics using the race of the mother. As a result, bureau demographers calculated a revised set of figures for 1990 and previous censuses reflecting this new classification approach. Because of the rise of intermarriage and the preponderance of Black males in such partnerships, these revisions substantially lower the estimate of the differential undercount. It is difficult to know which set of estimates is most reasonable. Furthermore, before demographic estimates can be compared with census data further "modifications" are required (see Robinson et al. 1993; and especially the discussion in Passel 1993).

Finally, we note that the 1990 figures include an estimate of undocumented immigrants on the order of five million, based on data on the foreign-born population obtained from censuses and supplements to the CPS. This number is subject to considerable uncertainty but

Table 6.2   Estimated Net Census Undercount from 1940 to 1990, as Measured by Demographic Analysis (Percentage)

	Year	Black	Non-Black	Differ-ence	Overall Net Undercount
Original estimates					
	1940	10.3	5.1	5.2	5.6
	1950	9.6	3.8	5.8	4.4
	1960	8.3	2.7	5.6	3.3
	1970	8.0	2.2	5.8	2.9
	1980[a]	5.9	0.7	5.2	1.4
	1990[b]	7.4	1.0	6.4	1.9
1990 revised estimates[c]					
	1940	8.4	5.0	3.4	5.4
	1950	7.5	3.8	3.8	4.1
	1960	6.6	2.7	3.9	3.1
	1970	6.5	2.2	4.3	2.7
	1980	4.5	0.8	3.7	1.2
	1990	5.7	1.3	4.4	1.8

Source: Data from Fay et al. 1988; U.S. Bureau of the Census 1991; Robinson et al. 1993.

[a]The figures for 1980 are based on the assumption that three million aliens were living in the United States at the time of the census.

[b]Preliminary calculation using same methodology as in 1980.

[c]Revised to reflect 1990 change in methodology in the classification of mixed-race births.

was up approximately two million from the comparable estimate for 1980.

In 1990, the Census Bureau also reported the undercount on the Hispanic population based on data from demographic analysis, but the data here are spotty, with uneven collection across states. The demographic documentation of the Hispanic population over time is severely limited by comparison with that for Blacks.

At first glance, the 1.8 percent net undercount figure appeared comforting to those who worried over the quality of the 1990 count, but what it did not mean was that the census correctly counted more than 98 percent of the U.S. population. Rather, 1.8 percent represented the net undercount, that is, the difference between the actual undercount (consisting of missed individuals or omissions) and the overcount (erroneous enumerations and duplications). As we noted earlier, careful observers knew that the 1980 undercount of 1.2 percent translated into an overall error rate of 7 percent. The increase in the net undercount hinted that it might be reasonable to expect that the percentage of people correctly counted was closer to 90 percent for the 1990 count (corresponding to a gross error of about 10 percent). Furthermore, the differential undercount between Blacks and non-Blacks and between Hispanics and non-Hispanics has been considered an important yardstick for the assessment of census accuracy and is a sensitive issue, as well, because allocations of political and budgetary resources to each of these groups are based on the population of each group as recorded by the census count. The 1990 differential undercount for Blacks was measured at 6.4 percent or 4.4 percent, depending on the methodology used, and this appeared to be the largest differential undercount since the Census Bureau began to measure it back in 1940.

In other words, the results of the demographic analysis confirmed what many already knew: it was becoming increasingly difficult for the Census Bureau to get the job done. There were increasing levels of distrust among the very same groups that seemed to be the hardest to count. And there had been an overall decline in the rate of survey response over the past decade, the causes of which may have had a significant impact on cooperation rates for the 1990 census. In this context, it was remarkable that the Census Bureau appeared to have succeeded in gathering accurate information on about 90 percent of the population of the nation. The problem was that the errors for the remaining 10 percent were not distributed evenly over population groups.

Following the release of the demographic analysis estimates, bureau demographers set to work on eleven demographic analysis evaluation projects (referred to as the D-studies, for demographic), each of which yielded an evaluation report. We provide a list of these reports in appendix E. These D-studies were intended to provide the first comprehensive evaluation of the individual components of the methodology (for example, births, undocumented residents, emigrants, Medicare data, inconsistency in racial classifications). Demographic Evaluation Project Report D11 drew the information on uncertainty together in the form of a total error model. A careful reading of these D-studies highlights the level of uncertainty and lack of statistical rigor in the formulation of interval bounds on the demographic analysis estimates. As we noted in chapter 4, the errors and uncertainties associated with undocumented immigrants and shifting racial identification combined with increasing intermarriage make the demographic analysis numbers increasingly problematic, except as a broad coverage evaluation tool.

As the results of the demographic analysis emerged, the staff on the Undercount Steering Committee continued their work to prepare the dual-systems estimates. These estimates could confirm the results of the demographic analysis and allocate the undercount to smaller units of geography. The work involved the preparation of what came to be called the production estimates for the 1,392 individual post-strata, checking the data for anomalies and problems, and then calculating the total adjusted population. This final step involved multiplying the undercount estimate factors by the census counts for each of the 1,392 poststrata in each of the seven million blocks in the census and then reaggregating these counts for the total adjusted population.

In late winter, as Census Bureau statisticians were analyzing the PES counts, the implications of the forced reduction in size of the PES, from 300,000 households to 165,000, were becoming clearer. The raw adjustment factors for the 1,392 poststrata were more variable than was originally anticipated, as were the variances of these estimated factors. As a consequence, bureau statisticians decided to insert a step into the estimation process involving "presmoothing" of variance estimates. This presmoothing used a second simple regression model before using these variances in the regression model of equation (5.5) of chapter 5. Presmoothing reduced the variability and seemed to produce "better" estimates at the poststratum level. When the results were applied to the nation as a whole, this step had the the effect of adding substantially to the net national undercount. This alteration to the pre-announced production process for PES data became another rallying point for the critics of adjustment. The alternative to presmoothing would have been to change the postratification scheme by reducing the number of poststrata and eliminating what turned out to be very small ones. Although the bureau was to examine this alternative after the decison making was complete, to do so in the spring of 1991 would have run counter to the bureau's public commitment to the prespecification of procedures.

On April 18, 1991, the Census Bureau released preliminary results from the PES and reported an overall undercount of 2.1 percent in 1990, confirming the earlier reports from the demographic estimates of a significant differential undercount affecting Blacks and Hispanics. We give the final version of these results detailing the net undercount by population group appears in table 6.3. The PES data and detailed information on adjusted counts were subject to scrutiny by bureau

Table 6.3 Estimated Census Undercount for 1990 as Measured
by the Postenumeration Survey (Percentage)

Group	Undercount	Differential Minority Undercount
Non-Black	1.7	
Black	4.8	3.1
Hispanic	5.2	3.4
Asian	3.1	1.0
American Indian	5.0	2.9

Source: U.S. Bureau of the Census 1991.

statisticians and members of the Special Secretarial Advisory Panel, as
well as a number of consultants. Their reports were due at the bureau
in mid-June, giving bureau staff and the Commerce Department exactly a month to reach a final decision.

The Census Bureau's internal evaluation of the PES results came
in the form of a set of P-studies (P for PES). We provide a list of these
reports in appendix E, following the listing of the D-study reports.
Most of these reports were designed to measure the previously identified principal sources of error in the PES, in part through results from
a PES follow-up, which took place in October and November 1990
and which attempted to resolve discrepancies between the census and
the PES. Others, such as report P13, explored some demographic-
based alternatives to the usual dual-systems estimator to account for
correlation bias. This report also explored the occurrence of negative
values in the 2×2 tables used for adjustment of PES poststrata (recall
the discussion associated with equation 5.4 in chapter 5). As it turned
out, 37 percent of the PES non-Black 2×2 tables and 26 percent of the
Black 2×2 tables in 1990 had such negative values. (For an extensive
discussion of this phenomenon in 1990, see also Bell 1993.) The extent of occurrence of such negative 2×2 table entries and downward
adjustments in the 1990 data surprised many and later became a focal
point for both technical criticism and public ridicule.

A final two-part report, P16, attempted to pull together all the
known and contemplated sources of error into a "total error" model,
based on methodology developed by Mary Mulry and Bruce Spencer
(1991) to evaluate the 1988 dress rehearsal results. In implementing
the total error model, bureau statisticians assessed the bias and added
uncertainty associated with each source of error, as well as covariation

between them. Although most of the final PES evaluation P-studies were dated July 1991, drafts of all of them were circulated to others at the Census Bureau and to members of the Special Secretarial Advisory Panel, and they played critical roles in the expert evaluation of the PES results. Thus, while other criticisms of the PES adjustment process surfaced after the bureau's decision-making process was complete, there was a reasonable assessment of the extent of most of the errors in PES well in advance of decision-making deadlines. In fact, the extent to which the critics of adjustment rely upon results of the bureau's P-studies is remarkable.

As the results of the PES became public, reaction split in line with the preexisting positions on the overall advisability of adjustment (as suggested in figure 6.4). Bureau officials quietly took satisfaction in the fact that they had produced credible PES results in the pressure-cooker time frame between the summer of 1990 and the spring of 1991. What had been beyond the realm of possibility in 1970 and 1980 was now a reality. Statisticians outside the Census Bureau who had been urging an adjustment cheered the results and began to lobby intensely for adjustment. But those who were dubious about the merits of dual-systems estimations techniques were not so sanguine about the

Figure 6.4

Source: Pat Oliphant, copyright 1991, Universal Press Syndicate. Reprinted with permission. All rights reserved.

PES results and began to raise objections to the quality and the overall capacity of this method to provide credible estimates of adjusted 1990 counts at the state and local levels. To add pressure to the debate, everyone recognized that an adjustment of the counts released in December 1990 would have an effect on congressional apportionment. Two more seats would switch if Secretary Mosbacher recommended adjustment of the 1990 count: Pennsylvania would lose a third House seat, and Wisconsin would lose one of its nine House seats. California would receive one of those seats, the second would go to Arizona. Ironically, perhaps, congressional districts for New York, which had brought the undercount lawsuit, would not be affected by an adjustment.

In June, the Special Secretarial Advisory Panel split four to four on their adjustment recommendations, with the experts drawn from the plaintiffs' list recommending adjustment and the government's experts opposing it. On June 21, the internal Census Bureau Undercount Steering Committee, which reviewed the final evidence from PES evaluation studies, voted seven to two in favor of adjustment. The two who opposed a recommendation to adjust did so "because they believe[d] that reasonably complete analyses of results ha[d] yet to be done." These two census statisticians said, however, that they did support the use of adjusted data for intercensal population estimates. Bureau Director Barbara Bryant supported the majority recommendation to adjust and forwarded it with her blessing to the Commerce Department. Later, she was quoted as saying that she believed an adjustment was warranted because it would improve the counts for a majority of states and for the places where the majority of the nation's population lives.

The Secretary's Decision

Even before the Commerce Department announced its decision, allegations of political interference were in the air. On the morning of July 15, 1991, the *New York Times* carried a story of calls made from the White House staff to members of the Special Secretarial Advisory Panel.

At 2:30 P.M. on July 15, 1991, Secretary of Commerce Robert A. Mosbacher ascended the stage of the Commerce Department auditorium with several staff members and stepped forward to the microphone. "After a thorough review," he announced, "I find the evidence in support of adjustment to be inconclusive and unconvincing. Therefore, I have decided that the 1990 census counts should not be changed by a statistical adjustment." Although Mosbacher's decision had been widely expected, according to the *New York Times,* it was immediately criticized as groundless and politically motivated. Mayor David Dinkins of New York City referred to it as "nothing less than statistical grand larceny" (*New York Times,* July 16, 1991). And Mosbacher's reception the next day in a pair of congressional hearings brought forth critical remarks from many of those who had been closest to the issue on Capitol Hill.

The Commerce Department decision not to adjust was accompanied by five thick volumes of supporting materials and analyses (weighing in at an estimated fifteen pounds), which immediately became the hottest item in Washington for census adjustment aficionados. These detailed materials attempted to marshal a strong case against adjustment, and they focused on arguments that built on and went beyond those found in the reports by the various statistical experts. Clearly the product of a major review within the Commerce Department, all of this documentation did not take place at the final moment. Rumors quickly circulated about which statisticians from the Census Bureau had actually written the attack on their bureau colleagues at the behest of the Commerce Department.

The secretary's report made a special point of emphasizing that the capture-recapture methods appropriate for fish and animal populations required special justification for use with human populations, ignoring to a considerable extent the extensive literature on the topic extending back over forty years. And for the more media conscious, the secretary took note of what had come to be called the "wily trout" problem, the inability of even the greatest fisherman (or census official) to catch (or count) those who would not be netted. The government (fishermen) could not be faulted for failing to do the impossible: counting the uncountable. Better to stick with the tried and true methods of the traditional enumeration rather than threaten the foundations of the republic with untried and potentially disruptive methods.

Ironically, perhaps, given his decision, Mr. Mosbacher did say that adjusted data would be used for intercensal estimates. This represented for many a way of allowing the proverbial camel's nose of adjustment methodology to slip in under the census tent and blunt the negative reaction from proponents of adjustment.

The Aftermath of the Decision

As the decision making was in its final stages, the New York plaintiffs recognized that Mosbacher would probably rule against adjustment. Thus, on July 1, they filed a motion in the lawsuit for an order permitting additional discovery in the event that the Commerce Department announced a decision against statistical correction. On July 11, the government responded, thus signaling that they, too, recognized that the undercount lawsuit would go to trial. Shortly after the July 15 decision, Judge Joseph McLaughlin set a trial date early in November and ordered expedited discovery.

As the census and its controversies faded from the memory of the general public, census officials and stakeholders in the count began to take stock of the 1990 count and its disputes. The count had faced major problems during the enumeration phase that most likely led to errors of various sorts in the enumeration. The differential undercount for Blacks and other minority groups appeared to have grown. The method of adjustment based on the use of a postenumeration survey offered what many statisticians believed to be a defensible approach to correcting the census counts. The adjustments proposed from the PES results (see Hogan 1993, 1052) added 5.27 million people to the resident population. Of the increase, 1.5 million people (29 percent) were Black, 1.2 million (23 percent) were Hispanic, 231,000 (4 percent) were Asian or Pacific Islander, and 99,000 (1.9 percent) were American Indian. In other words, more than half of the net undercounted population was minority, though only about a quarter of the population was Black, Hispanic, American Indian, or Asian or Pacific Islander. The panel of eight experts appointed to advise the secretary of commerce split on the issue of the usefulness of the PES methodology and the quality of it in practice in 1990. The secretary argued that the method was not defensible, especially for small areas. These questions would next be taken up in the courts.

Chapter 7

Out of the Limelight and into the Courtroom

Interest on the part of the general public in the intricacies of the census-taking process and even the decennial results tends to fade rather quickly after the census year. Among census stakeholders, interest remained high through the July 15, 1991, Commerce Department decision, because a decision to adjust would have led to revisions of all the data that were pouring out of the Census Bureau. With that possibility ended, most users returned to the data at hand, and the 1990 controversies began to pass into a haze of memory. For officials at the bureau, however, and the stakeholders in the undercount lawsuit, the decision merely framed the controversy to come. The New York plaintiffs claimed that Secretary Mosbacher had been wrong, and the census director and statistical experts in the bureau had been right, about adjustment. The legal evaluation of that decision would take another five years to play out. For the rest of 1991 and the first half of 1992, the New York lawsuit wound its way through pretrial depositions and motions. A thirteen-day district court trial took place in May 1992. Judge McLaughlin issued his decision in favor of the commerce secretary in April 1993. The plaintiffs appealed, and there was a hearing at the appellate level and then an appeals court decision to reverse the district court and remand the case in August 1994. The government appealed the circuit court decision to the Supreme Court, which held a hearing in January 1996 and issued a decision in March 1996 to let the district court decision stand. By the time the Supreme Court ruled in March 1996, plans for the 2000 census were well developed. The Commerce Department had become an agency in a Democratic administration, while the majority in Congress had turned Republican.

By that point, the controversies surrounding the 1990 count might have seemed rather remote, but their technical, legal, and political implications would play a major role in the emerging shape of things for 2000.

Pretrial Discovery

The New York plaintiffs were not surprised by the announcement of Secretary of Commerce Robert A. Mosbacher that the results of the 1990 census would not be adjusted to correct for what he acknowledged as an undercount of approximately five million people. Hence, they expected that the primary focus of attention in the controversy over correction of the 1990 census results would shift from Washington back to New York City and the courtroom of Judge Joseph M. McLaughlin. McLaughlin had presided over the original 1989 stipulation and order regarding the Census Bureau approach to adjustment and the 1990 enumeration. Although this stipulation agreement was not a formal decision against the Commerce Department position on the PES, it did support the original position of the Undercount Steering Committee statisticians within the bureau, and it did reinstate the PES as part of the decennial census methodology. Because the judge had facilitated the reinstatement of the PES into the decennial census plan, the plaintiffs now hoped that the court would see a parallel process occurring in the Commerce decision not to adjust. The secretary, in this view, had again disregarded the expert advice of the Undercount Steering Committee and the director of the bureau. The court should thus find the actions of the commerce secretary "arbitrary and capricious" and hence illegal under the Administrative Procedures Act. Such a decision would permit the court to order the secretary to adjust the decennial counts. As in 1989, the plaintiffs hoped to show that the best scientific advice of the bureau statisticians was disregarded by the political leadership of the Commerce Department.

The first indications of the federal government's position also became evident quite soon after the July adjustment decision. From the court's perspective, by the summer of 1991 the litigation was almost three years old. Judge McLaughlin set an early November trial date for the lawsuit brought in 1988 by the City of New York and other cities and states, and he ordered an expedited process of evidential discovery. The government appealed this order, arguing that depositions were unnecessary because the secretary had already provided the full basis for his decision in the five-volume report released at the time of his July 15 announcement. The federal government, in other words, was not interested in expediting a trial in the case, and they claimed that no trial was necessary at all. Rather, Justice Department attorneys argued, because the case involved merely a determination of whether the secretary's decision was arbitrary and capricious under the guidelines set by the Administrative Procedures Act, the court should simply rule on the administrative record alone. That record, they continued, was provided in full at the time of the secretary's July 15, 1991, decision. The plaintiffs countered by noting that the federal government's position put the cart before the horse. It was precisely the nature of the administrative record that was at issue in the case, a record, they argued, that was self-serving, inaccurate, and incomplete. Only a trial would make it possible for the judge to make a decision on the record. By late summer, therefore, the strategies that would frame the positions of the plaintiffs and defendants were evident in the legal maneuvering in preparation for the trial on the census lawsuit.

The government appeal had the effect of delaying all official trial-related activities into the fall. On October 27, 1991, Supreme Court Justice Anthony Kennedy denied the appeal requesting a stay of depositions. Judge McLaughlin immediately reset the trial for December 10, and the process of taking depositions resumed. Again, however, the case ran into further delays. In November, as the taking of depositions was under way, plaintiffs sought to depose Commerce Secretary Mosbacher, the key government official involved in the decision not to adjust. The government immediately moved to block this attempt on the familiar legal grounds that allowing the deposition of high government officials in the course of their duty is action that should be allowed in only the most compelling situations. Judge McLaughlin ultimately ruled for the government, but the delay led to yet another postponement of the trial. The plaintiffs also requested a complete set of adjusted data, down to the block level. These data were provided by the Commerce Department in the form of a collection of computer tapes, but under a protective court order that prevented their release for other purposes.

By early December, the plaintiffs had completed their first round of depositions but had yet to announce their list of expert witnesses. Observers recognized that the earliest date for the commencement of the trial would be the middle of February 1992.

Relatedly, at a November 13 hearing of the Senate Subcommittee on Governmental Information and Regulation chaired by Senator Herbert Kohl of Wisconsin, Commerce Deputy Under Secretary Mark W. Plant outlined a set of issues to be addressed before Secretary Mosbacher would be able to decide to follow through on the recommendation from the bureau to adjust the intercensal estimates. The list of issues sounded much like the secretary's objections to the PES-based adjusted data in his July 15 report. They included

- lack of robustness or stability in the models used to calculate an adjustment;

- removal of known measurement biases in the postenumeration survey results as estimated in the PES evaluation studies;

- resolution of differences between PES and demographic analysis estimates;

- thorough documentation and explanation of all components that make up the total level error in the PES;

- more information about the assumption of homogeneity regarding the probability of inclusion in the census.

Plant suggested that much research remained to be done and that it might not be accomplished in time to adjust the July 1, 1992, intercensal estimates. When asked by Senator Kohl whether he would use adjusted intercensal estimates if he had to make the decision today, Plant said he would recommend against such use. This brought a positive response from the senator. Wisconsin, Kohl noted, would not benefit from adjustment because it would lose relative representation as a result of the use of PES-based adjusted census figures and, in fact, would lose a seat in the House of Representatives if the 1990 census were adjusted.

Meanwhile, in the House of Representatives, the Subcommittee on Census and Population, chaired by Representative Thomas C. Sawyer, voted on November 18 along party lines to subpoena the full set of adjusted figures down to the block level. The purpose of the request was to allow the subcommittee to assess the strengths and weaknesses of current census methodology, independently from the Commerce Department. Speaking for the department, Under Secretary for Economic Affairs Michael Darby said that the department refused to release the adjusted data because they are "bad numbers" with "large numbers of random errors" and also because their release could disrupt the legislative redistricting in progress at the state level. On

December 6, Representative Sawyer ordered Secretary Mosbacher to appear before the subcommittee at a hearing scheduled for the following Tuesday, unless he turned over an unofficial set of the adjusted population data.

Mosbacher failed to show up at the December 10 hearing, and in his place he sent Under Secretary Darby, who said that the department would provide the subcommittee with "one-half" of the data, as well as numbers for blocks with one thousand people or more. Sawyer accused Mosbacher of putting himself outside the law: "No cabinet official has ever failed to appear . . . when withholding subpoenaed documents." There was no immediate decision on whether the subcommittee would seek to have Secretary Mosbacher held in contempt of Congress, though additional congressional hearings were planned for the new year. The chairman of the Democratic Party said that the secretary's "contempt for Congress is surpassed only by his contempt for the standards of accuracy and fairness in the first place" (*New York Times*, Dec. 11, 1991).

The intensification of the rhetoric of partisan sniping and the suspicion of the motives of the Commerce officials also was a result of the early maneuverings of the 1992 election season. On December 5, President Bush had announced that Secretary Mosbacher would leave the Commerce Department to become chairman of the president's reelection campaign. Less than two weeks later, Under Secretary Darby announced that he, too, had resigned from the department, to return to his teaching position at the University of California, Los Angeles. The effective date of Mosbacher's resignation remained uncertain, while Democrats called for holding the secretary in contempt. Darby indicated he would leave on January 4, 1992. Mosbacher's designated successor, Republican fund-raiser and campaigner Barbara H. Franklin, had not yet been active in census matters, and it remained to be seen what effect her arrival would have on the position of the Commerce Department regarding the adjustment issue and the disposition of the New York City lawsuit. But early commentary in a *New York Times* editorial (Jan. 1, 1992) indicated that Franklin's confirmation hearings would provide yet another forum for the airing of adjustment issues. "When Robert Mosbacher . . . refused last July to adjust the 1990 Census . . . he took a regrettable but defensible position," the *New York Times* fumed. "But when the same Robert Mosbacher, since designated as chairman of the 1992 Bush re-election campaign, won't give Congress the correction data, that's raw politics. . . . If Mr. Mosbacher can't grasp this simple point before he leaves, his designated successor, Barbara Franklin, ought to be asked at her confirmation hearings whether she too would deny the people something that is rightfully theirs."

That fall, several other lawsuits were brought against the Commerce Department in connection with its refusal to release the block-level adjusted census data for use by states in reapportionment of state legislatures. A federal court order in California directed the Census Bureau to provide the state with adjusted figures for reapportionment. In the fall, the Supreme Court ruled that the data need not be turned over until the trial in the lawsuit was held. Other states, including Florida, Massachusetts, and Montana, also sought access to adjusted data. Ironically, both California and Florida were part of the New York City lawsuit, and thus they had access to the adjusted data. They were not allowed to use these data for apportionment purposes, however, because the figures had been provided under a protective order of the court. Florida did pursue use of the data, however, and engaged statisticians to "reconstruct" the full set of adjusted counts from the unadjusted data reported by the bureau and the "one-half" of the data that was produced for the House subcommittees (Meyer and Kadane 1992).

The Trial

It took the first four months of 1992 to complete pretrial preparations for the New York suit, and the court reflected on these delays as the trial date finally arrived. At 10:00 A.M. on May 11, 1992, Judge Joseph M. McLaughlin entered a Manhattan federal courtroom crowded with lawyers and expert witnesses. "Good morning, ladies and gentlemen," he began. "This day has been a long [time] coming. I would like to say that I have been looking forward to it, but candor forbids that." Thus began the trial on the lawsuit brought by the City of New York and others seeking to overturn a 1991 Commerce Department decision not to adjust the results of the 1990 decennial census to account for the differential undercount of Blacks and other minorities.

Judge McLaughlin framed his notion of the history of the case in his opening remarks. He had presided over the original 1989 stipulation and order regarding the Census Bureau approach to adjustment and the 1990 enumeration, and he was finally to weigh the evidence on the appropriateness of adjustment. His opening statement essentially laid out the ground rules for the case (Fienberg 1992a):

> The plaintiffs requested that the court hold a trial. The defendants objected to conducting a trial, arguing that because the case arose under the Administrative Procedure Act (APA) the scope of the court's review should be limited to the administrative record. On February 18th of this year the court . . . concluded that the evidentiary hearing is necessary . . . for several reasons.
>
> First, there have been several allegations, some of them serious, that the administrative record is a self-serving . . . compilation of documents, assembled for the purpose of strengthening the defendant's litigation position. The court therefore must consider the integrity of the administrative record to ensure that these documents, and only these documents, were considered by the Secretary.
>
> The second purpose of the hearing is to enhance the court's understanding of the record, replete as it is with references to technical jargon and arcane procedures. To this end, the testimony of expert witnesses hopefully will prove helpful. Their testimony should also assist the court in determining whether the Secretary considered all the relevant factors in making his decision.
>
> Finally, the court is fully aware of the important constitutional questions this case presents.

The structure of the trial consisted primarily of testimony from a large number of expert statistical witnesses, nine for the plaintiffs and five for the defendants. The plaintiffs called all four of their members on the Special Secretarial Advisory Panel, Eugene Ericksen, Kirk Wolter, John Tukey, and Leo Estrada. They also called several additional statistical witnesses: John Rolph, of the Rand Corporation; Barbara Bailar, former associate director of the Census Bureau and executive director of the American Statistical Association; Franklin Fisher, an econometrician from MIT; Bruce Cain, political scientist from the University of California, Berkeley; and Stephen Fienberg. Defense witnesses included Kenneth Wachter, member of the secretary's panel; Peter Bounpane and Robert Fay, from the Census Bureau; Paul Meier, statistician from the University of Chicago; and David Freedman, statistician from the University of California, Berkeley. A final defense witness, Leo Breiman, of the University of California, Berkeley, did not testify. The plaintiffs objected, and the judge agreed, that he was not qualified to testify as an expert on surveys of human populations.

Opening Statements

In their opening statements, attorneys for the two sides of the litigation identified their positions on the issues and the roles of the experts they planned to call.

Speaking on behalf of the plaintiffs (in addition to the City of New York, plaintiffs or plaintiff-intervenors included six states, seventeen cities, four counties, the District of Columbia, and the Navajo Nation), attorney Robert Rifkind recalled the thirty-page report submitted to Secretary Mosbacher by Census Bureau Director Barbara Bryant in which she recommended the adoption of the adjusted data on the basis of her detailed and careful review of the bureau's evaluation of the PES results. He then summarized the extensive research program carried out by the Census Bureau throughout the decade of the 1980s, leading up to the PES. All this information, Rifkind claimed, was seemingly ignored by the secretary in his "official decision," and little or no information on it was included in the "so-called" administrative record prepared after the fact, under the supervision of trial counsel from the Justice Department. Rifkind continued:

> And on July 15th the secretary issued his decision and this case is about that decision. He says in his opening words, "Reaching a decision on the adjustment question has been among the most difficult decisions I have ever made."
>
> And well he might say so. Our evidence will show that it is utterly groundless, that all its convoluted obscurity is a sham, dressed up to look like scientific analysis but utterly fallacious, root and branch. Indeed, your Honor, if it were a brief submitted by counsel in this court, counsel would be subject to serious rebuke for serious and patent misuse of the record.
>
> We will focus both on what the decision omits and what it includes. What it omits is critical, and what it includes is erroneous. . . .
>
> Your Honor, the arbitrariness and capriciousness with which the secretary acted is enough to overturn his decision and reestablish the decision of the expert agency [the Census Bureau]. Although I think we do not need to demonstrate any motive on the part of the secretary, we intend to show your Honor that there is ample evidence of the real rationale at work in this decision, although not apparent in the decision document.

Rising to respond for the defendants (who included the Commerce Department and its secretary and under secretary, the president of the

United States, and two states as intervenors) was Justice Department attorney Michael Sitkov. After expressing his outrage at the inappropriateness of Rifkind's implications of political interference, Sitkov noted:

> Now, because this case is one under the APA, the Secretary's decision cannot be disturbed unless it is shown to be arbitrary and capricious. In other words, even if the court determines that Secretary Mosbacher's decision was wrong, the decision must be affirmed unless the court finds that it was totally unreasonable as well. And because this is a suit under the APA, the only remedy, in the event that the court finds the secretary's decision was unreasonable, is a remand to the Secretary with instructions to reconsider his decision. . . .
>
> Now these guidelines also provide that the census is to be considered more accurate than an adjustment unless it can be shown that adjusting the 1990 decennial census will result in a more accurate picture of the proportional distribution of the population of the United States on a state-by-state basis.
>
> That's the same test Judge Sprizzo applied in *Cuomo v. Baldrige*. That was the suit some of these plaintiffs brought to force an adjustment of the 1980 census. It's worth mentioning . . . that a number of the witnesses in this case were witnesses on that case, although a couple have changed sides.
>
> One thing that has not changed is that the case for adjustment is as weak today as it was then. Our evidence will make clear that the Secretary was right to decide that adjustment fails Judge Sprizzo's test and the Secretary's decision was not tainted in any way.
>
> First, I'm going to summarize what the evidence will show about how adjustment is done. And I think that's important, especially in this case, your Honor, because in some ways, adjustment is like a salami. You might like the way salami tastes, but you might not eat it if you saw how it was made.

Sitkov then proceeded to give an overview of the PES and adjustment methodology, emphasizing that the Census Bureau had relied throughout on statistical models that depended on critical and unjustifiable assumptions. In summation, he remarked:

> Finally, your Honor, we have argued and we continue to believe that trial is not only unwarranted in this case but that it's improper. The APA does not have one set of rules for important cases and another set for less important claims. The Supreme Court's most recent decisions on the APA make it clear that except in circumstances that aren't present here, judicial challenges and agency action are to be resolved on the administrative record. The record is insufficient if

it's not supportive of the agency's decision and the remedy is to send the decision back.

We submitted an administrative record of more than 18,000 pages in support of the Secretary's decision. The Court has never suggested that it's incomplete, that it's confusing or that it doesn't support the secretary's decision.

In this situation, there is no basis for a trial.

For the next two weeks, plaintiffs and defendants examined and cross-examined their witnesses with the aim of proving their interpretation of the secretary's decision. If the court agreed with the plaintiffs, then the secretary's decision was indeed "arbitrary and capricious" and should be overturned. If the court agreed with the defendants that the decision was within the scope of the secretary's proper authority, the decision against adjustment should stand. In other words, the testimony was to be considered in light of the extent to which it supported the legal claims of the parties and the legal issues alluded to by the judge in his opening remarks. And implicitly, both sides spoke to the question of precedent. For the defendants, the situation was much as it had been in 1980: there was simply no adequate method to adjust the census. From the plaintiffs' perspective, however, things were very different. For the 1980 census, the decision not to adjust was made in advance of the reporting of the data by the director of the bureau, Vincent Barabba, to whom the authority for the decision had been delegated by the secretary. The plaintiffs in *Cuomo v. Baldrige* were challenging the decision of the expert agency and its judgment. For the 1990 census, the decision not to adjust had been made by the secretary, counter to the recommendation of the Census Bureau. Plaintiffs were thus explicitly saying that the court and the secretary should defer to the bureau's judgment.

Witnesses for the Plaintiffs

The first witness presented by the plaintiffs was Eugene Ericksen, from Temple University. In well more than a day's worth of direct testimony, he outlined the problems the Census Bureau encountered in conducting the 1990 census, the implications of the lower-than-expected return rate for the mailed questionnaire on the quality of the data, the nature and extent of omissions and erroneous enumerations, and the qualitative information about the undercount provided by reports from ethnographic observers. He cited and explained the contents of a General Accounting Office (GAO) report (GAO 1991) that noted that there were as many as twenty-five million gross errors in the census (the sum of the estimated numbers of omissions and erroneous enumerations). The defendants objected to this particular line of testimony because the GAO document had not been "authenticated." The plaintiffs countered that it was "self-authenticating" and noted its special relevance in that it was not part of the administrative record. The judge then overruled the objections and allowed the report to be entered into the record as an exhibit. A similar objection was made to the reports from the ethnographic observers, which were also not included in the administrative record, and the judge ultimately admitted most of them as exhibits, as well.

Cross-examination of Ericksen ran for almost a full day and ranged over many topics. Much of the focus, however, was not on the primary areas of his direct testimony but rather on the methodology for smoothing of adjustment factors and on loss functions. Questions about details of regression models used in the smoothing process were interspersed with ones relating to the lack of information on smoothing in the report Ericksen had submitted to the the secretary in his role as member of the Special Secretarial Advisory Panel. This was followed by a series of questions regarding the model that Ericksen had proposed for use in adjusting the 1980 census and criticisms of it by Barbara Bailar, David Freedman, and William Navidi. The criticism involved in almost all the questions was that virtually all work on the PES involved statistical models of some sort, that all models involve assumptions, and that the assumptions for the 1990 PES were not correct (Ericksen acceded to all these points). At one point, defendants' counsel showed Ericksen a Census Bureau report on a model for total error and suggested that figures in one of the tables meant that one-third of the estimate of the net national undercount rate was a result of bias. Ericksen responded that such a ratio was misleading. He noted on redirect examination that even if the net national undercount was zero and the ratio of bias to undercount rate was thus infinity (instead of one-third), the ratio would say nothing about the effect of an adjustment on the way in which the differential undercount was distributed across the nation.

The second witness for the plaintiffs, called on the third day of the trial, was Kirk Wolter, of A. C. Nielsen and formerly chief of the statistical research division at the Census Bureau. He testified about the the research and evaluation activities on undercount reduction and adjustment at the bureau following the 1980 census and the process followed by the bureau in developing the PES for 1990 and assessing its technical and operational feasibility. This process included the identification of the major sources of bias or error in the PES and how they would be controlled. As Wolter reviewed the contents of a bureau memorandum, he explained that "it was certainly my view, the view of the Undercount Steering Committee that the decision would be made by the Census [Bureau] director. The decision was made by the Census [Bureau] director in 1980."

When he took the stand the next day, Wolter explained the trade-off between sampling error and control of nonsampling error that comes with taking a sample instead of conducting a census, and he described alternative approaches to undercount adjustment, including reverse record checks, the use of administrative records, and so on. He went on to note, "After conducting a number of scientific evaluations of each of these methods in the early 1980s, the Bureau ultimately rejected all of the[m] for one reason or another and decided, quite clearly, I should say, that the PES had the best chance of success in 1990."

Wolter's direct testimony ended with a review of the total error model used to assess the effectiveness of the PES for adjustment purposes. On cross-examination, Wolter was asked about the various evaluation reports on the PES known as the P-studies and about how various errors or problems in the PES would affect his judgment of its appropriateness for adjustment. Then he was asked to examine his published commentary on a paper by Freedman and Navidi (1986) criticizing the work of Ericksen and Kadane (1985) on a possible approach to adjustment in 1980, at which point the following exchange ensued:

Q: If you would, take a look at your comment, Dr. Wolter, on page 24.

Plaintiffs' counsel: Excuse me. Our copy is missing a page. . . . Do you have another copy?

Witness: I seem to be missing every other page. I don't seem to have 24, 26, 28. There is an undercount in this book.

Defendant's counsel: We will see if we can adjust it, Dr. Wolter.

The court: Let's smooth it.

Following a brief recess, questioning on Wolter's commentary on Freedman and Navidi resumed, and Wolter was asked if the assumptions in 1980 and 1990 were similar (Wolter had criticized the work for 1980). He responded that in 1990, the context, the PES design, and the data were all different.

The third expert witness for the plaintiffs was John Rolph, of the Rand Corporation.[1] He had served on the CNSTAT Panel on Decennial Census Methodology in the 1980s. He discussed how the panel had evaluated the research on undercount adjustment during the decade and why it had ultimately recommended that the bureau proceed with plans for the PES and a possible adjustment. Then he described, at length, the statistical methods used to smooth the adjustment factors, methods that can be viewed as empirical Bayes procedures (at which point the judge asked, "Is that B-A-Y-E-S, from Bayes' Theorem?"). Finally, Rolph was asked to comment on some of the wording in the secretary's decision:

Q: "One of the most problematic parts of the adjustment process was the bundle of statistical techniques contained in the smoothing process."
Do you see that?

A: Yes, I do.

Q: Do you agree with that?

A: I definitely agree that smoothing is a bundle of statistical techniques, indeed virtually everything or much of what the Census Bureau does is, in fact, statistical techniques. They carry out surveys, they take censuses. So smoothing certainly is a bundle of statistical techniques as I have attempted to explain. What I strongly disagree with is whether there is anything problematic with it, so I very strongly disagree with that statement.

Cross-examination of Rolph focused yet again on the assumptions in the regression models used for smoothing the adjustment factors and the extent to which the process actually used by the Census Bureau was prespecified. The suggestion in more than one question was that model selection, smoothing, the smoothing of variances, and the deletion of outliers were novel statistical techniques that had not been subjected to careful scrutiny. The witness responded to the contrary.

The final witness of the first week of the trial was Leobardo Estrada, a demographer at the University of California, Los Angeles. He began by describing work he had done at the Census Bureau during the 1970s on pretesting items on race and ethnicity for the 1980 census. He then testified about his recommendations as a member of the Special Secretarial Advisory Panel—specifically, on the results of demographic analysis and how they should be used. In particular, he noted that demographic analysis estimates of the differential undercount could not be used for a fine-grained analysis. Rather, they were intended for broad comparisons, both historically and across population subgroups:

Q: Given the strengths and the limitations that you were just telling us about, is Secretary Mosbacher's use of the demographic analysis a proper one?

A: Absolutely not. The guidelines . . . indicate that the proper use is the patterns and changes over time. Scant attention was given by Secretary Mosbacher to exactly those issues from which we have the most confidence, and almost all of the discussion of demographic analysis is focused upon these individual isolated undercoverage percentages for very specific groups.

Cross-examination of Estrada returned to the issue of the secretary's observations of contrary findings from the demographic analysis. He continued to insist that they were exactly the type of detailed comparisons for which demographic analysis is ill-suited.

When the trial resumed the following Monday, the plaintiffs called Franklin Fisher, an econometrician from the Massachusetts Institute of Technology, who proceeded to testify about the Census Bureau's loss function analyses. He began by describing a simple example of how a squared error loss function trades off bias and variance; he then used the example to represent an analogy with the loss function analyses performed by the bureau in the so-called P-studies and others also reported on by Secretary Mosbacher in his decision. He noted that the loss for the PES-adjusted data was smaller than for the raw enumeration data at the state level as well as at lower levels of geography for several different loss functions. He testified more generally as to the appropriateness of the bureau's work. When directed to a statement in the secretary's decision "that the proportionate share of about 29 states would be made more accurate and [that of] about 21 states would be made less accurate by adjustment," Fisher characterized it as "the product of what I can only describe as a cascade of errors. It is not true." He then went through the sequence of errors step by step. He also introduced two different ways to do correctly what the secretary claimed to have done, and he noted that for each, the relevant test favors the adjusted data over the unadjusted data. Fisher was also asked if his conclusions would hold if the variances from the total error model were inflated. He responded that they would hold even if the variances were increased by a factor of seven, whereas the secretary implied that they would change with an increase by a factor of two or three. Finally, Fisher was asked about a last-minute report prepared by the bureau on a test of hypothesis requested by Under Secretary Darby. He noted that it, too, supported the use of adjusted data, and its contents had been mischaracterized by Secretary Mosbacher in his decision.

Fisher's cross-examination began in midafternoon and continued into Tuesday morning. Defendants' counsel asked a number of questions about smoothing and the P-studies, and Fisher claimed limited knowledge about the methodologies in use. Considerable time was taken up with a dispute over the admissibility of various documents and analyses reported on by Fisher, because they were prepared for him by others after his deposition had been taken early in April. He claimed that the analyses could not have been performed earlier because the required data had not been provided by the government and that he had responded accurately at the deposition about his plans for further analyses. The judge reserved his ruling on the defendants' objection, pending the preparation and submission of affidavits by the two parties.

At midmorning on Tuesday, plaintiffs called Bruce Cain, a political scientist from the University of California, Berkeley, and qualified him to testify on political aspects of statistical analyses of census data and redistricting. Cain described the effect of the use of unadjusted data on apportionment for the California legislature, noting that the undercount in some districts was as high as 8.7 percent, while other districts were erroneously overpopulated by 2 to 3 percent, in contrast with the target maximum variation of 0.5 percent set by the redistricting guidelines. He also demonstrated a direct relationship between legislative district undercount and minority percentages. When asked to comment on the secretary's interpretations that adjustment posed risks to the technical independence of the bureau's professionalism, Cain responded, "I think he's got it wrong," and went on to explain his reasons in graphic detail. He also noted that the secretary was clearly misleading in focusing on the effects of adjustment on congressional apportionment, when everyone conceded that the effects on legislative redistricting were more important by far. On cross-examination, Cain was questioned about the knowledge the secretary had about the political partisan implications of his decision, a point that was also pursued on redirect.

The next witness, following lunch, was Barbara Bailar, executive director of the American Statistical Association and former associate director of the Census Bureau for statistical standards and methodology. She testified about the 1980 decision not to adjust, made by Bureau Director Vincent Barabba, and the reasons for her opposition to adjustment a decade earlier. She then described the work done at the bureau on approaches to adjustment during the 1980s, leading up to the 1987 decision by Under Secretary of Commerce Robert Ortner against adjustment in 1990 and her subsequent resignation from the bureau. Throughout, she attempted to explain how problems in 1980 were addressed in the procedures that the bureau proposed to set in motion for a decision on adjustment in 1990. In passing, she explained that she now understood that every census block does not have to be improved by an adjustment for it to be superior to the raw enumeration—a reversal of the position she had erroneously taken in 1980. Under cross-examination, Bailar was asked, in particular, about statements she had made in a comment on a 1985 paper by Ericksen and Kadane about problems with their proposal for an adjustment. She replied repeatedly that the methods she was discussing then were different from those used by the bureau in 1990 and that most of the problems with the earlier approach had been adequately addressed in 1990.

John Tukey, professor emeritus from Princeton University, began his testimony on Wednesday morning. In brief direct testimony, he spoke about his work as a member of the Special Secretarial Advisory Panel. He then explained that accuracy at the block level was "not a significant issue" and proffered a semitechnical explanation of its impact. He also spoke about prespecification (stating that the procedure followed by the bureau in 1990 "was as fully specified as our knowledge and understanding at the time before the data were analyzed would permit"), robustness ("all of these [results] clearly indicated an absence of undue sensitivity"), and assumptions ("you would be wrong to think of assumptions as something like hypotheses in elementary geometry, as things which were supposedly essential to reach the conclusion. . . . There are assumptions that have helped to guide the choice of analysis. . . . But typically the real world is not too far from these and the procedures are satisfactory"). On cross-examination,

Tukey was asked about the "reasonableness" of statisticians opposed to adjustment, the lack of prespecification for parts of the smoothing method, the impact of a recently discovered coding error on his recommendation for adjustment, and assumptions associated with different aspects of the PES procedures:

Q: Isn't it also your view, Professor, that the statistical procedures involved in the 1990 dual-system estimates have no assumptions?

A: If you want to take me that far, I will go that far.

Stephen Fienberg, then of York University in Canada, was the final witness for the plaintiffs.[2] His testimony lasted for somewhat more than a day and focused on several broad themes: (1) the long history of the capture-recapture, or dual-systems, method and its use to measure the size of human populations; (2) the bureau's own use of dual-systems approaches, beginning with the 1950 census, and the decade of research on the topic in the 1980s; (3) the work of CNSTAT's Panel on Decennial Census Methodology and its dissolution in 1989 as a result of lack of cooperation and support from the Commerce Department; and (4) the errors, biases, misrepresentations, and extreme assumptions used to support the secretary's decision not to adjust ("He ignored the evidence adduced by the Census Bureau and instead relied upon alternative after alternative that I find implausible. . . . I think [he] unfairly rejected the evidence presented by the Bureau, which to me strongly supported the use of the corrected census counts based on the postenumeration survey"). Cross-examination followed the familiar pattern of discussion of assumptions, especially those related to smoothing, and included a recounting of statements he had made in publications about the role of statistics as evidence in the courts and about an exchange with David Freedman on the use of statistical methods, published in the mid-1980s.

The Government Defense

The first witness for the defendants was Peter Bounpane, of the Census Bureau, who began his testimony on Thursday afternoon. He described the key steps in the 1990 census process, including promotion and advertising efforts, special outreach programs, and local review. He then focused on the PES and explained both his reservations about its use for adjustment and the form in which he had expressed his reservations to the secretary. Bounpane was one of the two members of the Undercount Steering Committee who had recommended that the 1990 enumeration not be adjusted. He also had provided a memorandum to the commerce secretary just before the July 15, 1991, decision, indicating his reservations to an adjustment.

At this point, Bounpane was asked about evaluations of the PES that had been done following the secretary's July 15 decision and if he still felt that the estimate of an undercount of five million people was "correct." "No, I don't think it is," he replied and proceeded to describe the work of the Committee on Adjustment of Postcensal Estimates (CAPE). One of the CAPE evaluations had led to the discovery of a computer coding error involving erroneous enumerations, which had led to an overstatement of the undercount rate of 0.4 percent; the undercount was consequently reduced from 2.1 percent to 1.7 percent. The next morning, under cross-examination, Bounpane conceded that the impact of the computer error on the differential undercount was small and that many of the other errors in the PES that he had described in his direct testimony were already included in the bureau's estimate for the bias in the adjusted counts. He was also asked about parts of the secretary's decision, which he had helped to draft.

The next witness was Robert Fay, also of the Census Bureau, who oversaw the computation of variances for the raw adjustment factors and all variances and covariances used in the evaluation studies. Fay also had served on the bureau's Undercount Steering Committee of the bureau and had supported its recommendation to the director to proceed with an adjustment. Although he supported the decision, he testified, he still thought that a major residual issue was uncertainty in the smoothing process. At that time, he had formed "a judgmental interval" that the variances were understated by a factor of 1.7 to 3.0. He was then asked about his work on this topic following the July 15 decision. At this point, Fay described a bootstrap calculation of variances that produced a doubling of the original values but did not include additional sources of potential variability. Finally, he was asked if he still favored adjustment, to which he responded no. Under cross-examination, Fay denied that the bureau had been biased in favor of adjustment as it viewed the results of the PES, as alleged by Secretary Mosbacher. When he was asked to consider an alternative to the smoothing model, which had been proposed by David Freedman, he said that it was not preferable to the one used by the bureau.

The final witness in the second week of the trial was Paul Meier, from the University of Chicago. He began his testimony by describing a long-standing interest in census issues and why he considered it inadvisable for the census to be anything other than a head count. He objected, in principle, to the use of complex statistical methodology for census taking that might be subject to challenge from others, and he claimed that many of the choices made among alternatives were arbitrary. Finally, he was asked to characterize the dispute before the court (with reference to another decision on census adjustment), and he responded that the court was not well placed to judge whether a statistical analysis was competently done. On cross-examination, when Meier was asked about different aspects of the adjustment procedure, he continued to object to them on principle but did not provide details regarding their failings.

When the trial resumed the following week, the defendants called Leo Breiman from the University of California, Berkeley. After a brief introduction of his background and experience, counsel tendered him as an expert in the field of statistics and asked that he be admitted as an expert witness. Plaintiffs' counsel objected, on the grounds that Breiman's expertise was not in the areas about which he was planning to testify, that is, nonsampling errors. This led to extended discussion and additional questioning of the witness, after which the court ruled that it would not accept Breiman's testimony.[3]

Following a brief adjournment, the defendants called Kenneth Wachter, from the University of California, Berkeley, to testify, especially about his work as a member of the Special Secretarial Advisory Panel and more broadly about the accuracy of adjusted census counts.[4] Wachter began by discussing the demographic analysis (DA), and he compared its results with those from the PES, noting discrepancies, which he attributed to correlation bias. Wachter then turned to the assumption of homogeneity and the bureau's poststratification scheme. He said that heterogeneity was not adequately reflected in the bureau's total error model, and he described an alternative approach to poststratification (using information from the census itself to decide on the groupings of states) developed by Henry Woltman at the Census Bureau and the substantial difference this repoststratification would have made on the unsmoothed adjusted counts. He also described the results of a computer simulation study that demonstrated, he claimed, greater heterogeneity at the local-area level than that measured at the poststratum level. Cross-examination of Wachter began with his simulation study and an explanation of how the numbers in it were generated. He confirmed that the study did not indicate how much improvement would be achieved by adjustment under conditions of perfect homogeneity, and he presented an instance from his study in which the use of estimates with heterogeneity yielded an improvement over perfect homogeneity. At this point, the court adjourned for the day.

When the court reconvened the next morning, Wachter again took the stand and responded to questions on the use of loss functions (he favored their informal use), combining demographic and PES-based estimates (he was opposed), smoothing, and his use of unit-counting loss functions in his computer simulation study (the only measure of loss reported).[5] He was presented with the following example:

Q: Let us now envision a United States of five states A, B, C, D, and E, which in the census are counted with populations as follows: state A has 7 million people; states B, C, and D have 5 million people each; state E has 3 million people. An adjustment is again proposed under which each of the states, A, B, C, and D would have 6 million people, state E would have 5,999,999 people. You will not be surprised to know that the truth is that each of the states has 6 million people.
I take it, Dr. Wachter, that, again using a unit counting approach, looking at distributive accuracy, you would conclude that the census count is more accurate, is that correct? I have a calculator if you need it.

A: 25 altogether, so we have 20 percent in B, C, and D. . . . The shares of B, C, and D are correct in the census, and the shares of A and E are incorrect. So unit counting gives that result. . . .

Q: And once again unit counting tells you in this example that the census count is more accurate from a distributive point of view, is that right?

A: That's right.

Cross-examination continued on various points related to the details of Wachter's two reports on repoststratification and on the computer simulation.

The final witness for the defendants was David Freedman of the University of California, Berkeley.[6] He began by describing the trade-offs that would be necessary among potentially conflicting criteria that might be used to evaluate the results of the PES and the census. He stressed the impact of sampling error on the PES-based estimates, saying that one cannot tell whether most of the states are "improved" or not by the proposed adjustment. Freedman then turned to the smoothing process, describing it in detail, exposing its assumptions, and explaining why he believed that most of the assumptions were not reasonable. He outlined some alternative assumptions and approaches to smoothing and described several reanalyses, with different assumptions, different approaches to variable selection, with and without the smoothing of the variances, with and without ratio adjustments, and so on. In each reanalysis he found big differences from the results of the Census Bureau analysis, and he claimed that they were illustrative of the lack of robustness of the smoothing procedures.[7]

The other main topic of Freedman's testimony was the inadequacy of the bureau's loss function analyses.[8] Freedman believed that they overtly favored adjustment; he then described his own reanalysis of the loss function results, looking at differences in state contributions to the overall risk. The following exchange captures the essence of his conclusions:

A: For most of the states, the gains from adjustment are so small that when you plot them on this figure, their bars just blur into the vertical line.

Q: How would you describe California's effect on the results in the table?

A: California, I think, is the dominant source of the apparent gain . . . in accuracy from adjustment.

Q: In your opinion, is a loss function a good way to summarize the gains in accuracy from adjustment?

A: No, I don't believe it is. . . . It seems to me that we have a situation here with one or two big outliers, as we call them. You just don't summarize data like that by adding up the numbers, at least not without looking at them.

Freedman concluded with a criticism of Franklin Fisher's calculations and tests, claiming that there was a serious theoretical mistake in them.

The final day of the trial, Thursday, May 27, began with the cross-examination of Freedman on the details of his calculations on smoothing. Then it turned to Freedman's position on adjustment and on the use of models more broadly, with counsel for the plaintiffs suggesting that Freeman's position was an extremist one, characterized by Paul Meier as "Freedman's hard-line defense against most statistical inference for observational data." On the issue of smoothing, Freedman was asked about prespecification and the extent of the bias it introduces (he did not attempt to measure this). Subsequent questions then probed the extent of the differences between the smoothing models used by Freedman and those used by the bureau. He was then asked to review the document that Fisher had relied upon for the formulas in his calculations. This led to an extended sequence of questions and answers about the details of Freedman's own calculations, which did not clearly resolve the question of whose calculations were correct or how they should be interpreted.

Rebuttal

The plaintiffs presented only one rebuttal witness, John Rolph. He reinforced the extent of prespecification of the smoothing and presmoothing procedures, and he described a series of Census Bureau memorandums in which many of the alternative approaches suggested by Freedman had been considered and found to be less appropriate than the approach ultimately adopted. He also described various sensitivity analyses considered by the bureau before it finally applied the results of the smoothing. He distinguished these in spirit and approach from Freedman's alternative analyses. He concluded by noting that Freedman's testimony had not caused him to change his opinion that smoothing had been properly done by the bureau.

Aftermath

By the time the trial ended, the transcript ran to twenty-six hundred pages of highly detailed testimony. Final briefs were filed at the end of July. The points of contention between the two sides were revealing and posed something of a paradox. The City of New York plaintiffs argued that the Census Bureau did an excellent job of developing the new methods for correcting for the differential undercount. They saw its work as professional, reliable, and above politics. The Commerce Department, plaintiffs claimed, constantly intervened and attempted to undercut the efforts of the professionals. The government defendants, in contrast, argued that the secretary rightfully overruled the bureau because its work was inadequate to solve the problem, contained errors, and was not to be trusted.

The plaintiffs' strategy was to focus on what was known at the time of the secretary's decision and to ask the judge to overrule the secretary in light of what was known in July 1991. New analyses, such as those performed by the defense expert witnesses, were beside the point, they claimed. So was the discovery of the computer error when new approaches to stratification were tried after the decision. Although it lowered the overall undercount estimate, that error did not fundamentally change the differential undercount. The Justice Department strategy was to undermine the work of the statisticians in the Census Bureau as best it could by arguing that the secretary correctly put the brakes on the use of an untried statistical innovation. Thank heavens the secretary recognized the limitations of the bureau methods, the attorneys noted—even if he did not have the evidence in hand in July 1991. The discovery of the computer error, and Freedman's reanalyses of the presmoothing, using alternative specifications, showed the wisdom of the secretary's position. The plaintiffs claimed that the defendants wanted to have it both ways: first, they argued that the judge could and should rule on the administrative record alone, and then they chose to ignore what was in the record and introduce new evidence. The defendants proudly acceded to that charge.

Finally, both sides impugned the credentials of the other. The plaintiffs noted that all their experts had worked on the technical aspects of the adjustment methodology covered in their testimony and had all published directly or indirectly on that work. They claimed that such experts could properly judge the quality of the work of the PES, noting that although departures from assumptions were important, they were relative and had to be understood in context. On balance, the PES-adjusted counts were still superior to the raw enumeration. The government experts said that departures produced unacceptable biases, and that the plaintiffs' experts disagreed even among themselves on the quality of the PES. As a result, the PES and an adjustment based on it were fatally flawed. The plaintiffs' experts relied almost completely on the work done by the bureau in conducting and analyzing the PES up through the secretary's decision. The defense experts chose to disregard or criticize much of the bureau's work and relied heavily on their own analyses, developed after the secretary's decision. And finally, the plaintiffs noted that all but one of their experts did all their work on a pro bono basis. The Commerce Department's outside experts were paid substantial fees by the government for their work.

Changing Personnel, Continued Controversy, and Congressional Interest

Prolonged litigation tends to leave behind a strange trail. The New York City case was originally brought in 1988 against the Commerce Department, Under Secretary Robert Ortner, and Secretary William Verity. The adjustment decision was made by Secretary Robert Mosbacher and supported by Under Secretary Michael Darby and Deputy Under Secretary Mark Plant. In 1987, the director of the Census Bureau was John Keane and supporting his recommendation to proceed with the PES was Associate Director Barbara Bailar and Kirk Wolter, chief of the Statistical Research Division. Bailar was succeeded by Robert Groves, who participated in the bureau's deliberations in 1991. Throughout these deliberations, Louis Kincannon was deputy director of the bureau. By mid-1992, all had left their government positions. No one from the Commerce Department was called for testimony by the defendants in the case (the court refused to compel former secretary Mosbacher to testify), although two Census Bureau statisticians did testify.

The adjustment issue also continued in relation to the question of what to do with intercensal estimates. Intercensal estimates are designed to update the results of the decennial census by incorporating information on population change from Census Bureau surveys and other sources. In July 1991, Secretary Mosbacher had announced his intention to "incorporate, as appropriate, information gleaned from the Post Enumeration Survey into [the] intercensal estimates" (see appendix F), and some announcement on procedures was anticipated in advance of the release of intercensal estimates on July 1, 1992. That release was based on unadjusted data. After the testimony of Census Bureau officials at the trial, observers had anticipated such a delay because of the lawsuit and the negative comments from the Commerce Department regarding any use of adjusted data. At an August 5 congressional briefing organized by Senator Herbert Kohl of Wisconsin, a Census Bureau representative described several alternatives for intercensal estimation, assuming that the July 15, 1991, decision by the secretary of commerce was not overturned by the courts (see Fienberg 1992a, 38):

- Incorporate the results of the PES into the base for intercensal estimates at all levels of geography.

- Incorporate the PES results into the intercensal base at the national
  and state levels. At the substate level, use a simple synthetic estimate based on the percentage of state-level estimated undercount.

- Incorporate the results of the PES into the intercensal base for na-
  tional- and state-level estimates but not for substate levels.

- Use as the base for intercensal estimates for all levels of geography
  a simple average of the 1990 census count and an estimate incorporating the results of the PES.

- Do not incorporate the PES results into the intercensal estimates
  for any jurisdiction.

The Bureau also published a notice in the *Federal Register* seeking
comments on these alternatives and announcing a public hearing
scheduled for August 31, 1992, and deferred the decision until December. The call for public commentary (as opposed to the seeking of
informed technical statistical advice) raised the specter of continued
politicization of census activities—at least in recent memory, there was
no precedent for such an action on the technical details of ongoing
bureau activities. As someone close to the issue was overheard to re-
mark in the halls of the American Statistical Association meetings in
Boston, "The next thing you know, the bureau will file a notice in
the *Federal Register* calling for public comments on second-stage ratio
adjustment in the data released from the Current Population Survey."
What was not widely shared at this point in time was the August
7, 1992, report of the Committee on Adjustment of Postcensal Estimates (U.S. Bureau of the Census 1992a), which detailed the work of
the bureau statisticians carrying the results of the PES adjustment beyond the July 15, 1991, decision. The CAPE report did several things:

- For the first time, it documented the computer-processing error
  detected in late 1991 and referred to by many of the government
  witnesses at trial in 1992. The effect of the error was to reduce the
  estimate of the net national undercount by 0.4 percent, from 2.1
  percent to 1.7 percent.

- It made some additional refinements and corrections in the undercount estimates.

- It refined the estimates of bias in the dual-systems estimates.

- It attempted to address the concerns expressed regarding the smoothing model by revising the poststratification scheme, reducing the number of poststrata from 1,392 to 357.

- It compared the July 15, 1991, adjusted counts with the newly revised ones and concluded that there was strong agreement at most levels of geography.

- It carried out a variety of loss function analyses to determine whether the revised adjusted counts were superior to the enumeration counts for intercensal purposes.

- It described the internal decision-making process on intercensal estimation.

The language regarding criteria to evaluate adjustment in the CAPE report continued to resemble that used by the secretary of commerce in 1991, and the specter of the just-completed New York City trial still cast a long shadow over the methodology and its uses. Some of the salient results in the CAPE report were subsequently incorporated into Hogan (1993), where they were seen for the first time by the broader professional community.

Elections, Apportionment, Decision

The redistricting for the November 1992 federal and state elections used unadjusted census counts. The elections ended the twelve-year Republican control of the White House and executive branch of government. Confounding the political pundits, William Jefferson Clinton beat George Herbert Bush. With a Democratic majority in Congress, Clinton promised a wide variety of legislative reforms, most notably plans for national health insurance and for bringing real diversity to high federal office. He signaled his shift with early appointments of minorities and women to high federal posts. The secretary of commerce position went to Ron Brown, former head of the Democratic National Committee and one of the Democrats' most visible African American political leaders. By the early months of 1993, expectations ran high of dramatic changes in social and economic policy. Once again, the political winds of change swept through Washington. Director Barbara Bryant prepared to leave the Census Bureau in January, and career officials waited for the changing of the guard at the Commerce Department and at their own helm. The bureau was relatively low on the priority list of the new administration, and there were few indications of who the next director would be. Again, officials braced themselves for the initiatives of a new administration.

In April, eleven months after the trial, Judge McLaughlin decided the census undercount suit. He issued an opinion ruling in favor of the Commerce Department, but on relatively narrow grounds: Because the decision not to adjust came under the Administrative Procedures Act, plaintiffs had to demonstrate that the decision was "arbitrary and capricious." Judge McLaughlin found the plaintiffs case failed to meet this standard, but he went on to note that they "made a powerful case that discretion would have been more wisely employed in favor of adjustment. Indeed, were this court called upon to decide this issue *de novo*, I would probably order the adjustment" (*City of New York v. U.S. Department of Commerce* 1993, 928–9).

Initially, in a rather paradoxical outcome, Judge McLaughlin's decision and the change of administration in Washington appeared to put the controversies surrounding the 1990 census to rest. The judge upheld the authority of the Commerce Department secretary and agreed that his July 1991 decision not to adjust could stand. But, as he had throughout the case, he also noted that it was imprudent at best, and increasingly suspect at worst, for the federal government to claim that it could do nothing to remedy the differential undercount. A de novo review by the court would have supported adjustment, and, he warned, it would be best for the officials in Washington to guarantee that the years before the next census be used to improve the adjustment methodology and avoid further litigation. The change in leadership at the Commerce Department would seem to guarantee that department officials would look differently at the issues of the decennial census—at least for the next four years.

But as in previous years, the census undercount controversies had yet to play out completely. The New York plaintiffs, unhappy with the judge's decision, prepared to file an appeal. There was also the matter of the intercensal estimates. In December 1992, the Census Bureau, acting in the waning days of the Republican administration, had announced the decision not to adjust the intercensal estimates using the PES results. And though the emerging plans in the bureau looked to a new concept for 2000 called "the one-number census," which would include statistical adjustment and other innovations (see chapter 9), observers were far from sanguine about the capacity of the bureau to plan its own destiny for 2000.

Accordingly, the New York plaintiffs appealed McLaughlin's decision, and at a January 1994 hearing before a panel from the Second

Circuit Court, they argued that the district court had erred in applying an arbitrary and capricious standard of review. The case should be remanded, New York argued, for reconsideration under a constitutional claim of equal representation according by the Fifth and Fourteenth Amendments. The appellate court responded positively to this request and ruled in favor of those who challenged the accuracy of the counts from the 1990 decennial census.

The ruling came in early August 1994, as most of the Washington government bureaucracy was away on vacation and statisticians across the country were preparing for the annual joint statistical meetings across the border in Toronto, Canada. The federal appeals court issued a "stunning" opinion that left everyone wondering what would happen next. Writing for the majority, Judge Amalia Kearse vacated the judgment of District Court Judge Joseph McLaughlin. That decision alone left most observers surprised. But Judge Kearse in her opinion went much further, arguing that, at the original trial, the plaintiffs had carried their burden of proof, showing that the secretary of commerce, in his refusal to adjust the census based on the PES, had failed to make "an effort to achieve equality as nearly as practicable." She went on to note:

> The burden thus shifted to the Secretary to justify his decision not to adjust the census in a way that the court found would for most purposes be more accurate and would lessen the disproportionate counting of minorities. . . . When the official answer is that it is preferable to undercount minorities, that answer must be supported by an official showing that that result (a) furthers a governmental objective that is legitimate, and (b) is essential for the achievement of that objective. (*City of New York v. U.S. Department of Commerce* 1994, 1131)

In vacating the lower-court judgment, the appellate court remanded the case for further proceedings "not inconsistent with this opinion." Thus, while the appellate court did not quite order adjustment, it raised the requirements by forcing the government to show why an adjustment should not be mandated.

The appellate opinion also discussed a claim, raised at earlier stages of the litigation and again on appeal by the States of Wisconsin and Oklahoma, to the effect that a statistical adjustment is barred by the Census Act. Citing legislative history surrounding the 1976 revision of that act, the court concluded that statistical adjustment and the sampling incorporated within it were not only not barred by the Census Act but, in fact, were meant to be encouraged.

The opinion was not unanimous. Judge William Timbers dissented and expressed concern that the court's opinion conflicted with those recently issued in two other circuit courts.

Although Judge Kearse's decision vacated the original decision of Judge McLaughlin, the case was not over. The next move was up to the plaintiffs, led by New York City. They could request a renewal of the trial or a directed judgment in favor of adjustment. The federal government also considered its options: (1) to argue compelling government objectives that preclude an adjustment, (2) to appeal the decision to the Supreme Court, or (3) to reach a settlement of some sort with the plaintiffs. In September 1994, the Justice Department decided to let the decision stand, but both Wisconsin and Oklahoma indicated their intent to appeal the decision as defendant-intervenors.

Meanwhile, officials in the statistical system outside the Census Bureau quietly introduced sampling-based adjustment into survey designs. The Bureau of Labor Statistics incorporated adjusted population figures into the labor force results from the monthly Current Population Survey. The Census Bureau planned a 1995 test of a one-number census, incorporating sampling for nonresponse and some form of sampling-based adjustment. If such a one-number design were used in the 2000 census, the methods for correcting the differential undercount would no longer be separable from the rest of the census enumeration procedures.

To the Supreme Court

The political winds shifted again in November 1994 as Republicans swept to the majority in both houses of Congress. Now, the partisan political differences between Congress and the executive branch that had surrounded the controversies in the 1990 count reappeared, but with the cast of characters reversed. The new Republican congressional majority came to Washington intent on changing the way government worked. Newt Gingrich's "Contract with America" promised smaller government, the abolition of useless and unresponsive government agencies. The new majorities looked with suspicion on the "established" agencies of government. Early proposals looked to the abolition of the Commerce Department and the devolution of many of its functions. Statistical programs, to these cost cutters, seemed like an extravagant waste of taxpayer resources. Many of these themes had been heard in previous years, but in 1994 they posed a new and uncertain environment for the Census Bureau and its plans.

It was in this environment, in September 1995, that the States of Wisconsin and Oklahoma appealed the Second Circuit Court decision to the Supreme Court. The Justice Department, representing the Commerce Department, reversed its decision of September 1994 and also appealed to reinstate the authority of the secretary of commerce. The Supreme Court agreed to hear oral arguments and scheduled a hearing for January 1996.

The Arguments in Brief

Before the Court heard oral arguments, the parties submitted briefs describing the legal and constitutional bases for their claims. Although Oklahoma was one of the appellants, its brief to the Supreme Court rested in part on the argument that Title 13 of the U.S. Code "expressly prohibits the use of sampling for the count used in the apportionment of Representatives," a position counter to that expressed by the Second Circuit Court in its decision to reverse. The brief concluded with the argument that "there is no constitutional right to census accuracy. Thus, the decision not to adjust the census did not violate the Constitution."

Wisconsin, which would lose a seat if the House of Representatives were reapportioned under an adjusted set of census counts, argued in its brief that "the recognition of a judicially enforceable right to the most accurate census practicable conflicts with Congress' express and historically exercised authority to direct the manner of taking the census." Furthermore, Wisconsin argued, the Second Circuit Court had "misapprehended the relation between census accuracy and equality of representation," and "the use of statistical estimation techniques to "correct" the results of the enumeration census . . . penalized states, like Wisconsin, whose high rate of voluntary census participation corresponded to high rates of voter participation." The federal government's brief, the most detailed of the three, argued that the secretary of commerce "acted within the range of discretion afforded by the constitution in declining to make a statistical adjustment" and that "judicial review must reflect appropriate deference to his decision."[9]

The New York City response to these arguments noted that census taking in the United States historically does not reflect the monolithic tradition suggested by the petitioners, and it argued that the adjustment correction approach represented the natural culmination of decades of statistical attention to the differential undercount problem. The brief made reference to the constitutional uses of census data and then argued that the secretary's decision was not consistent with the constitutional language and goal of equal representation. Thus, the brief concluded, the circuit court was correct in deciding that the secretary's decision should be subject to strict scrutiny and not be given the deference suggested by the petitioners.

Armed with these briefs and responses from the petitioners, counsel and the Supreme Court justices entered the courtroom on January 10 for one hour of oral argument and questioning. The seven and a half years of litigation would once again find dramatic moment, this time in an hour of highly charged debate, boiled down to the essence of the narrow question that had framed the case from the beginning. All sides were cognizant of and made reference to the profound constitutional issues of equity underlying the case. But all sides were also cognizant of the narrow legal question the Court would actually decide. What standards should guide the actions of the secretary of commerce? Did his actions deserve strict scrutiny or deference? And, therefore, had the district court judge properly ruled that the actions of the secretary of commerce were not "arbitrary and capricious" and could stand?

The Supreme Court Hearing

The hearing was scheduled for January 10, 1996, during a week that saw a major snowstorm bring Washington and the northeast corridor of the United States to a standstill. Because of the storm and the closure of airports and the federal government, the courtroom was not full. In fact, Justice John Paul Stevens had not been able to make it back to Washington from Florida in time for the hearing. But those in attendance included several participants in the original trial, former Census Bureau Director Barbara Bryant, and a number of government officials. The solicitor general of the United States, Drew Days, was scheduled to begin the arguments at the hearing, followed by the Wisconsin attorney general, James Doyle. Attorney Robert Rifkind, representing the City of New York, would respond.

The justices entered the courtroom promptly at 10 A.M., and Solicitor General Days was barely under way in his presentation when the questioning from the justices began (*Wisconsin v. City of New York* 1996, Oral Argument):

General Days:	The true total population of the United States is unknown and unknowable. At every 10 years for the last 200, the United States Government has been making the best effort possible to count every person it could. . . . The 1990 census was no exception. By all accounts, it was the most well organized and most thorough census in history, accounting for 98.4 percent of the population. Since at least 1790, people informed about the census-taking process—
Justice Rehnquist:	If the true population is unknown, how can one be sure that the most recent census accounted for 98.4 percent? (*Laughter.*)
General Days:	Well it's an estimation, Mr. Chief Justice. It's the best we can [do].

And so the hearing proceeded, with most of the justices aggressively interrupting the planned presentations by counsel with questions and comments.

As the exchange between Rehnquist and Days made clear, the primary issue before the Supreme Court was the question of the authority of the secretary of commerce to make the decision not to adjust, given the evidence that was before him. Solicitor General Days, in particular, was concerned with defending the authority of the secretary of commerce to make decisions about the conduct of the decennial census. Days suggested that the court of appeals decision would open the door to a variety of lawsuits challenging the authority of federal officials in the conduct of their usual business. "What the respondents have really invited the courts to do in this case," Days noted, "—and certainly the court of appeals seems to have accepted the invitation—was for the courts to take sides in a statistical dispute among statisticians and demographers about the propriety of a statistical adjustment." "We do not," he continued, "think that's the type of dispute that properly belongs in Federal court."

Justice Ruth Ginsburg pressed Days on the implications of his position on the use of statistical estimation in future censuses. Quoting from the opinion of the district court judge, she asked Days if "the use of adjustment in the next census is probably inevitable." When Days answered, "I don't think there's any determination at this point to do a PES in the way that was suggested in this lawsuit" in 2000, Ginsburg pressed the point further. "Do you know," she asked, "what was the source of the trial judge's confidence that the use of an adjustment after the enumeration would be inevitable?" Days responded that he was "not certain." As he began to explain, noting that "after he heard thirteen days of testimony from experts of the highest caliber," Justice Antonin Scalia completed his sentence with, "He was punchy." The courtroom filled with laughter. Days then continued that the trial judge felt "that the statistical science was moving forward and there would probably be the ability of the Census Bureau to rely more heavily than in the past on this."

The justices also questioned whether modern methods of counting followed the intent of the framers in creating the population census and whether a consensus exists among expert statisticians on the best methods to reduce the differential undercount. The justices were reluctant to second-guess the secretary's position because they were not convinced that the experts agreed that the adjusted counts were actually more accurate. Justice Scalia took the dimmest view of statistical estimation, agreeing with the position of the Wisconsin attorney general, James Doyle, that adjustment was improper. But all the justices repeatedly questioned the attorneys about the comparison on the unadjusted and the adjusted counts.

Even Robert Rifkind, who responded on behalf of the City of New York and most of the others who originally brought the lawsuit, conceded that the statistical community was not of one mind. When asked whether "a reasonable person could make a different set of value choices from the ones which I personally prefer," Rifkind admitted that such different choices presented problems for his case. He agreed that, "[as] Dr. Bryant said, reasonable men can differ, reasonable persons can differ [on adjustment]." But then he went on to note, "I must say that I don't envy the position Dr. Bryant was in when she had to utter that statement. She was standing next to her boss, and it's a common thing for non-lawyers to say when they're standing next to their bosses." This brought forth laughter once again in the courtroom. Rifkind kept returning to the fact that no authority found the unadjusted count better than the adjusted census and that the adjusted count did, in fact, reduce the differential undercount. Furthermore, he argued, the secretary in his decision changed the rules from the original stipulation order, and "that is suspect and requires further attention from a court."

As the justices continued to press Rifkind about the constitutional claim he was making in support of the Second Circuit Court decision and the specific harm claimed, the hour ended, and the hearing was suddenly over.

The Decision

With surprising speed, the Supreme Court rendered its decision in a unanimous opinion issued on March 20, 1996, just a little more than two months after the oral hearing. The Court held that the secretary's decision "conformed to applicable constitutional and statutory provisions" and "was not subject to heightened scrutiny." The Court thus reversed the circuit court decision and in effect decreed that the unadjusted census counts would remain the official numbers for 1990.

The opinion, delivered by Chief Justice William Rehnquist, not only reviewed some of the history of the differential undercount but also attempted to describe the dual-systems approach to estimation, using an analogy to counting pumpkins in a pumpkin patch:

> The particular variations of the "dual system estimation" [method] . . . considered by the Bureau are not important for purposes of this opinion, but an example may serve to make the "dual system estimation" [DSE] more understandable. Imagine that one wanted to use DSE in order to determine the number of pumpkins in a large pumpkin patch. First, one would choose a particular section of the patch as the representative subset to which the "recapture" phase will be applied. Let us assume here that it is a section exactly 1/10 the size of the entire patch that is selected. Then, at the next step—the "capture" stage—one would conduct a fairly quick count of the entire patch, making sure to record both the number of pumpkins counted in the entire patch and the number of pumpkins counted in the selected section. Let us imagine that this stage results in a count of 10,000 pumpkins for the entire patch and 1,000 pumpkins for the selected section. Next, at the "recapture" stage, one would perform an exacting count of the number of pumpkins in the selected section. Let us assume that we now count 1,100 pumpkins in that section. By comparing the results of the "capture" phase and the results of the "recapture" phase for the selected section, it is possible to estimate that approximately 100 pumpkins actually in the patch were missed for every 1,000 counted at the "capture" phase. Extrapolating this data to the count for the entire patch, one would conclude that the actual number of pumpkins in the patch is 11,000.

Sadly, while Justice Rehnquist's description does capture the notion of scaling up from a sample to the population, it misportrays dual-systems estimation, because it does not explicitly include a matching stage. In his explanation, Justice Rehnquist implicitly assumes that of the eleven hundred pumpkins included in the second or recapture count, one thousand were counted (that is, matched) in the first count. In the notation of chapter 4, he assumes that all of the one thousand pumpkins counted in the first count would fall in cell a of the 2×2 table and that none fall in the b cell (see table 4.5). In such a situation, his calculation of the true population would be correct. But as we noted in chapter 4, the dual-systems method generally demonstrates that some pumpkins in the first count would be missed in the second count, cell b, and that some pumpkins counted in the second count would be missed in the first count, cell c. Thus the true population of pumpkins in the sampled patch would exceed the eleven hundred pumpkins counted in the second count, and the statistician would also wish to estimate the number of pumpkins missed both times (the d cell). Finally, Rehnquist does not consider the possibility of erroneous enumerations in the first count.

Similarly, Justice Rehnquist's description of the accuracy of the census counts is off the mark. As we have explained, the oft-repeated comment that the Census Bureau was successful in counting 98.4 percent of the population (see Bryant and Dunn 1995; Choldin 1994) focuses solely on net census population undercount and ignores the extent of erroneous enumerations and omissions from the census. Finally, the opinion's argument that prior adjustments, in 1970 and 1980, based on sample surveys and imputation "took place on a dramatically smaller scale" than the adjustment considered in 1990 seems somewhat of an exaggeration.

The Supreme Court decision avoided a formal ruling on the question raised by Wisconsin and Oklahoma, namely, that the reference in the Constitution to an "actual enumeration" would preclude the use of any form of statistical adjustment or sampling. The opinion left that issue in limbo. In a footnote, Chief Justice Rehnquist merely said, "We do not decide whether the Constitution might prohibit Congress from conducting the type of statistical adjustment considered here." The issue remains salient as we look toward the 2000 census.

The Aftermath

The Supreme Court decision brought the legal controversies surrounding the 1990 census counts to an official end. By the spring of 1996, no further legal challenges to the basic enumeration remained. Many commentators in the statistical community and among the political groups involved in the litigation interpreted the Supreme Court decision as a review of the accuracy of the dual-systems approach to adjusting the census. From such a perspective, the court ruled against adjustment.

But a closer look demonstrates that all along the controversies were fundamentally about questions of law, not about questions of statistical method. From the federal government's perspective, the New York City case was about the delegation of authority from Congress to the Commerce Department to administer the census and the deference typically granted to government officials while doing their jobs. The counterposition of the litigants who brought the suit was also fundamentally about a matter of law. The City of New York charged that federal government officials had a special obligation under the Constitution to provide an equitable count of minorities and residents of urban areas. A census method that did not provide such a count was suspect. New York was not able to convince the Supreme Court of the virtue of this position. As the *New York Times* noted in a page-one story on January 11, 1996, on the day following oral argument, "Whatever the merits of a statistical adjustment as a question of policy, the Court is not about to order it as a matter of constitutional law."

The professional world of statistics was not so innocent a bystander to all this legal argument. The alignment of statistical experts on both sides of the dispute ironically had the oft-observed effect of vitiating the statistical arguments, leading to the possibility, as we will see, of more controversy and more litigation in 2000. The lawyers for the Commerce Department and the States of Wisconsin and Oklahoma (as well as a number of members of Congress) interpreted the difference of statistical opinion as a denigration of sampling, at least for this purpose, rather than as a difference in the interpretation of the value of numerical versus distributive accuracy in the PES adjustment, or even about the possibly inadequate size of the PES. They ended up arguing that sampling was not a proper census methodology—a dangerous course indeed, given 2000 census plans being developed by the Census Bureau.

In this sense, the results of the legal deliberations have already had a profound impact on the quality of government data and the ability of the Census Bureau to pursue its mandate to collect high-quality data for policy purposes. And in a sign of things to come, everyone in the courtroom in January 1996, including the justices themselves, also implicitly framed their arguments in terms of 2000. The published opinion clearly had implications for the 2000 census, but crucial features of planning for 2000 were left in limbo by a brief one-sentence footnote in the opinion. Rehnquist's footnote in effect deferred the legal evaluation of sampling and adjustment in future censuses. But the challengers were already visible. Wisconsin attorney general James Doyle, when pressed on whether Wisconsin would oppose a 2000 census plan that included sampling, hedged his remarks by noting he was "not a statistician" but added, "I do not believe that you can arrive at the census of Wisconsin based on counts of people that you have made in Illinois, Indiana, and Michigan" (*Wisconsin v. City of New York* 1996, Oral Argument). It would be in this legal and political environment that planning for the millennial census would proceed.

The Measurement of Race and Ethnicity and the Census Undercount: A Controversy That Wasn't

To this point we have not examined the classification of race and Hispanic origin in the census. The figures in table 6.2, for example, derive from the method of demographic analysis, which we described in chapters 2 and 4, where the the census results, grouped by age, race, and sex, are compared with a reconstruction, using information from a variety of sources including vital registration data. In demographic analysis, the classification of U.S. residents by race is taken as a given.[1] In many ways, this is how the information was treated in the 1990 postenumeration survey as well, especially in connection with the attempt to adjust for differential undercount. In other words, the answers to the following two questions on the census short form were treated as factual and without error:

4. Race. Fill ONE circle for the race that the person considers himself/herself to be.

- White
- Black or Negro
- Indian (Amer.) (print the name of the enrolled or principal tribe)
- Eskimo
- Aleut
- Chinese

- Filipino
- Hawaiian
- Korean
- Vietnamese
- Japanese
- Asian Indian
- Samoan
- Guamanian
- Other AIP (Asian or Pacific Islander) (print one group, for example: Hmong, Fijian, Laotian, Thai, Tongan, Pakistani, Cambodian, and so on)
- Other race (print race). . . .

7. Is this Person of Spanish/Hispanic origin?   Fill ONE circle for each person.

- No (not Spanish/Hispanic)
- Yes, Mexican, Mexican-Am., Chicano
- Yes, Puerto Rican
- Yes, Cuban
- Yes, other Spanish/Hispanic (print one group, for example: Argentinan, Colombian, Dominican, Nicaraguan, Salvadoran, Spaniard, and so on).

But close examination of the questions from the census, their historical origin, and the problems associated with their collection reveals a much murkier picture.

There are two interrelated issues here. First, we know from research on survey design and response variation that a researcher can generate different response rates for individual racial and ethnic categories by changing the form and details of the question. In 1987, for example, the Census Bureau, as part of its pretests for the 1990 census, conducted a split-ballot experiment involving 515 respondents, which took the two census questions and looked at the effect of reversing their order. The respondents in this study were asked to complete the census form for themselves and for members of their families, and they were randomly allocated to receive either the "census form" version or the version with the questions reversed. The result was 1,446 completed questionnaires, 703 using the standard order and 743 using the reversed order. The big differences came in the number of people completing the Hispanic origin question. The reordered sequence yielded a much higher response rate for the Hispanic origin question (increasing it from 82 to 91 percent) while changing only slightly the nonresponse to the race question. Furthermore, closer examination showed that nonresponse for those who answered the race question was related to the race of the respondents. Finally, putting the Hispanic origin question first also reduced the proportion of individuals who checked "other" as their race.[2] The results of this and subsequent studies demonstrate the fluidity that respondents attach to race and ethnicity labels and the difficulty that the Census Bureau and others have in capturing complete and unambiguous information on race and ethnicity.[3]

Second, there has been a loud and rather confusing recent discussion of the significance or salience of race and ethnicity as social markers. Some scholars and public officials have framed a significant critique to all racial and ethnic categories, challenging long-held views of the viability, advisability, and usefulness of race-based statistics in particular. Others have argued for the extension and deepening of statistical information on the racial and ethnic characteristics of the population and have advocated finer-grained classifications and more-detailed questions. All this discussion throws into question just what we mean by a differential undercount of minority populations in the census, and thus how to correct for it.

Because the responses to these questions on race and Hispanic origin are directly implicated in the adjustment processes considered for 1990 and planned for the census in 2000, in this chapter we take a break from our narrative on the 1990 census adjustment debate and take a hard look at the issue of the measurement of race and ethnicity and the debates it has engendered. We also pose these questions because the most obvious evidence of the differential undercount is the continuing series of high undercount rates for minorities relative to the rest of the population. Yet the opponents of adjustment have claimed successfully that it is not appropriate to adjust the official census figures. They have argued (1) that the adjustment procedures are not sufficiently accurate to allocate the missed people to states and localities, and (2) that it could be constitutionally inappropriate to adjust the census for the minority undercount, even if the procedures were improved. This latter claim, that it may be inappropriate to correct for the differential minority undercount, even were it possible to do so, directs us back to the core constitutional purposes of the census itself and the measurement of "equity." The tangled issues of the measurement of race and ethnicity and their use in the demographic analysis of the American population need to be scrutinized to understand how "counting by race" became part of American statistical traditions and, in turn, have influenced the controversies surrounding accuracy and fair representation that have bedeviled recent censuses.

The Classification of Race and Ethnicity

"Standards for Maintaining, Collecting, and Presenting Federal Data on Race and Ethnicity," promulgated by the Office of Management and Budget (OMB), defines the official federal government methodology for collecting and reporting survey data on the race and ethnicity of the American population. These standards were revised in the fall of 1997 from the 1977 Statistical Policy Directive 15, which itself represented a codification of earlier disparate practices among federal agencies. The current standards have five categories for data on race: American Indian or Alaska Native, Asian, Black or African American, Native Hawaiian or other Pacific Islander, and White. There are two categories for data on ethnicity: Hispanic or Latino and Not Hispanic or Latino (see appendix H). The 1997 revision emphasizes that self-reporting by individuals is the preferred method of gathering data. It also requires that respondents "be offered the option of selecting one or more racial designations. Recommended forms for the instruction accompanying the multiple response question are 'Mark one or more' and 'Select one or more.'" The policy is a minimum standard for the federal government; the census, in particular, collects and reports considerably more detail on race and ethnicity than the OMB standards require.

The current functions of the classification are defined in the policy: namely, "to provide a common language for uniformity and comparability in the collection and use of data on race and ethnicity by Federal agencies." They are to be "used for all Federal administrative reporting or record keeping requirements that include data on race and ethnicity," including "for civil rights and other compliance reporting from the public and private sectors and all levels of government." The logic of the classification does not derive from an interest in providing a thorough categorization of the ethnic and racial origins of the American population. Rather, it emerged from the "new responsibilities to enforce civil rights laws" in the federal government in the 1970s. The classification was designed to provide data "to monitor equal access in housing, education, employment, and other areas, for populations that historically had experienced discrimination and differential treatment because of their race or ethnicity." The Office of Management and Budget emphasizes that "the categories represent a social-political construct designed for collecting data on the race and ethnicity of broad population groups in this country, and are not anthropologically or scientifically based"; in addition, they "are not to be used as determinants of eligibility for participation in any Federal program" (Office of Information and Regulatory Affairs 1997b; for additional background, see Evinger 1995, 7–14; and Funderburg 1994).

The current directive was the result of a four-year review process. During that time, a wide variety of individuals and groups commented on, defended, and critiqued the classification. New groups of people asked to be identified in the classification. Advocates for separate categories for Cape Verdeans, Arabs, Muslim West Asians, Middle Easterners, Creoles, and multiracial Americans argued that the existing classification did not properly identify their group. Others pointed out a number of paradoxes in the ways the American government conceptualizes race.

- On the one hand, we are told by modern anthropologists and geneticists that there is no scientific basis for a concept called race; on the other hand, we know that a substantial number of geneticists engage in research on genetic differences among population groups.

- Federal policy requires universities to report student admissions by race and ethnicity in order to comply with affirmative action regulations. The presumption of such regulations is that admissions of the racial and ethnic groups should be roughly proportionate to their numbers in the "qualified" applicant pool. Then again, research that investigates the alleged differences in "intelligence" among population groups, such as the research in Herrnstein and Murray's (1994) recent book, *The Bell Curve*, has been excoriated and attacked as racist.

- It is illegal to require information on race as part of an employment application, but federal law requires employers to report the race of applicants. (Such data are typically collected by voluntary and anonymous self-reports from applicants, ignoring problems of nonresponse.)

- It is difficult to explain why we can "see" that some people are black and some are white, and with a bit of investigation we can link this distinction to the color of their parents, yet we are told that this "racial" difference may not be genetically based.

Given these paradoxes, it is not surprising that Americans express truly conflicted opinions about issues of race and ethnicity, at once affirming diversity and the multicultural background of the population, and the right of Americans to define their ethnic origins, and in the next breath condemning the divisiveness of identity politics based on those distinctions or proclaiming the unity of Americans despite their varied origins. (See, for example, Arthur and Shapiro 1996; Gregory and Sanjek 1994; Hacker 1995; Lubiano 1997; and Thernstrom and Thernstrom 1997.) The testimony at the hearings and public debates on the revision of the OMB classification captured these positions with particular sharpness, as representatives of traditional civil rights organizations took positions opposed to those from constituencies requesting a new designation in the policy. Politicians, the media, and academic authorities weighed in on the issue. The proposal for the creation of a "multiracial" category in the official classification drew major commentary, especially in the summer of 1997 after the young golf champion Tiger Woods commented on the Oprah Winfrey television show that he had referred to himself as "Cablinasian" when growing up. (See, for example, Wright 1994; "Black America and Tiger's Dilemma" 1997; O'Hare 1998; and Fisher 1998.)

The multiracial category found unlikely support from some conservatives. *Washington Post* columnist George Will, for example, advocated that a "multiracial" category be added to the existing OMB categories. He argued that the new category "would serve civic health by undermining the obsession with race and ethnicity that fuels identity politics." He then went on to identify a number of prominent Americans with multiracial origins. Yet even as he advocated the new category, he noted that "race and ethnicity are not fixed" and "can be, to some degree, matters of choice." "Perhaps it would be best to promote the desegregation of Americans by abolishing the existing five categories," he mused. Finally, he concluded that the new category "could speed the dilution of racial consciousness" (*Palm Beach Post,* Oct. 5, 1997).

Some established civil rights organizations did not express support, or even opposed, a new multiracial category. The National Association for the Advancement of Colored People (NAACP), for example, opposed the creation a "multiracial" race category in the OMB classification.[4] "The NAACP has great sensitivity on the issue of multiracial categories," testified Harold McDougall in May 1997.

We support the right of individual self-identification and support self-determination in defining one's racial makeup. But the census may not be the correct place to make such a personal statement, particularly in light of the fact that repercussions in census numbers impact the lives of many people. Provisions of the Voting Rights Act, for example, are specifically directed at correcting past discrimination (particularly in the deep South) where African-Americans were denied their constitutional rights. With some figures showing 70 percent of African-Americans as possibly fitting into a multiracial category, will we be able to identify black voters in terms of fair representation?

The answer to the rhetorical question was no, though McDougall made it clear that he was more concerned with maintaining the possibility of producing data in the appropriate reporting categories than he was with preventing an individual from identifying more than one racial or ethnic origin.

And academics traditionally concerned with racial and ethnic characteristics of individuals and groups have begun to advocate the elimination of the concept of race identification in government statistics altogether, even while couching their positions in ambivalent and conflicted language. The American Anthropological Association (AAA) made its claim to authority to speak on the issue by noting that "anthropology as an academic discipline has been dealing with issues of human variation for over 100 years. There has always been debate within the discipline about the exact nature of humankind." In its statement on proposed revisions of the OMB's Statistical Policy Directive 15, the AAA urged the federal government to phase out the use of the term *race* altogether and shift to the use of the term *ethnic origin* to define the social and cultural background of Americans. "The concept of race is a social and cultural construction, with no basis in human biology," the AAA noted. Furthermore, "race can simply not be tested or proven scientifically," and "many Americans do not understand differences between race, ethnicity, and ancestry categories in surveys and fail to distinguish between them."Addressing the question of biological differences among humans, the AAA noted that "probably the clearest data on human variation come from genetic studies. Genetic data do show differences between groups, and these can potentially trace an individual's likely geographic origin. This can be helpful in such applications as health screening. Nevertheless, the data also show that any two individuals within a particular population are as different genetically as any two people selected from any two populations in the world" (American Anthropological Association 1997; see also Smedley 1993).

The anthropologists recognized that "eliminating the term 'race' presents an opportunity and dilemma" because the categories are still required "in order to be vigilant about the elimination of discrimination." "Yet ultimately," they continued, "the effective elimination of discrimination will require an end to such categorization, and a transition toward social and cultural categories that will prove more scientifically useful and personally resonant for the public than are categories of 'race.'" They proposed that the race question remain in the 2000 census with a new title, "race/ethnicity," and that the term *race* be eliminated in the census of 2010.

In short, the evidence that has emerged during the most recent review of federal standards for collection of data on race and ethnicity poses an even greater problem for the discussion of the undercount. If the categories by which the differential undercount is measured themselves have no scientific basis and should be phased out, how can the federal government ever find a solution to the problems of measurement and "correction" for a differential undercount of minorities? And if individuals respond differently depending on the order in which questions are asked or the context in which they are asked, is there any validity to our data on the differential undercount? And why, from our current perspective, has such an important issue as underenumeration of portions of the population in the census been framed on a set of classifications that are either suspect or themselves flawed? The answers to these questions are embedded in the oblique references to the history of discrimination and civil rights compliance in the text of the OMB standards and hence to the history of the classification of race, ethnicity, and national origin in the census itself.

History of Racial Classifications

Anthropologists have noted the intellectual origins of "racial" classifications in their own discipline in "early European folk taxonomy that linked perceived biological and behavioral differences with a ranking, in terms of superiority, of races" (American Anthropological Association 1997). These classifications, in turn, emerged during the European expansion and world migration in the early modern era and are particularly visible in the development of the Americas. Using race as a means of classifying the population has a long statistical tradition in the United States. Beginning with the first census in 1790, the federal government has always measured race in some form or another, although the labels have changed, as have the purposes justifying its measurement. To set the current discussion in an appropriate historical context, it is thus useful to review the history of racial questions on the decennial census. That history, in turn, informs the logic and uses of the current OMB standards for data collection.

The United States at its founding in the late eighteenth century was the first "new nation" in the world, a nation of immigrants and, more ominously, a nation in which some people conquered, enslaved, and exploited other people in the process of nation building. It is this complex historical legacy that resonates through the debates about racial and ethnic classification and makes the controversies surrounding the differential undercount a flashpoint for many of the most difficult issues of equity in contemporary American life.

Racial classifications are embedded in the original "constitution" of the American state. Although the Declaration of Independence emphatically proclaims that "all men are created equal," and the Constitution grounds political authority and sovereignty in the "People of the United States," the actual language of Article I of the Constitution embodies a less equitable principle (Anderson 1988).

When the framers actually wrote the formula for allocating political representation among the states "according to their respective numbers," slaves "counted" as only three-fifths of a free person, and "Indians not taxed" were not counted at all. These decisions thus required the decennial census—the new instrument created to count the population—to classify the population into free, "other persons" (that is, slaves), and "Indians not taxed." Because the preexisting racial shorthand of White, Black, and Red underlay the civil categories, very quickly a classification by "color" supplanted the civil statuses in statistical compilations, though the translation of civil status to color was not exact. Free people were presumed to be white but could also include "the free colored." "Whites" also included indentured servants, who were not "free." Slaves were Black or mulatto but not White. After the Civil War, the Thirteenth Amendment nullified the three-fifths rule, but the federal government continued to count the population by race. Discrimination in civil, social, political, and economic opportunity on the basis of racial origin was practiced by federal, state, and local governments and by private employers and organizations and was legal until the period of "second Reconstruction" and the civil rights revolution of the 1950s and 1960s. "Indians" were designated as "civilized Indians" and "Indians not taxed" until 1924, when Congress awarded citizenship to all American Indians born in the United States.

In tables 8.1 and 8.2, we list the actual categories in the census over a period of fifty years. They demonstrate the evolution of the complexity and detail of the questions over time and the origins of the system in the civil statuses of "free," "slave," and "Indian not taxed." Figures 8.1 to 8.3 provide visual evidence of the size of the various groups, most importantly indicating that the proportion of the population that was classified as being other than White or Black did not rise above 5 percent of the population until 1980 (see Nash 1974; Allen 1994; Ignatiev 1995; Shoemaker 1997; and Davis 1991).

From 1790 to 1840, the census was taken using a "household" schedule, which asked the head how many individuals in the household were in various age, race, and sex cohorts. From the very outset, the federal statistical system and the population census defined three of the six categories currently listed in the OMB standards, that is, whites, blacks, and Indians. Along with sex and age, they were the basic variables characterizing the American population. In later years, revisions in racial classification would be built atop these existing three categories. From 1850 to the present, the race of each individual was identified according to the categories listed in table 8.2. Figure 8.4 summarizes the shifting number of race categories asked at each census and displays the changing definition of the overall classification (from *color* to *race*). We note also that some racial categories were eliminated over the years. There is a pattern of increasing differentiation of the categories from the mid-nineteenth century to the early twentieth century, during which time the number of categories grew from three to ten. There is also a long-term tendency for categories designed to identify groups of people who were racially mixed, such as mulatto, to be subsumed into one of the larger groups (see Mencke 1978; Williamson 1980).

The expansion of the number of race categories after 1850 and the inclusion of a large number of new questions on nativity and immigration status identified many of the new demographic groups that migrated to the United States after the mid-nineteenth century (see table 8.3 and figure 8.5). Chinese immigrants began to arrive in the United States in the mid-nineteenth century. By 1870, the census listed a category for "Chinese" as a new "color" and also recorded Chinese nativity under the question on place of birth.

American naturalization law from the 1790s to the 1940s restricted citizenship to immigrants who were "White," and thus it had

Table 8.1   Census Race Categories, 1790 to 1840

Year	Race Category
1790	Free white males of 16 years and upward, including heads of families under 16 years Free white females, including heads of families All other free persons Slaves
1800 and 1810	Free white males, divided into 5 age cohorts Free white females, divided into 5 age cohorts All other free persons, except Indians not taxed Slaves

1820	Free white males, divided into 6 age cohorts
	Free white females, divided into 5 age cohorts
	Slaves
	  males, divided into 4 age cohorts
	  females, divided into 4 age cohorts
	Free colored persons
	  males, divided into 4 age cohorts
	  females, divided into 4 age cohorts
	All other persons, except Indians not taxed

1830 and 1840[a]	Free white persons
	  males, divided into 13 age cohorts
	  females, divided into 13 age cohorts
	Slaves
	  males, divided into 6 age cohorts
	  females, divided into 6 age cohorts
	Free colored persons
	  males, divided into 6 age cohorts
	  females, divided into 6 age cohorts

Source: Wright and Hunt 1900, passim.

[a]The federal government used a two-sided schedule: in 1830, the age/sex breakdowns for Whites were on the front of the schedule and those for slaves and the free colored on the back; in 1840, the age/sex breakdowns for Whites and free colored were on the front of the schedule and those for slaves were on the back.

Table 8.2 Census Race Categories, 1850 to 1990

Year	Census Race Categories		
1850[a]		B	M
1860[a]		B	M (Ind.)[b]
1870	W	B	M, C, I
1880	W	B	M, C, I
1890	white	black	mulatto, quadroon, octoroon, Chinese, Japanese, Indian
1900	W	B	Ch, Jp, In
1910	W	B	Mu, Ch, Jp, In, Ot, (+ write in)
1920	W	B	Mu, In, Ch, Jp, Fil, Hin, Kor, Ot (+ write in)
1930	W	Neg	Mex, In, Ch, Jp, Fil, Hin, Kor (Other races, spell out in full)
1940	W	Neg	In, Chi, Jp, Fil, Hin, Kor, (Other races, spell out in full)
1950	W	Neg	Ind, Jap, Chi, Fil, (Other race—spell out)
1960	White	Negro	American Indian, Japanese, Chinese, Filipino, Hawaiian, Part Hawaiian, Aleut, Eskimo, (etc)
1970	White	Negro or Black	Indian (Amer), Japanese, Chinese, Filipino, Hawaiian, Korean, Other (print race)
1980	White	Negro or Black	Japanese, Chinese, Filipino, Korean, Vietnamese, Indian (Amer), Asian Indian, Hawaiian, Guamanian, Samoan, Eskimo, Aleut, Other (specify)
1990	White	Black or Negro	Indian (Amer), Eskimo, Aleut, Chinese, Filipino, Hawaiian, Korean, Vietnamese, Japanese, Asian Indian, Samoan, Guamanian, Other API, Other race

Source: Wright and Hunt 1900; U.S. Bureau of the Census 1979, 1993a.

Note: The categories are given in the order they appeared on the schedule. If abbreviations were used, the abbreviation is listed. Otherwise, the full term is written out.

[a]In 1850 and 1860, free persons were enumerated on the schedule for "free inhabitants," and slaves on the schedule designated for "slave inhabitants." For the free schedule, the

Figure 8.1   Proportion of the U.S. Population, White, 1790 to 1990

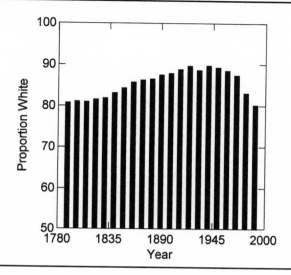

the effect of dividing immigrants who wished to remain in the United States and become citizens into two different civil statuses. Those who were considered "White" could naturalize, and a series of court cases in the late nineteenth and early twentieth centuries defined who was "White by law" and thus eligible for citizenship. Chinese and other Asian immigrants who were classified as not "White" were excluded from naturalization and became "aliens ineligible for citizenship." The Chinese Exclusion Act of 1882 barred further Chinese immigration. Japanese immigrants began coming to the United States in the late

---

instructions told the enumerators, "in all cases where the person is White leave the space blank in the column marked 'Color.'" For the slave schedule, the listed categories were B or M.

[b]Although this category was not listed on the census form, the instructions read:

5. Indians.—Indians not taxed are not to be enumerated. The families of Indians who have renounced tribal rule, and who under State or Territorial laws exercise the rights of citizens, are to be enumerated. In all such cases write "Ind." opposite their names, in column 6, under heading "Color." . . .

9. Color.—Under heading 6, entitled "Color," in all cases where the person is white leave the space blank; in all cases where the person is black without admixture insert the letter "B"; if a mulatto, or of mixed blood, write "M"; if an Indian, write "Ind." It is very desirable to have these directions carefully observed.

Figure 8.2   Proportion of the U.S. Population, Black, 1790 to 1990

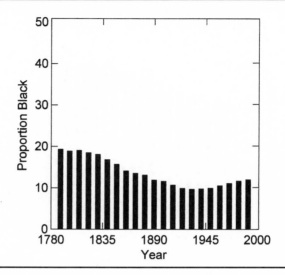

Figure 8.3   Proportion of the U.S. Population, Neither White nor Black, 1790 to 1990

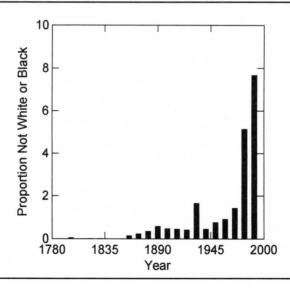

Figure 8.4   Census Race Categories, 1820 to 1990

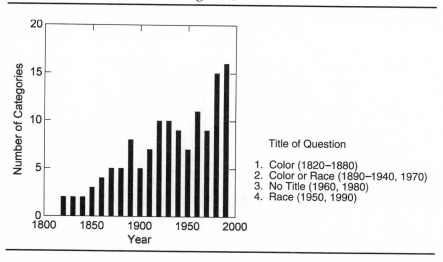

Title of Question

1. Color (1820–1880)
2. Color or Race (1890–1940, 1970)
3. No Title (1960, 1980)
4. Race (1950, 1990)

Table 8.3   Frequency of Questions on Immigration and Nativity, 1820 to 1990

Type of Question	Frequency
The country of origin of the person	
(a) Where the person was born (1850–1990)	15
(b) The country of parents' or "ancestors'" origin	
Place of birth of parents (1870–1970)	11
Ancestry (1980–90)	2
Citizenship status (1820–30, 1890–1950, 1970–90)	14
Language status	
(a) Ability to speak English (1890–1930, 1980–90)	7
(b) Mother tongue (1890, 1910–40, 1960–90)	9
When the person arrived in the United States (1890–1930, 1970–90)[a]	8

Note: Between 1820 and 1990, seventeen censuses asked questions on immigration and nativity of the foreign born. The most common questions were on place of birth (asked fifteen times) and about citizenship (asked in some form fourteen times).

[a] At the 1920 census, also included when person was naturalized.

Figure 8.5   Census Questions on Immigration and Nativity, 1820 to 1990

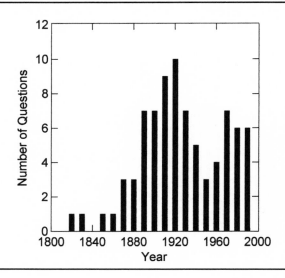

1880s, and "Japanese" was added as a response to the "race or color" question in 1890. "Filipino," "Hindu," and "Korean" were added in 1920. During World War II, restrictions on naturalization of Asian immigrants were repealed. The amalgamation of the disparate Asian "racial" categories into the Asian and Pacific Islander group was a result of the creation of OMB Statistical Policy Directive 15 in 1977 (Haney Lopez 1996; Daniels 1990; Takaki 1993; Omi and Winant 1994).

The historical antecedents of the "Hispanic" category tell a different story (see table 8.4). The first notable Hispanic residents of the United States were neither a definable racial group nor an immigrant group but rather the roughly eighty thousand residents of New Mexico and California living in lands annexed to the United States as a result of the Mexican War (from 1846 to 1847). In the twentieth century, immigrants from Mexico, Puerto Rico, Cuba, and Latin American nations migrated to the United States. These groups merged to form a large and growing population, which the Census Bureau identified as of "Spanish culture and origin."

Hispanic Americans have resisted being classified as a racial group, and were so classified in only one federal census (in 1930), when the Census Bureau listed "Mexican" as a possible answer to the "color or race" question. Mexican Americans objected to the practice, and it was

Table 8.4   Census Questions on Spanish or Hispanic Origin
or Descent, 1970 to 1990

Year	Question
1970	Is this person's origin or descent?
	Mexican
	Puerto Rican
	Cuban
	Central American
	Other Spanish
	No, none of these[a]
1980	Is this person of Spanish/Hispanic origin or descent?
	No, not Spanish/Hispanic
	Yes, Mexican, Mexican American, Chicano
	Yes, Puerto Rican
	Yes, Cuban
	Yes, other Spanish/Hispanic
1990	Is this person of Spanish/Hispanic origin?
	No, not Spanish/Hispanic
	Yes, Mexican, Mexican American, Chicano
	Yes, Puerto Rican
	Yes, Cuban
	Yes, other Spanish/Hispanic, print one group . . .

Note: The census asked a specific question on "Spanish origin or descent" in 1970 on
the 5 percent sample as a second part of the sample question on place of birth. In 1980,
a question on "Spanish/Hispanic Origin or Descent" appeared on the short form. In
earlier years, individuals of "Spanish/Hispanic origin or descent" could be identified
through a combination of questions on place of birth, place of birth of parents, and
mother tongue. In 1930, the Census Bureau listed "Mexican" as a category for the answers to the question on "color or race" (see table 8.2). It was not repeated in later
censuses.

[a]This question appeared in the 1970 5 percent sample long-form.

not repeated. Nevertheless, a constellation of information from questions on nativity and mother tongue have made residents of "Spanish
origin or descent" identifiable in statistical compilations in the years
before the official creation of the "Hispanic" ethnic category in 1977.

  This brief history does not exhaust the full story of racial and ethnic classification in the federal statistical system, but it does indicate
that the overall purpose of the classifications from the founding of the
republic through the mid-twentieth century was to separate those

people who were entitled to the full measure of opportunity and participation in the society from those who were not so entitled because
of their racial, ethnic, or national origin. Over the years, Americans
pressing for a nonracialized society challenged such classification and
treatment, and the history of the nation can be told as the debate about
the history of the inclusion or exclusion of the various elements of
the population from full participation. Over time, the boundaries of
participation expanded, most notably as Americans rejected race-based
slavery as a labor system and endorsed probably the most liberal immigration policy in the world—particularly until the early twentieth century. Nevertheless, after the official abolition of slavery and the Fourteenth Amendment's ringing endorsement of the requirement that all
Americans receive the "equal protection of the laws," at the turn of
the century the Supreme Court sanctioned differential treatment on
the basis of race if the policy or practice was "separate but equal."
Accordingly, the statistical system continued to build racial classifications into the emerging data systems of the nation, including systems
of administrative records, immigration records, and vital registration
systems, as well as the census. It would be in this officially sanctioned
world of Jim Crow that government officials first discovered the differential undercount. In the 1950s and 1960s, the nation challenged its
racialized past and passed a series of landmark laws designed to guarantee equal opportunity and access to the benefits of the society. The
Civil Rights Act of 1964 banned discrimination in employment and
public accommodations. The Voting Rights Act of 1965 and its later
amendments sought to expand political participation of racial groups
excluded from voting and office holding. Federal Executive Order
11246 required all federal contractors to comply with nondiscrimina-
tory employment practices and develop administrative systems to
monitor compliance. The Housing Act of 1968 and later amendments
banned discrimination in housing markets. Suddenly, the racial classifications in the federal statistical system were called upon to meet the
needs of the civil rights enforcement machinery and the emerging
claim of the "right" of Americans to define their own identity.

Civil Rights and Self-Identification

It might seem a bit of a paradox that racial classification of the population got a new lease on life after the civil rights revolution of the
1960s. Civil rights activists and legislators, after all, had struggled long

and hard to dismantle the system of overt Jim Crow discrimination by race and to guarantee voting rights, public accommodations, economic and educational opportunity, and housing choices to people long barred from full citizenship because of ethnicity, race, or color. Yet the early efforts to institutionalize a full equal-rights agenda were not particularly successful. Efforts at school desegregation and employment change were particularly frustrating. Hence, officials instituted new administrative systems to monitor the implementation of equal rights in the major sectors of American life and to enforce sanctions for noncompliance. Organizations representing Black, Asian, Hispanic, or American Indians insisted that the federal government continue to report statistics on the ethnic or racial identity of Americans and to promote "affirmative action" policies to end the legacy of discrimination. Such new agencies as the Office of Federal Contract Compliance Programs in the Department of Labor, the Equal Employment Opportunity Commission, and the Office for Civil Rights in the Department of Education thus mandated that employers, schools, and other public agencies report the racial and ethnic distribution of their clients, employees, or students. (See Graham 1990; Skrentny 1996; Eastland and Bennett 1979; and Peterson 1995.)

The civil rights revolution of the 1960s also coincided with changes in research practice that made self-identification the preferred response method in survey research. By 1970, the census was taken by mail, and thus people puzzled out the "right" answers to questions alone in their own homes. Especially when it comes to classification schemes, as noted at the outset of this chapter, minor variations in presentation of questions (not just the wording) can yield substantially different responses, and an individual may respond quite differently to the same question in different contexts, for example, replying to the census or applying for a job. This is especially true in the present context for those who have multiple group identifications. Some 9.8 million people checked "other race" in response to the race question on the 1990 census. Two percent of the population did not answer the race question. The Census Bureau estimates that 97 percent of those who checked "other race" were Hispanics. An additional quarter of a million people identified multiple-race responses, such as "Black/ White," "Eurasian," or "Amerasian" (Edmonston, Goldstein, and Lott 1996, 23).

The pressure for statistical information to monitor civil rights enforcement has combined with the self-identification rule to shape the current racial and ethnic classification in OMB's standards for data on race and ethnicity. There is tension between the choices presented by the boxes in a census questionnaire, which define the possible answers according to administrative requirements, and the complex lived identities of individuals. But if everyone paid homage to a rule of self-identification, then people could claim the right to "be what they are" and not fit in established categories.

Relationship of Race Classification to Undercount Controversies

The classification of race and ethnicity in the census and the broader federal statistical system reflects the history of discrimination in the larger society, efforts to redress that discrimination, and the newer subjective claim to self-identification. The undercount controversies, framed as they are with patterns of differential undercount by race, resonate with that history, as well. It is useful then, once again, to review the history of the technical discovery of the undercount in the context of the history of statistics of racial and ethnic groups in the society.

It is perhaps a particular irony of the legacy of American statistical practice that the differential undercount of hard-to-count groups in the population was discovered and labeled as a minority, or nonwhite, undercount.[5] Defining and measuring a census undercount requires a statistical conception of the possibility of measuring underreporting using a second count or source of information on the population. In the nineteenth century, there were scattered protests by local areas that the census count was too low, protests usually fraught with partisan accusation. The Census Office actually reenumerated Philadelphia and New York in 1870 as a result of such protests. But these efforts took place before the concept of probability had taken hold in the statistical sciences and did not lead to any further innovation in bureau practice in counting. City leaders claimed the first count was flawed and needed to be redone, and they were pleased when the second count was higher than the first. Neither they nor the census officials conducted a person-by-person or district-by-district comparison of the two counts to evaluate coverage, as would be done today.

The discovery of the undercount following the fall 1940 draft registration was another matter entirely. By the late 1930s, bureau officials had begun to integrate sampling into census practice, and they had developed the concepts of sampling error, nonsampling error, and bias. The bureau's internal work and Daniel Price's (1947) published analysis focused on the methodological implications of the undercount for census practice. The officials looked for alternative record systems and variables that would allow finer-grained analyses of the data and would, in turn, allow them to evaluate coverage further. As noted, the draft registration comparison involved geographic and race comparisons: namely, a comparison of the census counts for draft-age men by race and state with those of the actual registrations. The race data were available in the registration system because Jim Crow policy segregated the American military by race.

In later years, as demographers studied the undercount, they turned to vital records of births and deaths to compare with census data. Again, a race classification was available in the system, along with age and sex, allowing for its use to segment the population into more detailed demographic subgroups for analysis. Geographic analyses were not possible because Americans routinely migrated among states. The tradition developed in a period of relatively limited foreign immigration, allowing the demographers to approximate a closed population—particularly for nonwhites.

For the first thirty years following the discovery of the census undercount, the data systems available to analyze the count tended to preclude the analysis of undercount by state and encouraged the analysis of the undercount at a national level by race, age, and sex. Yet as Allen Schirm (1991) has shown, had officials adjusted the counts from the censuses from 1940 to 1980 using what are today the best estimates of adjustment developed retrospectively, the adjusted numbers would have changed the apportionment of seats in Congress by at least one seat for four of the five census years. Only in 1960 would the apportionment as implemented have remained the same. (This analysis applies demographic estimates for undercounts for Blacks and Whites and then corrects for this differential separately state by state.)

The persistent differential undercount of racial minorities is also a persistent differential undercount of states and local areas that affects congressional apportionment. This fact became abundantly clear in the course of the litigation during and after the 1990 count. What does change if one reconceptualizes the differential undercount by race to a differential undercount by state is the consistency of the political impact on apportionment. Schirm's analysis also demonstrates that it is not obvious which states will win and which will lose a congressional seat from census adjustment. In fact, in perhaps the supreme irony, Schirm's data show that New York State would never have been a winner from census adjustment using today's best estimates of adjusted census counts from previous censuses and would, in fact, have possibly lost a seat in 1940 and in 1980. Other potential losers in various years under various scenarios included Massachusetts (1950), Oklahoma (1970), and Colorado, Pennsylvania, Tennessee, Iowa, and Kansas (1980). Possible winners included California, Georgia, Indiana, and Texas (1980), Connecticut (1970), Tennessee (1950), and Alabama (1940 and 1980).

Schirm also notes that other decisions about counting particular population subgroups in a particular place—for example, college students—or whether to include a group at all—for example, overseas populations allocated back to a state—also have an impact on apportionment. He notes that the "revisions currently undertaken by the Census Bureau as a matter of course and the resolution of issues by the exercise of administrative discretion can have the same effects on apportionment as adjustment" (ibid., 538).

In short, an adjustment for the differential undercount by race increases the population count for geographic areas with higher proportions of minorities relative to those geographic areas with smaller proportions of minorities. But those adjusted population counts do not necessarily lead to predictable increases in minority political representation at the level of Congress. Furthermore, the changing demographics of the American population make it hard to predict which groups in the population will be undercounted in the future and thus calls for an undercount measurement method that is flexible and supple enough to capture those changing demographics by geographic area. In that sense, the race variable, like the age, sex, or housing status variables used to measure and adjust for local-area undercounts, is a tag needed to identify people counted in the survey and in the census. It is an effective marker. The 1990 PES was a sufficiently fine-grained instrument with adequate markers to reveal for the first time that other groups besides Blacks were undercounted, including a 12 percent undercount of reservation Indians, a 6 to 9 percent undercount of Hispanic urban renters, and a 2.8 to 6.9 percent undercount of non-Hispanic White and other renters outside urban areas (Hogan 1993).

More broadly, any procedure for measuring and adjusting undercount in the future will have to be sufficiently sophisticated to provide adjustments for congressional apportionment and sufficiently accurate to earn the political support necessary for implementation. The changing racial composition of American society and the changing racial classification scheme have added a new level of uncertainty to the undercount measurement. Jeffrey Passel, a former Census Bureau official and one of the chief researchers on the changing racial and ethnic demographics of the country, has noted that "in little more than a generation, the United States has shifted from a predominantly White society with a Black minority to a more heterogeneous society. The Black population now accounts for only half of the minority population and will become the second-largest minority within 15 or 20 years" (Passel 1993).

In such an environment, a postenumeration survey with dual-systems estimation is the only method for correction that promises success, precisely because it employs two measures of counting that are proximate in time and thus are less likely to be complicated by changes in an individual's demographic status.

A Small Postscript

As we began the research for this book in the mid-1990s, the remaking of the classification scheme for race and ethnicity promised to be at least as controversial as the plans to adjust the census for the differential undercount. Yet, except for the occasional session at professional and social science research conferences, the revisions published in October 1997, and now being implemented by federal statistical agencies, have been barely noticed on the public radar screen. At the same time, the issue of census adjustment has been repeatedly the subject of public controversy and has twice been the topic of major lawsuits argued before the Supreme Court. What distinguishes the two issues, and how they have played out?

At this point, we simply identify a few salient features of the revision of the standards for classification of data on race and ethnicity. First, the revision has been carried out by the Statistical Policy Office in the OMB and has involved all of the statistical agencies as well as representatives of a diverse collection of civic and professional groups and other government agencies at federal, state, and local levels. The process relied on an interagency committee that oversaw and developed the review, monitored almost four years of research activity, and summarized and published extensive reports and recommendations for public commentary before OMB announced the final revisions.[6] Although not everyone agreed on the final result, virtually all of those involved agreed that some revision was required and that the ultimate authority lay with OMB. Second, the research program to explore the implications of alternative classification schemes was broadly based and involved cognitive laboratory research followed by direct statistical experiments of alternative wordings in multiple government surveys (see, for example, Tucker et al. 1996). There were some disputed interpretations, but by and large the research findings remained uncontroversial. Third, the entire process was kept at arm's length from the ongoing disputes over adjustment of the decennial census. Thus, few members of Congress and the press have yet to appreciate the extent to which the issues are joined. The current retrospective efforts to criticize the 1990 adjustment methodologies virtually never mention the topic of error and uncertainty in racial classification in the Census Bureau.

Chapter 9

Toward Census 2000

T he reader will have already observed (from chapters 3 and 5) that the modern Census Bureau works on at least two censuses at once: the previous one and the next one.[1] Hence, the procedures and policies for the upcoming census are in development as the publication and analysis of the previous one are still ongoing. Thus one must look to the early 1990s for the beginning of the planning for the 2000 census. Census 2000 planning began during the Bush administration, during Barbara Everitt Bryant's tenure as census director and Robert Mosbacher's tenure as commerce secretary. At the July 15, 1991, announcement of the decision not to adjust the 1990 count, for example, key Commerce Department officials were already projecting the implications of the PES research and other 1990 research for the 2000 census. At the news conference at which Secretary Mosbacher made his announcement, Michael Darby, under secretary of commerce for economic affairs, also announced that the Commerce Department and the Census Bureau intended to continue the research program into adjustment and how to incorporate adjustment "into the intercensal program." When asked how he would respond to "various minority groups" who could "feel even more disenfranchised when you do the census again in the year 2000," Darby replied, "We have major planning—and the Secretary made very clear that part of that planning effort is trying to figure out how to do an adjustment correctly for the year 2000."[2]

In other words, years before the actual outcome of the New York litigation was clear, officials in the Bush administration took the initial steps that shaped the plan for 2000. In the second half of 1991 and in 1992, the bureau staff developed an internal administrative and planning schedule for innovations they wished to test for 2000, worked with the Democratic Congress to pass legislation to recruit from the larger statistical community the expertise needed to develop those innovations, and organized an extensive campaign to promote understanding and discussion of the decisions to be made for 2000. Within the bureau, a technical committee and a policy committee began to articulate plans of a broad range of possible changes to the enumeration methods to be used to take the 2000 count. These included innovations that were extensions of ongoing research, such as the creation of user-friendly forms, sampling for nonresponse follow-up, increased use of administrative records for counting the population, and refinements of the PES methodology. The bureau also proposed several radical new proposals for counting (see Miskura 1992; U.S. Bureau of the Census 1992b), including a system of continuous measurement of the population, which might ultimately obviate the need for a decennial count altogether.[3] These activities occurred largely out of public view.

On the public front, on October 15, 1991, Commerce Secretary Mosbacher "announced the establishment of an advisory committee to ensure that there is full participation in public discussions of the nature of the census for the year 2000" (U.S. Department of Commerce 1991). The executive director of the Council of Professional Associations on Federal Statistics, Katherine Wallman, was selected to head the committee, made up of representatives of twenty-five organizations of census stakeholders, the postmaster general, and the chair and ranking minority members of the four congressional committees with census oversight responsibilities. Relatedly, the House and the Senate passed a bill authorizing a new three-year independent study of alternatives for the decennial census of the year 2000, to be conducted by the Committee on National Statistics at the National Academy of Sciences (NAS). On October 24, President Bush signed the Decennial Census Improvement Act of 1991, and Congress authorized funding for the study in the bureau budget. Meanwhile, the Census Bureau requested the Committee on National Statistics to carry out a separate study focused on census methods. Members of the two resulting panels, the Panel on Census Requirements for the Year 2000 and Beyond and the Panel to Evaluate Alternative Census Methods, were appointed over the months and began meeting in June 1992. Former Office of Management and Budget (OMB) official and economist Charles Schultze headed the Requirements Panel.[4] Norman Bradburn, of the National Opinion Research Center, headed the Methods Panel.

By the time the new National Academy of Sciences panels began meeting, Census Bureau officials, professional stakeholders, and key members of Congress had begun to shape a basic framework of issues for the 2000 count. In the context of the ongoing litigation, all parties were cautious about making dramatic public statements, promising too much, or proposing radical changes. Nevertheless, by mid-1992 there was general consensus in the bureau leadership, Congress, and the professional community that the 1990 count procedures could be improved significantly, particularly by additional use of sampling, that the escalating costs of the last three censuses needed to be brought under control, and that a good deal of technical work was needed to facilitate a final 2000 census design. Different parties placed varying emphasis on particular possibilities, but there was little concern that the range of possibilities the bureau had defined were improper or overly narrow. Schedules for testing, planning, and decision making were developed and coordinated with the NAS panels. They included content tests of revised user-friendly schedules in 1992, stakeholder meetings in 1992 and 1993, reports from the NAS panels in 1994, tests in 1995 of the most likely design alternatives for 2000, and an announcement of the 2000 design in late 1995 or early 1996. All parties recognized that the ongoing litigation from 1990 could have an impact on 2000, but the agenda at hand was primarily technical and bureaucratic. It involved encouraging the understanding of and finding solutions to the seemingly intractable problems of nonresponse, escalating costs, and problems in the new estimation procedures. Drawing from bureau and professional materials, census aficionados were already beginning to bandy about the new buzzwords for 2000: "integrated coverage measurement," "the single-number census," and "sampling for nonresponse follow-up."

What was not clear in late 1991 and 1992 was the impact political changes in the executive and legislative branches would ultimately have on the debates on the 2000 census design. In 1991 and 1992, all parties had adjusted to the process of planning under divided political control of the national government. There was at the time a Democratic Congress and a Republican president. Looking backward, all could see that Democrats had dominated the legislative branch since the 1930s, with only brief exceptions. Republicans had been dominant in the executive branch for twenty-eight of the last forty years. Those patterns showed no sign of changing. What was already clear from the census litigation of 1990 and earlier decades was that the courts looked critically on decision making that could be seen as politically motivated. Whatever the ultimate decision on the prudence of not adjusting the 1990 count, the emerging litigation had already demonstrated that an abrupt decision to cancel a statistical innovation that had broad professional support, such as Commerce Under Secretary Ortner's 1987 cancelation of the PES, would have trouble surviving judicial scrutiny. Hence, it was incumbent on all parties to work out a 2000 design that could garner broad political and technical support.

In late 1991 and early 1992, it also did not seem that the Democrats had much of a possibility of capturing the White House. President Bush's fortunes stood quite high in the polls in the aftermath of the successful prosecution of the Gulf war. The field of Democratic challengers did not seem terribly strong. Yet by the summer of 1992, Bill Clinton had emerged as the Democratic nominee and was showing surprising strength in campaign polls. Hammering away at the problems with the economy and the deficit and the "extravagances" of twelve years of Republican leadership, his "It's the economy, stupid" slogan turned out to be a winning approach. In November 1992, Bill Clinton won the presidency amid a heady atmosphere of generational change. The 1960s generation of Clinton supporters entered the White House in an upbeat liberal mood, calling for diversity in government, national health insurance, and a variety of postponed liberal initiatives.

Within the Office of Management and Budget, Katherine Wallman became chief statistician, returning to the Office of Statistical Policy that she had left after the Reagan administration took over in 1981. The appointment signaled the possibility that perhaps the Clinton administration would be making changes in statistical policy. And quickly, new initiatives emerged, such as the consideration of the revision of the standards for data on race and ethnicity (discussed in chapter 8).

The Clinton administration had a similar opportunity to review the leadership at the Census Bureau, as the bureau again faced the changing of the guard. Barbara Everitt Bryant submitted her resignation, along with all the other political appointees of the Bush administration, though she offered to stay. Two working days before she was to leave, commerce officials asked her to stay until the incoming administration had a nominee in place. She declined. Harry Scarr, then deputy director of the bureau, was appointed as acting director, pending the decision by the Clinton administration on a replacement for Bryant. Scarr, a career civil servant, had served as the first director of the Bureau of Justice Statistics and had joined the Commerce Department in 1982. He had served on the under secretary's staff and moved to the bureau to become acting deputy director in 1992, succeeding

Louis Kincannon (*New York Times,* Nov. 21, 1995; "The Census and You" 1992). Ronald Brown replaced Barbara Franklin as commerce secretary, and the Commerce Department began the search for a new Census Bureau director. As usual, the Census Bureau post was a relatively low priority, particularly once the Clinton administration ran into a firestorm of negative publicity over the proposed appointments of much more highly visible positions for Zoe Baird, Kimba Wood, and Lani Guinier. The scuttlebutt in Washington was that the Clinton administration was in search of a member of a minority group to head the bureau, but no name emerged. It would take the Clinton administration almost two years to settle on a nominee: Martha Farnsworth Riche, director of policy studies of the Population Reference Bureau. Her name became public in the second half of 1994, and she was confirmed in October of the same year.

For the first two years of the Clinton administration, Census Bureau officials labored on the plans for 2000 in relative obscurity and continued to develop the proposals prepared under the Republicans in 1991 and 1992. No dramatic new leadership took the helm of the agency. Scarr did not seek headlines or the attention of Congress. Judge McLaughlin's 1993 decision upholding the decision not to adjust provided the bureau with a measure of stability. If a set of plans for 2000 could be developed that had the support of the bureau leadership, stakeholders and professionals outside the bureau, and the department leadership, the bureau could avoid the controversies that had plagued the 1990 count. By the end of 1994, the Panel on Census Requirements and the Panel to Evaluate Alternative Census Methods had completed their reports (Steffey and Bradburn 1994; Edmonston and Schultze 1995); both called for a "redesigned census" that would make use of statistical estimation. The 2000 census should be a "one-number census" that would build "integrated coverage measurement" into its procedures. The panels saw their proposals as mechanisms to improve accuracy while reducing the cost of the count. The bureau, which had already been working in this direction, agreed and built many of the proposals in the reports into the spring 1995 census tests.

The major components for initiatives for the 1995 census tests aimed to solve the problems that had plagued the 1990 count, particularly skyrocketing costs, the low mail-response rate, and the problems with the PES. Another initiative focused on the redesign of questionnaires, to make them easier to read and to answer. Bureau statisticians developed new procedures to allow households to get a second form if they needed it. The size of the PES was slated to increase dramatically, to solve the problem of a data set with too few cases to make valid inferences.[5] To reduce costs, the bureau proposed a number of technological innovations in data capture and tabulation and, most importantly, sampling for nonresponse follow-up. The Achilles' heel of the complete count was the problem of sending out enumerators to get responses from every household that did not respond by mail. Officials knew that data quality declined dramatically and errors increased the further from the April 1 census day the data were collected.[6] If funds could be used to hire higher-quality enumerators who could get data on a sample of these nonresponders in a shorter period of time, then the overall quality of the census count would improve.

But the Census Bureau would find, once again, that it was not master of its own fate. The larger policy proposals of the first Clinton administration were in domestic policy, including bringing the deficit under control, strengthening enforcement of civil rights laws, reforming the welfare system, and building a national health insurance system. Despite Democratic control of both houses of Congress, Clinton's proposals did not fare well. By the summer of 1994, he faced major defeat as his plans for national health insurance collapsed, and Republicans mounted an effort to wrest control of Congress from the Democrats. Newt Gingrich, onetime congressional maverick and a campaigner as energetic as Clinton, developed a conservative agenda, which he called the GOP Contract with America, and molded together a coordinated group of challengers to the "big spending, liberal Democrats" in Congress. In November, the Republicans won both houses of Congress, and conservative euphoria and energy became the dominant mood in Washington. Census plans turned out to be an early casualty.

The arrival of the Republican congressional majority signaled major changes in the political landscape for the 2000 census plans. When the Republicans abolished the Committee on Post Office and Civil Service, and with it Representative Sawyer's Subcommittee on the Census, Statistics, and Postal Personnel, the oversight jurisdiction for the census shifted to the Committee on Government Reform and Oversight, which was created by merging the Post Office, Civil Service, and Government Operations Committees and the Committee on the District of Columbia. Within the Committee on Government Reform and Oversight, jurisdiction for most statistical and information activities was assigned to the Subcommittee on Government Management, Information, and Technology, chaired by Representative Steve Horn (Rep.-Calif.) and with Representative Carolyn Maloney (Dem.-N.Y.) as ranking minority member. Jurisdiction for the census, however, was assigned to the Subcommittee on National Security, International Affairs, and Criminal Justice, chaired by Representative Bill Zellif (Rep.-N.H.) and with Representative Karen Thurman (Dem.-Fla.) as ranking minority member. Zellif held only one or two hearings, and most of the work during the 104th Congress was done at the full committee level. Representative Harold Rogers (Rep.-Ky.) became chair of the Appropriations Subcommittee for Commerce, State, Justice, and the Judiciary, and it soon became clear that he looked with much greater skepticism at Census Bureau and professional claims for the emerging 2000 design. In particular, Rogers wanted to know why the bureau did not just get rid of the long form questionnaire, the 17 percent sample of the population asked to answer detailed questions, which, he felt, seemed intrusive at best and led people to neglect completing the form altogether (*New York Times,* Aug. 23, 1995; Elving 1991, 286). The bureau found itself in the congressional hot seat once again, trying to defend an emerging 2000 census design, including major new uses of statistical estimation, to a suspicious and often hostile Republican leadership.

During 1995, as the 2000 census tests were under way, Census Director Martha Farnsworth Riche began to promote the draft proposals for the "reengineered" 2000 census (U.S. Bureau of the Census 1995). Riche, a new face on the hill because of her recent appointment, was in fact promoting a design for 2000 that had been several years in the making and was not, in its broad outlines, viewed as terribly controversial among members of the professional statistical community. There were plenty of technical and operational questions to be answered before the 2000 design would be finalized, but, as Riche and other bureau officials emphasized, these questions would be addressed during the tests scheduled in the upcoming years. Besides the 1995 tests of the new census design, for example, the bureau had scheduled content tests for 1996, including a Race and Ethnicity Targeted Test, and a dress rehearsal for 1998.

Bureau plans fared poorly in the context of the Republican congressional agenda, as did bureau requests for appropriations to test aspects of the new design. Bringing the budget deficit down was a major Republican goal, and the emerging consensus among the Republicans with census oversight was that the Census Bureau had embarked on a plan that was too elaborate and did not merit their support. In the context of tight budgets, the bureau should plan on pruning the design further. Representative Rogers, for example, returned to a theme that Republicans had been raising since the early years of the Reagan administration—namely, that the collection of statistical data should be privatized or, at the very least, paid for by the agencies in the federal government that needed the information (*New York Times,* Aug. 23, 1995; *Washington Post,* Sept. 29, Dec. 5, 1995).

Throughout 1995, the emerging differences between the views of the congressional Republicans and the bureau leadership were overshadowed by the larger struggles between Congress and the executive branch over the various elements of the Contract with America and cutting the federal budget. In the fall of 1995, the confrontation reached a crisis point, as the two sides deadlocked over the passage of a fiscal 1996 budget. For four days in November 1995, and then for almost a month between mid-December 1995 and mid-January 1996, the federal government shut down because Congress and the president could not agree on a plan to balance the federal budget. Hundreds of thousands of federal workers were furloughed, and much of the routine business of the federal bureaucracy stopped. Republicans had hoped to demonstrate dramatically to the American people that the country could well afford to trim federal operations, and they hoped that the shutdown strategy would solidify support for their balanced-budget proposals. The Democrats in Congress and the Clinton administration labeled the move irresponsible and blamed the Republicans for any inconveniences the public endured. As it turned out, public opinion broadly supported the president's position. By winter 1996, the confrontations over the shutdown led to a plan for a balanced budget by 2002, including painful cuts in popular federal programs, but also to the resurgence of Clinton's political fortunes and a dramatic slowing of the momentum of Gingrich's Contract.

Announcement of the 2000 Census Design

It was in the context of these larger political changes, and the Supreme Court review of the 1990 census lawsuit, that the bureau made the formal announcement of the 2000 census design. On February 28, 1996, the Census Bureau and the Commerce Department announced that the 2000 census plans included "statistical sampling" at two different levels. Census Director Riche announced "twin goals of reducing costs and increasing accuracy" and the major innovations to meet them, including "simple, easy-to-read forms," an "open process that diverse groups and interests can understand and support," and "a much greater use of widely accepted scientific statistical methods." "Sampling," Riche continued, "is first and foremost among them" (U.S. Bureau of the Census 1996b).

The bureau announced its intention to use a complex set of methods to enumerate the population, grounded in a basic mail enumeration. It would send a mail questionnaire or enumerators to all addresses in the nation. In recent censuses, all addresses slated for mail enumeration had received only a single questionnaire. In the 2000 census, households would receive as many as four replacement questionnaires and reminders. The temporary Census Bureau offices around the country would keep a daily running tally of the questionnaires as they were returned and checked in for completeness. Because officials knew that a substantial portion of the households would not return their questionnaires—the mail response rate had been 63 percent in 1990 and was expected to be even lower in 2000—they focused special attention on integrating new methods of capturing information from the nonresponders into the total census plans.

As in previous censuses, the bureau planned to send enumerators to households that did not respond. But for the 2000 census, it proposed to use sampling as a fundamental methodological technique to contact households that did not respond promptly. To save money and concentrate resources, the bureau proposed to follow up on a sample of those addresses that did not respond, to complete the first phase of the count. During NRFU, or nonresponse follow-up, the bureau would use enumerators to contact the households in the sample by phone or in person.

The final phase of the 2000 enumeration, according to the bureau, would be a nationwide postenumeration survey of 750,000 housing units, which would be matched to the questionnaires received in the mail enumeration and nonresponse follow-up. This stage was specifically designed to provide a measure of the quality of the data from the mail enumeration and NRFU and to measure the differential undercount of hard-to-count groups. From all these operations the bureau would build estimates of all local-area populations and aggregate them for the total population, to provide what they called a "one-number census that is right the first time."[7]

In announcing the plan, Census Bureau officials emphasized that it had been several years in the making and that it implemented the recommendations from the two panels from the National Research Council's Committee on National Statistics. It evolved out of research the bureau had conducted since 1990, Riche noted, and, most critically, reflected the results of the research from the 1995 census tests. The bureau prepared "nearly fifty evaluation reports" from the 1995 tests, describing the host of new efforts they had made to simplify the census for the public, improve the accuracy of the count, and save money. The evaluation reports summarized a wide variety of tests—on the development of address files, coordination efforts with the post office or local officials in hard-to-count areas, the acquisition and use of administrative records, the use of repeat questionnaires and reminder cards, alternative questionnaires, the quality of coding operations, and the use of computer-assisted telephone interviews (CATI) and reverse CATI techniques.

Nevertheless, the Census Bureau's design for 2000 did not receive an enthusiastic response in Congress. Congress and the public have long accepted the results from statistical sampling for population surveys other than the census, such as the unemployment rate that comes from the Current Population Survey. But the controversies surrounding sampling methodologies designed to adjust for the differential undercount cast a cloud on the new plan, which officials would find hard to dispel in the months ahead.

The day after the bureau announced its 2000 plans, key members of Congress reacted to the new design in a hearing before the House of Representatives' Government Reform and Oversight Committee. Both Republican and Democratic representatives that day opposed the use of sampling, equating it with opinion polls used in their own political campaigns and describing it as "crude." Senator Herb Kohl (Dem.-Wis.) commented that "there appears to be no scientific method for determining who is included [in a sample] and who is not. We are asked to believe that this sample will be more accurate than the census, but we are given little reason to believe that" (U.S. House 1996). His fellow Wisconsin representative, Tom Petri, a Republican, echoed his views, comparing "a real head count" with a "quick, easy, and cheap method of throwing up our hands and relying on scientific guesswork" (ibid.). Tom Sawyer (Dem.-Ohio), former chair of the House Subcommittee with census oversight responsibilities, challenged these views and was more generally supportive of bureau plans. Barbara Bailar, Charles Schultze, and James Trussell testified in support of the plan, as well. Nevertheless, the bureau clearly did not have a mandate in Congress supporting the new design. And in perhaps the most dramatic written statement presented to the committee, University of California statisticians Kenneth Wachter and David Freedman voiced the fear that implementation of the 2000 plan could cause fundamental damage to the count. "We now know," they wrote,

> that if Secretary of Commerce Mosbacher had decided to use the statistically adjusted numbers as 1990 Census counts, a seat in the House of Representatives would have been shifted from Pennsylvania to Arizona by an error in a computer program. . . . The coding error epitomizes the problems of statistical adjustment in 1990. . . . In 1990, the complexity of their modeling systems made it hard for the Bureau to detect big mistakes and uncertainties, until long after critical decisions had been made. . . . Unfortunately, the Bureau's plans for Census 2000 add further layers of complexity onto the complications of 1990, and leave the final numbers even more vulnerable to statistical error. (Ibid.)

This particular statement, about the effects of the computer error, has now been repeated so often that it is taken as gospel by most statisticians and politicians. There was, indeed, a computer error, and it was discovered in the fall of 1991 as the parties were headed toward trial in the litigation brought by New York City against the Commerce Department. Its occurrence was taken by several witnesses for the defendants as evidence against adjustment. Wachter and Freedman's 1996 congressional testimony was the first to suggest that it would have *erroneously* shifted a seat in Congress from Pennsylvania to Arizona, but they offered no detailed calculations in support of this allegation. In his report of the analyses of the 1990 postenumeration results, Howard Hogan (1993) explained that the Census Bureau made several changes to the PES data and the adjusted census counts subsequent to the secretary's 1991 decision, as part of the bureau's ongoing research program. Among these was a set of corrections for errors associated with the computer editing of erroneous enumerations. This was followed by a change in the stratification scheme from the 1,392 poststrata chosen in advance of the 1991 decision making to 357 poststrata, to eliminate the smoothing component of the estimation process. Hogan presented the results of all these steps combined on the state population counts. If one were to use these numbers for apportionment instead of the original adjusted counts released in 1991, one would draw a conclusion similar to that of Freedman and Wachter (treating the new figures as if they were correct). Unfortunately, similar calculations based on the correction of the computer error alone, fail to support the Wachter-Freedman conclusion. What this discussion does illustrate is the sensitivity of the official apportionment formula to very small changes in counts, something that is widely understood among political scientists. This is why it was and continues to be important for the bureau to announce its procedures, for example, for poststratification, in advance of data collection and analysis. But the sensitivity of the apportionment formula to small count shifts is hardly an argument against adjustment.

At any rate, it soon became clear that even supporters of the Census Bureau plan felt that there were still serious operational and statistical questions to be answered before the 2000 design would be complete. In a more congenial political climate, the bureau could have used the second half of the decade to work the kinks out of the design, outside the harsh glare of the press and the carping of suspicious critics. But given the lingering effects of earlier controversies and the highly partisan nature of Washington politics, the bureau did not have that luxury. As in recent years, bureau staff had to conduct their business in front of the cameras as well as in the field and in the more decorous world of scientific forums.

In their analyses of the 1995 test results, for example, the bureau acknowledged that there was a variety of questions still to be decided about how to take the 2000 census. Chief among them were some of the knottier problems of estimation methods and sample design, for both NRFU and the PES. In the past, such an acknowledgment would have been accepted as a matter of course. As the bureau introduced new ideas and methods, choices needed to be made and the alternatives needed to be tested. But now every unresolved statistical issue could be used by those opposed to sampling and adjustment as a pretext for arguing against a change.

The first problem the Census Bureau faced was a semantic one. Although sampling methods formed the basis of both NRFU and the integrated coverage measurement (ICM) stages, they were fundamentally different operations. To make its case to Congress and the public, the bureau would have to be very clear about which stage was under discussion at any particular point and why the two kinds of sampling were necessary. Sampling for NRFU is fundamentally about producing better-quality estimates for the nonrespondents. It reduces the costs and time associated with what the bureau knows from past censuses are the diminishing returns garnered from trying to complete the count of nonrespondents. The bureau proposed, in line with well-known sampling methodologies, that an intensive and timely effort to acquire accurate information on a sample of nonrespondents would ultimately produce more accurate data than a sloppier, more expensive, and less controlled effort to reach all of them. The exact nature of sampling for NRFU and how it would best fit with other facets of the bureau's design took considerable time and professional debate to work out; in fact, not until the summer of 1997 would the final version be publicly unveiled.

The ICM stage of the Census 2000, on the other hand, is essentially equivalent to an expanded postenumeration survey operation like that of 1990. It would be a completely new and independent count of a sample of addresses and was designed to produce a sample of households that have been counted twice (that is, matched back to the original enumeration) and a sample of households counted only once (that is, missed in either the original enumeration or the postenumeration survey). The purpose of this stage is to "correct" the results of the initial attempt at enumeration and NRFU by providing estimates of undercount, overcounts, and erroneous enumerations. Integrated coverage measurement is intended to provide the information necessary to produce the "one-number census that is right the first time."

For ICM, by contrast with sampling for NRFU, the Census Bureau could develop and publicize its sampling strategy for the postenumeration survey well in advance of the census. Within some limitations, the bureau could define costs in advance and schedule the operational phase. Although much larger than other highly accepted federal household surveys, such as the Current Population Survey, the PES as a 0.75 percent sample of all households was fundamentally similar to them. The methodological controversy surrounding the PES and ICM, however, occurred at another point: namely, over whether to switch to a technique called CensusPlus or to continue with dual-systems estimation (DSE) to produce the one-number census. Again, the 1995 tests shed light on the problems.

The chief conceptual difficulty associated with DSE is the leap of faith required to convince the public that there were people missed in both the original enumeration (E-sample) and the postenumeration (P-sample) and that the "one-number census" should be adjusted upward by the estimate of those missed both times. To statisticians, this does not represent a leap of faith at all but rather a fact of life borne out by repeated applications of DSE methods in the past. The only issue for statisticians is how they estimate the upward adjustment. Although DSE is based upon well-known counting methodologies and is well documented in the statistical literature, as we described in chapter 4, the political problem for the bureau was that key stakeholders still had not accepted the method in the context of census taking.

CensusPlus attempted to avoid the problem of estimating people missed in both the *E*-sample and the *P*-sample, that is, the "fourth cell" in the 2×2 table (the *d* cell in table 4.5). Instead, it assumed that the ICM-based sample count could resolve the mistakes and omissions in the first enumeration and provide an estimate of the "true" population. It was intuitively easier to explain to a lay audience, and it was capable of producing final census estimates several months earlier than would a process using dual-systems estimation. Given the requirements of the bureau to report the census results by December 31, 2000, the simpler methodology was inherently appealing. There was simply one problem: the method relied on an untenable assumption, which could be shown to be demonstrably unworkable in the census context.

The evaluations of the 1995 census test of CensusPlus gave proof to the concerns voiced by many statisticians in advance. CensusPlus made a "poor showing" in the 1995 tests, and, as bureau statisticians reported, "DSE performed much better than CensusPlus. CensusPlus did not work operationally. The Bureau will test it again in 1996 'with many refinements.'" But, officials cautioned, "if CensusPlus does not work in the small test we are conducting in 1996, it will not work in 2000" (Vacca, Mulry, and Killion 1996).

In the months after the announcement of the 2000 plan, congressional committees, the advisory committees for the bureau, and other key stakeholders began to evaluate the details of the design. As these stakeholders responded, the bureau announced adjustments to specific parts of the design, although its broad structure remained constant. Spokespersons for minority groups, for example, were highly critical of the bureau's initial proposal to use the county-level response rate as the trigger for the nonresponse follow-up stage. Such a design, the critics charged, might mean that in a diverse and populous county, some census tracts would have response rates greater than 90 percent when NRFU began, but others might have only a 30 percent response rate. The quality of the data for such low-response tracts—if sampled on the same basis as those with much higher initial-response rates— would be poor. The Census Bureau agreed. On September 12, 1996, therefore, Under Secretary of Commerce Everett Ehrlich announced that the bureau would use tract-level response rates to implement NRFU. This was not to be the last such change in NRFU plans.

This and other changes allayed the concerns of some statisticians, who voiced support for the plan and pressed Congress to give the Census Bureau the authority and autonomy to make the technical decisions. Professional statisticians, in particular, pointed out that sampling was an integral part of modern statistical practice. In September 1996, for example, the ASA's Blue-Ribbon Panel on the 2000 Census made a public statement affirming that "sampling is an integral part of the scientific discipline of statistics." "Congress directed the Bureau of the Census to develop plans for the 2000 Decennial Census that (1) reduce the undercount, particularly the differential in the undercount across population groups, and (2) constrain the growth of costs," the statement continued. "Because sampling potentially increases the accuracy of the count while reducing costs, the Census Bureau has responded to the Congressional mandate by investigating the increased use of sampling. An additional benefit of sampling is that its appropriate use can also reduce the response burden on the population. We endorse the use of sampling for these purposes; it is consistent with best statistical practice" (American Statistical Association 1996).

Such positions did not assure the bureau's critics opposed altogether to the use of sampling in the plan. The response from the House Committee on Government Reform and Oversight, published on September 24, 1996, was highly negative. The majority recommended that "the Bureau should not use sampling methods to complete or adjust the actual enumeration of the 2000 Census, which is constitutionally mandated for purposes of apportionment." It further recommended that Congress should "clarify existing Federal statutes with regard to the use of sampling to make statistical adjustments to the census for apportionment purposes" (U.S. House 1996).

Congressional Intervention: Déjà Vu All Over Again

As we noted earlier, the grumblings about the use of sampling and statistical methods in the 2000 census began even before the outcome of the controversy over the 1990 census had been settled. The September 1996 report of the House Committee on Government Reform and Oversight claimed that the use of sampling for nonresponse follow-up and statistical adjustment (parts 2 and 3 of the bureau's one-number census approach for 2000) would yield local data that would be subject to substantial error, perhaps more so than in a traditional census. This language was somewhat ironic, in that it implied that the bureau's plan would yield more accurate data at higher levels of aggregation, the very issue that was the focus of litigation in 1990. At any rate, these activities were quickly followed by the introduction of a bill before the Senate that would require the bureau to carry out a traditional census without sampling and adjustment. This bill died in committee with the adjournment of Congress.

In the fall of 1996, Bill Clinton won reelection to a second term as president. Republicans maintained control of both houses of Congress, although their majority in the House was reduced from seventeen seats to only eleven. Hence, when Congress returned in the early months of 1997, the political landscape for the census had not changed dramatically. The effort to hold the line against sampling and other statistical evils was taken up anew in 1997, as Republicans introduced similar bills in both the House and the Senate.

Again, there was a barrage of congressional discussion and media coverage of the issue. And again, the emerging positions did little to provide definitive guidance to convince Congress either to defer to the professional expertise within the Census Bureau or to make an ironclad case to the public that sampling was to be banned. In March and April 1997, for example, in testimony before the Senate Committee on Governmental Affairs on the 2000 census, Census Director Martha Farnsworth Riche, Charles L. Schultze, chair of the National Academy of Sciences Panel on Census Requirements for the Year 2000 and Beyond, Commerce Secretary William Daley, and Under Secretary Everett Ehrlich reiterated their support for the Census Bureau's design, warning that accuracy would be lost by a return to the 1990 census design, and then noted that improvements were still being made to respond to specific criticisms leveled at the designs for the 2000 census. On the antisampling side, Wisconsin attorney general James E. Doyle testified in support of an "actual head count" (Senate 1997, 29). Former assistant attorney general Stuart Gerson catalogued the background surrounding the legality of sampling and noted that Section 195 of Title 13 governing the Census Bureau had not conclusively been found to bar sampling in the decennial count. The University of Pennsylvania statistician Lawrence Brown testified that he had recently reviewed the bureau's design and, though he had some technical reservations about sampling for nonresponse follow-up, he felt, "that the current plans are a very significant improvement over those in effect up to as recently as a month ago. Nevertheless, if economic considerations permit, in short, if Congress could find the money, I would prefer to see a full follow-up rather than the current sample response follow-up plan" (ibid., 53).

Committee chairman Fred Thompson (Rep.-Tenn.) pursued the point and pressed Brown further on whether he would recommend against all sampling. Brown responded that he was not referring to the plans for integrated coverage measurement. He continued, "The ICM plan needs to be continually worked on and refined, and if it is done really well, it should work, and if there are flaws, as there were last time, it will be problematic" (ibid., 54).

As the testimony continued, Thompson expressed frustration with the "inconclusion" (sic) and "uncertain territory" facing Congress on the issue. "This is obviously a question that is going to be with us for the next several days, the next several years," he concluded, "but this particular question on this particular census is something we are going to have to come to terms with shortly if we come to terms with it all in Congress" (ibid., 63).

House Republicans found their vehicle to press their objections to sampling further in the spring of 1997, as floods ravaged the upper Midwest and Congress was focused on curtailing U.S. peacekeeping efforts in Bosnia-Herzegovina. They attached the antisampling language to a section of a high-profile piece of legislation, H.R. 1469 (Title 8, 2000 Decennial Census),[8] beginning with the statement,

> The Congress finds that—
> (1) the decennial enumeration of the population is one of the most critical constitutional functions our government performs;
> (2) it is the goal that the decennial enumeration of the population be as accurate as possible, consistent with the Constitution;
> (3) the Constitution clearly states that the census is to be an "actual enumeration" of the population, and Section 195 of Title 13, United States Code, states that sampling cannot be used for purposes of the apportionment of Representatives in Congress among the several States;

and continuing later with,

> Section 141(a) of Title 13, United States Code, is amended by adding at the end the following:
> "Notwithstanding any other provision of law, no sampling or any other statistical procedure, including any statistical adjustment, may be used in any determination of population for purposes of the apportionment of Representatives in Congress among the several States." (House 1997)

As with the confrontations over the budget the previous year, congressional Republicans embarked upon a high stakes game of political brinkmanship. They believed that President Clinton would not risk political capital by vetoing a popular piece of legislation in the name of arcane issues of census policy. Again, they misread Clinton's resolve. He vetoed the bill, forcing continued discussions on the 2000 census design. The compromise plan, which accompanied the revised legislation on flood relief and overseas peacekeeping, deleted the census language. The bureau was permitted to continue to plan for sampling in 2000 but was required to submit a full report on the design, as well as the pros and cons of sampling.

The Census Bureau Reports to Congress

In the summer of 1997, the Census Bureau produced a detailed planning document for Congress entitled "Report to Congress: The Plan for Census 2000" (U.S. Bureau of Census 1997) with a detailed description of planned methodologies. This was the first report of this sort by the bureau, and it offered the defenders of the 2000 design the hope that the bureau had finally managed to provide the evidence needed to sway Congress to support sampling for 2000.

The bureau report focused on the necessity of adapting census methodologies in response to societal changes. In so doing, it reiterated a theme of both the panels of the Committee on National Statistics dealing with census 2000 (Edmonston and Schultze 1995; Steffey and Bradburn 1994). The CNSTAT Panel to Evaluate Alternative Census Methodologies also echoed this theme in its second interim report in June 1997: "Change is not the enemy of an accurate and useful census; rather, not changing methods as the United States changes would inevitably result in a seriously degraded census" (White and Rust 1997).

One of the new revelations in the bureau report was a radically revised plan for sampling for nonresponse follow-up, in which NRFU would become a complete replacement for the traditional enumerator-based follow-up procedures used in previous censuses. Instead of trying to reach all of those who did not return their mailed-out forms, the bureau now planned to take a sample of the residual housing locations and attempt to follow up only with those living in these locations. Technically, the population of interest is the population of nonresponders to mail-out/mail-back questionnaires. We can divide that population according to census tract and draw separate samples for each tract in the nation. The sampling rate would depend on the rate of return from the mail-out/mail-back phase. The goal was a combined response rate of 90 percent of the population of the housing units in the tract. Thus, a tract with a 60 percent response rate in the first phase would have a sampling fraction of three in four for the nonresponders, to boost its combined response rate to 90 percent. A tract with an 85 percent response rate would have the nonresponders sampled at rate of one in three. All tracts with response rates in excess of 85 percent (anticipated to be a rare event) would also be sampled at a one-in-three rate; thus, their combined response rates would exceed 90 percent. For each tract, the bureau would then estimate the counts for the final 10 percent or less of housing units by using the information gathered from the sample of nonresponding households. Such a sampling plan traded off increased accuracy, in the sense of reduced bias for those in the sample, against the increased uncertainty associated with sampling errors. The reduced bias comes from the elimination of large numbers of erroneous enumerations that were traditionally the result of coverage improvement programs implemented long after census day. The use of better-trained interviewers would also reduce omissions, but most likely to a much lesser extent.

The Census Bureau's 1997 report also included information on the types and sizes of expected statistical error rates with and without statistical sampling, from the nation as a whole all the way down to the census-block level:

> If Census 2000 is conducted using a traditional enumeration, without the introduction of sampling, the Census Bureau expects an average error rate of at least 1.9 percent at all levels of geography from the census tract level up to the national level. In contrast, the Census Bureau's plan for Census 2000, a plan involving the introduction of a limited use of sampling, has the following expected average error rates: 0.1 percent at the national level, 0.5 percent at the state level, 0.6 percent at the Congressional district level, and 1.1 percent at the census tract level.
>
> The Report also discusses error rates at the census block level. The 1995 Census Test did not provide meaningful error rates at the block level. The block error rates measured in the 1995 Census Test reflect two facts, that the test had lower rates of sampling than will be used in Census 2000, and that some blocks had few people. Even traditional methods of enumeration have seemingly high block-level error rates: the 1990 Census had an average block error rate of almost eight percent. Fortunately, with or without sampling, such substantial error at the census block level does not mean substantial inaccuracy when blocks are aggregated. At all geographic levels important to political representation and funds allocation, Census 2000 will provide more accurate results than physical enumeration alone. (U.S. Bureau of the Census 1997, xi)

210   Who Counts?

These figures on error rates deserve further explanation. The Census Bureau simulated biases and sampling errors using overcount and undercount estimates from the 1990 census and sampling errors from the 2000 census sampling for its nonresponse follow-up design. Thus, at the national level, the results from the Census 2000 plan and a traditional census with "improved procedures" are expected to differ by 1.8 percent, the 1990 net national undercount estimate. But the purpose of sampling for NRFU and ICM is not really to "fix" the net national undercount. Rather, the goal is to estimate how census errors are distributed across the population and to discover how to correct for them. Thus, the real improvements in any simulation would show up at the state and substate levels. Table 9.1, taken from the bureau report, adds to the national estimates values for the level of an "average" state, congressional district, and census tract, with accompanying 90 percent confidence intervals.

This report to Congress by the Census Bureau also provided the first public description of 1990 census error rates at relatively low levels of geography. The 8 percent reported rate at the block level is a few percentage points less than the gross error (the sum of the overcount and undercount) in the census that was widely discussed in the technical literature. In essence, this 8 percent figure confirms that overcounts and undercounts do not cancel each other out at the block level.[9] For the 1995 test census results, the report detailed the bureau's attempt to measure block-level sampling error directly, in terms of coefficients of variation,[10] which were surprisingly large, and so the report came with caveats and qualifications. For example, the sample sizes were smaller than the Census 2000 design would require. And

Table 9.1 Census 2000 Estimated Error by Geographic Level (Percentage)

	National	State	Congressional District	Census Tract
Census 2000 plan	0.1	0.5	0.6	1.1
		(0.2, 0.5)	(0.3, 2.3)	(0.6, 2.4)
Traditional census	1.9	1.9	1.9	1.9
		(0.4, 3.2)	(−1.2, 7.0)	(−1.2, 6.2)

Source: U.S. Bureau of the Census 1997, 44.

Note: The range of error at the census-tract level has been "trimmed" so that it does not include the most extreme outliers—the highest and lowest 3 percent.

these figures were affected by large percentage errors in some very small blocks, including one in Paterson, New Jersey, of size one. As a consequence, the block-level error rate from the 1995 census test was substantially greater than the expected error rate using the Census 2000 design and simulations from 1990 data.

Unfortunately, within weeks of the publication of the original report, the bureau was forced to admit that there were mistakes in the calculation of select error rates, and they had to revise and reissue the table in August. Critics of the Census 2000 design immediately pounced on the mistakes as evidence of incompetence, at best, and malfeasance at worst, within the agency. Like the "computer mistake" that so undermined bureau claims of quality in the 1990 PES, this mistake in a highly publicized report left the agency more beleaguered than before. Thus, although the corrected figures reported in August might seem quite reasonable to a statistician, they were used by those in Congress opposed to sampling as yet another argument against allowing the bureau to use sampling in the 1998 dress rehearsal, let alone in the 2000 census itself.

In the fall of 1997, amid a variety of skirmishes over the Census 2000 plan, the House set up a new Subcommittee on the Census within the Committee on Government Reform and Oversight, chaired by Representative Dan Miller (Rep.-Fla.), a former professor of economics at Georgia State University, and with Carolyn Maloney (Dem.-N.Y.) as the ranking minority member.

Congress Tries One More Time

In October 1997, the House of Representatives passed a bill that would suspend plans for sampling in the census until the federal courts ruled on its constitutionality, a move certain to derail the use of sampling in 2000. This bill was linked to the appropriations bill for the Commerce Department, in which the Census Bureau is situated, and President Clinton threatened to veto it if the ban on sampling in the census was also approved by the Senate. The resulting compromise, which was enacted into law in November 1997, allowed the Census Bureau to test both sampling and traditional methods in the 1998 census dress rehearsal and also allowed an expedited challenge to the constitutionality of sampling in the census to proceed through the U.S. courts (see appendix I for the detailed language).

But the language of the law was strongly prejudiced against the intelligent uses of sampling and statistical methods more broadly in the census context, and it set into place a new eight-person Census Monitoring Board to report to Congress on various matters but especially on "the degree to which efforts of the Bureau of the Census to prepare to conduct the 2000 census . . . shall be taken by means of an enumeration process designed to count every individual possible, and . . . shall be free from political bias and arbitrary decisions."

Four members of the oversight board were to be appointed by the Republicans in Congress (two by the majority leader of the Senate and two by the Speaker of the House) and four by the Democrats (by the president, with one recommended by the minority leader of the Senate and another by the minority leader of the House). The board has two cochairs, appointed by the two groups of four members, and separate staffs, each headed by an executive director, with a total budget of $4 million per year from fiscal year 1998 through fiscal year 2001. The board's first report, which is to include "its findings and recommendations as to the feasibility and desirability of using postal personnel or private contractors to help carry out the decennial census," was scheduled for April 1988 and was later deferred until 1999.

The eight-person Census Monitoring Board is certainly evocative of the Special Secretarial Advisory Panel that was established as part of the 1989 settlement in the New York City lawsuit (see chapters 5 and 6). But the new board appears to have even greater authority and a larger budget. Because it reports directly to Congress, it has become entwined with the renewed efforts to ban sampling and adjustment from the census plan for 2000.

And, though Congress may not yet be aware of the historical precedents for its actions, it is useful to conclude our review of the plans for 2000 with a short look back to the last time Congress constituted a "board" to monitor the census. That was in 1849 (see chapter 2), when, in anticipation of the need for changes in the 1850 census, Congress constituted the secretaries of state and interior and the postmaster general as a "board" to "prepare a bill for the 1850 census which the statistics of the country will require, and report that bill to Congress at the commencement of the next session" (quoted in Anderson 1988, 35). The board report was indeed a momentous one, both a response to the errors and controversies surrounding the 1840 census and a bold new plan for counting the population in 1850. As at present, the board proposals were a reflection of controversy, and generated further controversy, in Congress. The statistical advisers that the board turned to for advice, including the officials of the American Statistical Association, proposed the reform of the census instrument. In 1850, their proposals for an individual-level census expanded the scope of the count and initiated the partnership between the federal government and statisticians that has made the United States a major innovator in census-taking methodology ever since. It remains to be seen whether the current board will have the impact of its predecessor, but its very creation points to the stakes involved in census policy.

Chapter 10

The Saga Continues

Our story of the politics of census taking in contemporary America does not have an end. In fact, we have had some difficulty in completing this account because dramatic events continue to occur. In January 1998, for example, Census Director Martha Farnsworth Riche resigned, and James Holmes, Atlanta regional director of the Census Bureau, was appointed acting director. The Clinton administration nominated Kenneth Prewitt, a political scientist and most recently the president of the Social Science Research Council, for the director's position. Prewitt received Senate confirmation and took office in late 1998.

Appointments to the Census Monitoring Board were made in the first half of 1998, though the board did not begin to function fully until late in the year and has to date not had a major impact on resolving the controversies on the 2000 census.

New lawsuits, on the other hand, do have the potential to change the discourse about the 2000 census and census taking more broadly. In February 1998, two federal lawsuits were filed against the Clinton administration, asking the courts to stop the portions of the 2000 census plan that use sampling. The first suit, *U.S. House of Representatives et al. v. Department of Commerce et al.* (1998), was filed by House Speaker Newt Gingrich. The second, *Glavin, Barr et al. v. Clinton et al.* (1998), was filed by the Southeastern Legal Foundation in the name of individuals who claimed they would be harmed if the 2000 census were conducted as planned. Briefs were filed in these suits in the spring of 1998. Their filings provided much of the language for the myths we quoted in our prologue. The cases were argued in the summer of 1998, and both were decided in favor of the plaintiffs by district courts in the fall of 1998. The Clinton administration appealed both rulings to the Supreme Court. Oral arguments in both cases occurred on November 30, 1998.[1]

Both suits raised a number of objections to the 2000 census plan and reframed the constitutional, legal, and technical questions about the census. In the suits filed in the 1980s and early 1990s, the original plaintiffs were generally state and local officials who called upon the Census Bureau or the Commerce Department to adjust the census in light of the known differential undercount. In these earlier suits, the Census Bureau and the Commerce Department made arguments before the courts that such an adjustment was either unconstitutional or illegal. Federal courts had dismissed those claims, so the cases were litigated, as noted in previous chapters, on the technical questions of the feasibility or the accuracy of the adjustment and the relative authority and expertise of the Census Bureau and the Commerce Department to make the decision to adjust.

The current litigation reversed the players, so to speak: this time, the Census Bureau and the Commerce Department are defending their technical plans and authority to adjust, and the plaintiffs are suing to prevent an adjustment. In this new legal environment, the constitutional questions, and the intent of Congress in drafting various portions of Title 13, have been raised anew in opposition to adjustment.

Accordingly, plaintiffs in both suits included the claim that the Constitution requires an "actual enumeration" and that the 2000 census plan would violate the requirement for an actual enumeration in its use of sampling (as depicted in the cartoon figure 10.1). The suits also claimed that historical review of early census taking indicates that the Founding Fathers were aware of statistical estimation and rejected its use—particularly in the 1790 census.

The suits claimed that Section 195 of Title 13, the section of the federal code that regulates census taking, prohibits the use of sampling for the purposes of apportionment. The relevant portion of the code reads: "Except for the determination of population for purposes of apportionment of Representatives in Congress among the several States, the Secretary [of Commerce] shall, if he considers it feasible, authorize the use of the statistical method known as "sampling" in carrying out the provisions of this title."

In response to both claims, the same Justice Department that argued these claims in prior decades now argued that federal courts considering census undercount issues to date have ruled that sampling could be used in the decennial counting process and as part of an adjustment method to correct for undercount. None of the major

Figure 10.1

Source: Chip Bok, reprinted with permission from Creators Syndicate.

litigation from the 1980 or 1990 censuses found sampling for adjustment to be in violation of the Constitution.

The administration also pointed to Section 141 of Title 13, which orders that the "Secretary shall . . . take a decennial census of population as of the first day of April [of 1980 and later decades] . . . in such form and content as he may determine, including the use of sampling procedures and special surveys."

The Justice Department attorneys argued that the conflict between the two sections was a result of the intent of Congress in 1976 to ensure that sampling would become the preferred method of collecting population information, particularly since the 1976 legislation also authorized the secretary to begin collecting middecade census information in 1985. The Justice Department argued that the discretionary language of Section 141 permitted the secretary to use sampling as he saw fit, but did not require him to do so, for apportionment. The administration also argued that the plaintiffs in the suits did not have standing to sue before the census, because any harm they might incur was, at the time, hypothetical.

The district courts decided for the plaintiffs in both suits, on the grounds that Section 195 banned sampling for apportionment. The district courts did not rule on the constitutional question of whether the language of Article I, Section 2, banned sampling. All these arguments were repeated in the Supreme Court hearing of November 1998.

The Supreme Court hearing also revisited many of the more philosophical issues about accuracy and the responsibility of the respondent and the Census Bureau to ensure an accurate count. Dramatic exchanges reemerged between the attorneys and the justices. According to the summary published by Bulletin Broadfaxing Network (1998), for example, CNN reported that "Justice Stevens imagined an apartment building teeming with immigrants wary of being counted." In the ensuing testimony of Maureen Mahoney, the attorney representing the House of Representatives, the following exchange occurred:

Justice Stevens:	If you got no response, what's the Census Bureau to do?
Attorney Maureen Mahoney:	Your honor, they can't guess.
Stevens:	You'd put down zero then?
Mahoney:	That's right.

Elaborating on the point, the *Washington Times* (Dec. 1, 1998) reported, Mahoney argued that "it is better to have an inaccurate census that is legal than one using sampling which the lower courts have said is illegal" and added that the Census Bureau would be "deliberately trying not to find 10 percent of the population" if it used sampling estimates.

Technical Debate over Census 2000 Design Reemerges

Meanwhile, amid the legal activities, the new House Subcommittee on the Census, chaired by Representative Dan Miller, held several hearings in 1998, notably on May 5, September 9, and September 17, strongly weighted toward criticisms of the Census 2000 design and operational plans. And the Census Bureau made formal presentation regarding the technical details of Census 2000 at the Joint Statistical Meetings in August 1998. As a consequence, there is now a formal updated record of details on the bureau statistical plan and a reaction to it.

The Subcommittee on the Census hearing in May featured opponents to the 2000 census plan, including Philip Stark, a statistician at the University of California, Berkeley; Kenneth Darga, senior demographer for the Michigan Department of Management and Budget; and Jerry Coffey, formerly a member of the OMB statistical policy staff. Their criticisms, which harked back to the criticisms of Leo Breiman, David Freedman, and Kenneth Wachter, pointed repeatedly to the error in the PES, without exploring in any real way how the plans for Census 2000 differed from what had been done in 1990. Darga, in particular, misrepresented the nature of error in the census and resuscitated Breiman's charge that most of the net national undercount was the result of bad data.[2]

At the Joint Statistical Meetings in Dallas on August 13, John Thompson and Howard Hogan, both of the Census Bureau, made detailed presentations on the Census 2000 plan with a focus on the efficiencies and roles associated with statistical sampling, giving details of the statistical procedures linked to the integration of the components.[3] Examples of new details available for the first time included the operational procedure for identifying movers by working from the file of all current residents living or staying at the sample address at the time of the ICM interview plus all other persons who lived there on census day and have since moved. The current plan also provided for direct estimates of undercount by groups for each state and the use of "raking" to smooth adjustment factors across poststrata within states.

At the September 9 hearing of the Subcommittee on the Census, Under Secretary of Commerce Robert Shapiro and Acting Census Director James Holmes defended the bureau plans and responded to the criticisms of the Republican majority. Challenged that day by Democratic committee members to take testimony of experts in support of adjustment, the subcommittee scheduled another hearing just over a week later and this time invited five statistical experts who were critical of the Census 2000 plan: Leo Breiman, of the University of California, Berkeley; Lawrence Brown, from the University of Pennsylvania; Robert Koyak, from the Naval Postgraduate School; Martin Wells, of Cornell University; and Donald Ylvisaker of the University of California, Los Angeles.[4] These witnesses all argued that their criticisms of the 1990 adjustment were still relevant for the 2000 plan and that the adjustment methods would still put more error into the census than they would take out. Breiman stated, "The bottom line is that one cannot correct the errors in the Census by adding more errors to it" (Breiman 1998). Former census director Barbara Bryant, Stephen Fienberg, and Eugene Ericksen of Temple University also testified, and their comments were generally supportive of the Census 2000 design.

David Freedman and Kenneth Wachter have joined with several others, including three of the experts who appeared at the September 17 congressional hearing, in the preparation of a critique of the Census 2000 design that strikes a tone similar to that of earlier critiques of the 1990 adjustment we referred to in chapter 7. In the paper (Brown et al. 1998), they recount what they believe to be the failings of the 1990 methodology, and they claim that little will change in 2000 under the current plan. They pay scant attention to issues of errors in the census, however, and how the new design hopes to address them. And they end with a rhetorical flourish: "One of the oft-stated goals for Census 2000 is 'Keep It Simple.' . . . However, adjustment adds layer upon layer of complexity to an already complex census. And complex systems, from ocean liners to space telescopes, fail in unexpected ways.

"The results of adjustment are highly dependent on somewhat arbitrary technical decisions. Furthermore, mistakes are almost inevitable, very hard to detect, and have profound consequences" (ibid., 18). And they leave us with only the alternative of using demographic analysis estimates for a synthetic adjustment:

> Census figures could be scaled up to match the demographic analysis totals for subgroups of the national population. . . . The people in a demographic group who are thought to be missing from the census would be added back, in proportion to the ones who are counted— state by state, block by block. Current demographic analysis does not account for ethnicity, but the method could be adapted for that purpose. (Ibid., 17)

They offer no further details and make no mention of the desirability or feasibility of identifying erroneous enumerations in such a process or of how anyone could ever assess its accuracy.

Myths Unmasked

Such rhetoric, and stark exchanges such as the one from the oral arguments before the Supreme Court, illustrate why we began our story with a presentation of some myths about census taking. In the current charged political environment in Washington, D.C., absolutist statements about the rigid requirements of the Constitution and the law strike us as unhelpful. The long history of census taking, as well as the more in-depth examination of the controversies of the 1970s through the 1990s, certainly indicates that improving the accuracy of the count is not easy in a diverse, mobile, and politically divided society. But we think that the story of the careful development of new technical methods by many people over many years, and the long political debates about what to do about the undercount, lead to different conclusions. Hence, though it is not clear that there are compromises and solutions in sight to the intractable problems that beset the decennial count, we would like to recapitulate some of our argument as a mechanism for indicating how to proceed.

We have described the discovery of the differential undercount in the census, the development of a viable technical solution to its measurement, and the proposals for using statistical estimation to guarantee a more accurate decennial census. But it is not yet possible to trace a solution to the increasingly fractious political controversies that surround census planning and administration, including the controversy over the use of sampling procedures in the conduct of the 2000 census.

We noted at the outset that the framers of the Constitution created the census as a mechanism to apportion political power and tax dollars among the various constituencies of the population. The mechanism was to be automatic. Every ten years, the federal government would count the population and reapportion Congress on the basis of the results. And thus, every ten years, there would be winners and losers in the reallocation process, because the dynamism and diversity of the American population meant that states, locales, regions, and communities with growing populations would be winners and slower-growing or declining areas would lose political clout in Washington. Like elections, the census and reapportionment process shifts political power in the United States. And as with elections, the losers have to concede to the winners.

Over the past two centuries, the census has basically accomplished its goal. Congress has managed to reapportion successfully despite profound population growth and migration, ethnic and racial diversity, and political, social, and economic change. One can argue that the census instrument has served the country so well, in fact, that its impact on American politics is almost invisible. And, as perhaps an ironic result of its very success, when the census does become controversial, as in the current discussions about the differential undercount, sampling, and dual-systems estimation, there is little historical memory of prior census controversies or, in fact, the origins of the current one.

The concept of census undercounts is a function of the development of modern probability sampling methods and their use in statistical methodology. We have seen that census officials from the time of George Washington and Thomas Jefferson to the present have been aware of the extraordinary difficulties of counting a dynamic, diverse, and mobile population and that much of the concern for census accuracy has fueled improvements in census methods over the years. Until the 1940s, census officials had hunches but few tools to measure accuracy and certainly no mechanism to correct for undercounts, overcounts, or miscounts, beyond doing the enumeration over again. Beginning in the 1940s, statisticians and demographers perfected methods of measuring census accuracy, using the techniques of demographic analysis and dual-systems estimation. Sample data from the postenumeration surveys, statistical inference from sample to national rates, and comparison to the vital registration system through demographic analysis replaced the hunches and laments about census error with increasingly reliable point estimates of error and intervals of confidence about those estimates.

We have described the rise in the use of sampling, beginning with the sample long form in 1940 and the PES in 1950, as well as the special efforts in 1970. Although sampling has long been understood to be an efficient mode of data collection for a variety of purposes, its use as a methodological adjunct to supposedly traditional census enumeration methods awaited the demands placed on the census by the events of the 1930s, as well as the crucial developments of clustering and multistage sampling in the work of Jerzy Neyman and others. These technical developments made it possible to begin to fit the structure of sample designs with the structure of census operations, a theme that has continued to the present plans for the 2000 census. The overriding justification for the use of sampling methods, beginning in 1940 and moving forward to the present, has been to improve the accuracy and the quality of census counts and other data collection instruments. Part of the justification of the sample long form in 1940 was the reduction of respondent burden.

The purpose of the 1950 PES was coverage evaluation, with the goal of identifying areas to focus on for future administrative efforts to increase accuracy. At about the same time, the Census Bureau expended considerable resources to develop a statistical model for census error and began an organized effort to assess key components. The measure of correlated response error based on data collected from interviews led, for example, to the trial in 1960 of the mail-out/mail-back approach to enumeration, which worked to curtail the role of the interviewers. The bureau's strategy over the intervening years was to approach the problem of accuracy in a piecemeal fashion. With the recognition during the 1980s that most coverage improvement efforts had failed to address the differential undercount, attention focused anew on using the PES to correct the raw enumeration results. In the end, the 1990 design was a compromise, a traditional census complete with coverage improvement programs and a PES for possible use in correcting the count.

The sample size of the 1990 PES—of approximately 165,000 households—was itself a compromise between the original design of 300,000 households and the Republican administration's efforts to eliminate the PES altogether. Despite the generally acknowledged success of the 1990 adjustment as an improvement over the raw enumeration counts, the small sample size had two major impacts on accuracy: (1) the level of sampling error was a serious component of the overall census error; and (2) the data at low levels of geography were sufficiently sparse as to require smoothing of the adjustment results, even across state lines.

The public discourse on the 1990 census and adjustment has conflated sample-size problems with a more general condemnation of sampling in the context of census taking and has led to creation of the myth that sampling itself is a suspect enterprise. Wachter and Freedman's February 1996 testimony, quoted in the previous chapter, for example, depicts a census officialdom that has lost control of its methodology and has raised fears of numbers "vulnerable" to "statistical error." In the current context of partisan dispute, this testimony effectively drowns out their more measured endorsements of the bureau as "the world's finest statistical agency" whose officials "need and deserve Congressional support." Statements regarding the vulnerability of the proposed methodology for 2000 to such errors continue to appear in the work of these and other critics, as we noted earlier (see, for example, Brown et al. 1998, 6).

Similarly, the frequently repeated statement that "55 percent of the DSE national undercount estimate [in the 1990 census] is due to bad data or processing errors" (Breiman 1994) obfuscates the technical discussion needed of how to remedy the differential undercount.[5] And this is not simply rhetoric on the part of the critics: the error statement plays a subtle role in one of the formal arguments set forth about the lack of robustness of the bureau's 1990 loss function analysis arguments (see Brown et al. 1998), which are otherwise difficult to justify.

But such technical critiques and the rhetoric that surrounds them form only part of our story. The second piece of our tale is how the controversies surrounding these developments in the technical analysis of differential undercount emerged. We have tried to explain why the innovations in the measurement and adjustment of the decennial enumeration for differential undercount were not quietly integrated into census procedures, as has been the case with other innovations in counting. To understand this part of our story, it is useful to see the analogies to controversies at earlier points in the nation's history. As we noted in chapter 2, at points in the past, debates about census procedures also merged with national politics and led to political crises in "constituting" the people to be counted and, hence, in the apportionment of Congress. The first emerged over the interpretation of statistics on racial disparities in insanity rates in the 1840 census. The resulting controversies fed the growing sectional crisis of the 1840s through the 1860s and led Congress to appoint its first board of experts to propose reforms to the census in 1850. The second, the failure of Congress to reapportion itself after the 1920 census, is more relevant to our current dilemmas, because it was a direct result of the 1910 decision to fix the size of the House of Representatives at 435 members. Later Congresses managed to reapportion, but not without quietly acceding to massive malapportionment from the 1920s to the 1960s within congressional delegations. Between the 1920s and the 1960s, congressional districts in urban areas in the nation were as much as seven times larger than those in rural areas in the same state. In Illinois in the 1940s, for example, the largest district contained more than 900,000 people; the smallest, 112,000 (Anderson 1988, 208).

It is not a coincidence that the undercount controversies emerged on the heels of the Supreme Court "one person, one vote" decisions of the 1960s. Once the courts required congressional districts to adhere to the "one person, one vote" rule, not only did urban representation increase dramatically, but the accuracy of state populations with reference to one another, and in relation to within-state districting, also became important to the political life of the nation. The differential undercount of racial minorities, as we have noted in chapter 8, is also a differential undercount by state, and it is a differential undercount that impacts districting within states. At these lower levels of geography, the national net differential undercount of a few percentage points gets magnified many times over. As a consequence, the differential undercount is a partisan issue because of the political fact that minority groups in the United States vote heavily Democratic.

And thus the litigation that has emerged and the political splits within Congress pit Democrats against Republicans and apportionment losers against apportionment winners.

Thus, in an apparent paradox, as the technical capabilities of the Census Bureau to measure and adjust for the differential undercount have improved over the past three censuses, the political controversies over the legality and constitutionality of doing so have heightened. To resolve the controversies, one must separate the technical questions from the political questions and determine who has the responsibility and authority to address each.

Some Advice for 2000

The reactions to the proposal for Census 2000 thus fall into three categories: political, legal and constitutional, and technical. The political responses encompass Myth 8, that sampling is not scientific, and they also include the charge that sampling can be "manipulated," our Myth 6. We find these responses to be antiscientific and think that they should be given little or no credence. Sampling is scientific, and we might well describe it as one of the great statistical contributions of the twentieth century. The Census Bureau is highly professional, and to most of us who know it the notion that its sampling methods would be manipulated for some political purpose seems unthinkable. Furthermore, the process of Census Bureau oversight, not only via the Census Monitoring Board but also through panels at the National Academy of Sciences and the National Research Council and a collection of formal advisory committees, leaves little opportunity for manipulation, anyway.

Myth 6 in our prologue raised the possibility that the Census Bureau could "create" or "eliminate" "millions of strategically placed citizens with the stroke of a pen." We hope we have demonstrated how the extrapolation from a sample to the population from which it is drawn in fact properly attributes totals for people in a local area based upon the sample. Relatedly, the dual-systems method assumes that the researcher can estimate the number of people missed in both counts, that is, in cell d, or the fourth cell, of the 2×2 table (see table 4.5). Neither of these statistical procedures, however, means that the researcher can "skew" the sample adjustment for party advantage.

Unmasking Myth 6, however, also requires an explanation of why opponents of the 2000 census plan claim that the Census Bureau will "eliminate" people from the count. The charge is misguided and a misreading of the treatment of erroneous enumerations in the dual-systems method. An example should illustrate. In late 1998, the Census Bureau published on its website the official and adjusted counts from the redistricting files for the 1990 census, pursuant to what is known as Public Law 94-171 Data.[6] These data provide local-area breakdowns of the 1990 population by race and Hispanic origin, for the total population and for the population eighteen years or older (that is, the voting age population). One can thus compare the official and the adjusted 1990 counts for relatively low levels of geography and see the impact of the adjustment methodology on the original figures. Milwaukee County, Wisconsin, for example, had a high response rate to the census and would therefore be expected to show relatively small benefits from adjustment. In the city of Milwaukee, despite the city mail return rate of 76 percent, the PES adjustment would have added almost fifteen thousand people (2.3 percent) to the city's population.

But the adjustment would have actually "subtracted" 129 people from the category of adult whites in eight Milwaukee County suburbs. That is, in eight of the eighteen Milwaukee County suburbs (Bayside, Brown Deer, Fox Point, Glendale, Greendale, River Hills, Wauwatosa, and Whitefish Bay), the totals for whites eighteen years and older actually decreased in the adjusted counts. The total populations of these suburbs only dropped by seven people in the adjusted counts, however. Since, as we described in chapter 5, the Census Bureau subtracts erroneous enumerations from the original enumeration before calculating an adjustment factor, it is possible for an adjustment factor for a particular demographic group to be less than one and thus to reduce the adjusted count for that demographic group. But such reductions do make sense statistically. As we noted in chapter 6, bureau statisticians did not anticipate the impact that erroneous enumerations would have on the 1990 adjustment. The issue remains one for continued discussion in 2000.

Whether sampling is allowed by current statute and whether it is constitutional remain matters for the courts to rule upon, and these questions were the focal points of cases before the Supreme Court. For our part, we do not see the primitive counting methods of the framers of the late eighteenth century as controlling for demographers and statisticians of the late twentieth century. We do see the intent of the framers to develop an automatic and fair procedure for allocating political representation among the various elements of the society according to population to be one of the great innovations in democratic politics.

Thus, if the courts either permit or do not reach the question of the constitutionality of sampling, the larger political issues of census taking will remain to be decided. In such a situation, we propose several principles to guide the discussion.

First, the eight years of litigation framing the 1990 count point to the need to develop a consensus on methodology among stakeholders, policy makers—including Congress—and the social science community in advance of the census. It is then incumbent on the social science community, particularly those outside the bureau, to sell the plan to politicians, who, quite naturally, want to see the "experts" agree. Such a prescription requires that the statistical experts pay close attention to the technical controversies well in advance of the count, state objections to particular questions of controversy, contribute solutions where possible, and grapple with the very real question of how to do the best we can with the resources available.

Second, the Census Bureau should be permitted to produce one count, as it initially proposed. To be sure, the bureau and outside experts will and should evaluate the one-number census for its strengths and weaknesses, as they have in previous decades. But alternative data sets simply confuse and vitiate the credibility of any count and set the user to shopping for the statistic that suits the argument of the day.

Third, Congress needs to craft legislation quite different from that which it passed in the fall of 1997. The legislation must restore authority to the Census Bureau to manage the technical details of enumeration and sampling to fulfill the constitutional mandate for a census. This would not be a new approach to the handling of controversies over census taking. After all, following the paralysis of the 1920s, Congress delegated just such authority to the bureau in 1929.

Fourth, Congress may need to undertake an examination of some of the larger questions surrounding apportionment that underpin the current political controversy. There is evidence that census controversies will only become more intractable until Congress reviews its responsibility for defining the apportionment methodology and setting the size of the House. It has been almost a century since Congress has done so. In that time, the growth in the size of the population in the context of a fixed number of seats in the House may have begun to distort the political shape of our national politics.

Rein Taagepera and Matthew Soberg Shugart (1989) have surveyed the nature of electoral systems internationally, including the relation between population size and the number of seats in the most populous house of the national legislature (see also Kromkowski and Kromkowski 1991, 1992; Oberby 1992; Reader 1994). They describe the pattern of relationships between population size and legislature size most simply as the "cube root rule of assembly sizes" (figure 10.2). The best predictor of the actual size of the most populous house of a national legislature in stable developed countries is the cube root of the population in millions. Taagepera and Shugart also develop a theoretical model explaining their empirical results (1989, 173–83). Their models demonstrate that the United States, which has not increased the size of the House of Representatives since 1910, may in fact have a national legislature that is roughly two hundred members smaller than would be predicted by the pattern evident for the first 120 years of the republic or the current international pattern.

House members currently represent 572,000 people on average. After the 2000 census, if the House size remains at 435 members, the average member will represent approximately 630,000 people. By way of comparison, there are currently nine states with populations of less than one million. Twenty-four incorporated places in the United States have populations of more than 500,000 (U.S. Bureau of the Census 1996c, 28, 43). To reverse the argument, if the current House size were determined by the cube root rule of assembly sizes, each House member would represent roughly 431,000 people. If Congress does not revisit the question of the size of the House of Representatives, districts will grow each decade. By 2010, a century after Congress froze the size of the House, the 435-member chamber will represent more than 300 million people, up from 92 million in 1910. Much of the current controversy about the undercount may also be a result of the continuing shrinkage in the size of House delegations from various states. Nineteen states have seen the size of their congressional delegations drop since 1960. Thirteen states, all in the South or West, have larger delegations in 1998 than they had in 1960. Eighteen state delegations have remained stable, including four of the seven states with only one House member.

The final issues for 2000 are technical. Census taking in the United States is a complex task. The methods are elaborate and far from the notion of a simple head count. The added components associated with the two major uses of sampling proposed for incorporation into Census 2000 do increase the complexity. In complex systems, things can easily go wrong ("complex systems, from ocean liners to

Figure 10.2   Population and National Assembly Size for the United States from 1790 to 1980 and for Twenty Other Stable, Developed Countries in the 1980s

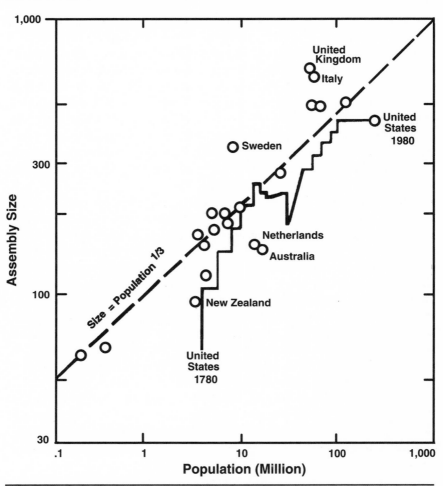

Source: Taagepera and Shugart 1989, 175. Reprinted with permission from Yale University Press.

space telescopes, fail in unexpected ways"), and the critics repeatedly point to the computer error in 1990, which "added a million people to the adjusted count" (see Brown et al. 1998). It could happen again, they claim. Although errors can occur, we hardly see this as a serious response to the current plan. The critics also suggest that sampling for nonresponse follow-up offers little opportunity to improve accuracy and simply adds to the complexity of the processing of census data in various ways. Again, we disagree, and we see this criticism as a consequence of the critics' failure to think in terms of error in the census and, in particular, to recognize the importance of dealing with erroneous enumerations.

But these same critics point to other complexities, such as the difficulty of matching enumeration and sample records that is a crucial feature of the integrated-coverage measurement approach. These and other features of the dual-systems estimation approach remain targets of statistical concern. Virtually all these technical issues relate to nonsampling error associated with the use of sampling in the census context, and many focus on the appropriateness of assumptions linked to statistical models and methods. These nonsampling errors are of real concern to the statisticians at the Census Bureau, and many are the focus of ongoing evaluation studies. Those who support the Census 2000 plan acknowledge the need to take stock of and control the sources of these nonsampling errors, but their assessment is that the Census 2000 plan offers the prospect of considerable improvement over the 1990 adjustment process (see, for example, White and Rust 1999, the report of the most recent Committee on National Statistics Panel on plans for the 2000 census).

The design for the 2000 census has built on these earlier efforts to use sampling to improve accuracy. The increase in the PES sample size allows better fitting of sampling with the design of the census. The lessons from 1990 should lead to improvements in the accuracy of the PES and thus in the dual-systems corrected counts. Sampling for nonresponse follow-up (SNRFU) could replace the faulty and inaccurate coverage improvement programs with a scientifically based survey that is expected to replace the biases in recent coverage improvement programs by a small component of sampling error. We note that the PES measures erroneous enumerations (EEs) and omissions, and there have been major disagreements (technical and otherwise) about the impact of the EEs on the adjustment process. A compelling feature of SNRFU is that it should reduce the level of EEs, a major component of the gross error. Moreover, to the extent that SNRFU reduces EEs, the PES/ICM will have much improved accuracy, because it will not have to cope with EEs to the same extent as it did in 1990. Finally, the integration of enumeration, SNRFU, and ICM means greater control over the census process and thus the prospect of the reduction of yet additional sources of error.

We agree with the leaders in Congress who point out that there are political implications of using one or another counting technique. Deciding to use integrated coverage measurement can move a seat in Congress from one state to another, as can a computer mistake. But we would like to direct attention to the discussion of how best to avoid mistakes and to enhance the accuracy of the census. Many other decisions about census or apportionment methodology also move seats among states. Deciding to count the overseas military in the apportionment totals may shift a seat. So may changing the apportionment formula or the size of the House. We expect that Congress will continue to focus on the details of census taking in the years ahead. Changing census methodologies may move seats in Congress between states, but only one or two, not the two dozen seats some claim.

In short, we should never forget that the census is about the apportionment of political power and resources—"moving power and money" (Bryant and Dunn 1995)—among the various population constituencies that make up American society. The framers of the Constitution knew as much when they instituted it two centuries ago. It behooves us to remember their legacy to us. The census and apportionment system works, though never quite as effortlessly as we would all like. The drama surrounding the possible adjustment of the 1990 census counts using statistical sampling and estimation methods is complete. The new drama for the 2000 census is already well under way. The play shows every indication of being an exciting one.

One Last Word

In late January 1999, the Supreme Court handed down a ruling in the two lawsuits challenging the Census 2000 plan, *Clinton v. Glavin* (1999) and *Dept. of Commerce v. House* (1999). The court held that the Census Act prohibited the proposed uses of statistical sampling to determine the population for congressional apportionment purposes. The court did not address the question of whether statistical sampling for apportionment was unconstitutional. The ruling invalidated the Census Bureau's plans to use statistical sampling for the nonresponse follow-up phase of the enumeration.

The decision did not end the controversies over sampling in the 2000 census since the ruling did not explicitly ban sampling in the census for uses other than apportionment. The major use of sampling in the Census 2000 plan would be via a postenumeration survey, the results of which could be used to adjust those from the "traditional" enumeration for purposes other than apportionment.

The court's decision invalidating the use of sampling for apportionment changed some of the technical demands on the design of the PES. The plan for the PES was intended to produce direct state estimates for apportionment and, thus, called for a very large sample of 750,000 households. With the court's decision, the bureau will need to spend more time in the field doing traditional follow-up, and, therefore, will delay the start of the PES. The sample is currently planned to include about 300,000 households.

There remain major differences of opinion regarding this use of sampling in the census context between the Congressional Republicans and the Clinton administration and some state and local governments. Hence we expect the constitutional questions to be raised again in litigation in the future and for Congress to continue to debate legislation to resolve the controversy.

Some Information on Sources of Census Error

The following list provides some examples of sources of error in the census enumeration process in 1990 and indications of their possible implications for the accuracy of the census enumeration counts.

1. *Missed Households*: Despite the enormous efforts to construct a master address file, which includes all housing units in the United States, the Census Bureau "misses" households. In 1990, 30.5 percent of omissions came from housing units that were not enumerated at all (U.S. Bureau of the Census 1997).

2. *Refusals*: Some housing units and their occupants refuse to participate in the census. Some of their occupants are "included" statistically, however, by some of the coverage improvement programs, such as the ones for parolees and probationers described later in appendix A.

3. *The appropriateness of census concepts and definitions*: During the 1980s, there was considerable discussion and empirical study of "housing units" and "families." The official census definitions of these terms for 1990 are often difficult to apply in practice, especially by respondents and enumerators in minority communities where nontraditional physical and family structures may be the norm. Individuals and households are often missed as a consequence. Also, individuals who are connected with multiple households may well be counted multiple times.

4. *Census day versus census operations*: Few if any people were enumerated at their household locations on April 1, 1990. (Recall that

233

this was a Sunday.) Yet many components of the census assume that people are correctly reported in the exact location where they resided on April 1.

5. *Use of household respondents*: One person completes the census form for each household. This person serves as a filter for information on others in the household and on household characteristics. Errors that enter into census data as a result of the "filter" applied by the household respondent are extremely difficult for anyone to correct.

6. *Problems of understanding connected with the wording of the instructions and questionnaire wording*: Many individuals in the population may have had difficulty in interpreting the instructions on the census form. For example, the census form is quite explicit that college students should be counted where they go to school. Nonetheless, many respondents believe that the students should be counted at home, and college students are often double-counted as a result.

7. *Recording error*: Individuals completing the census questionnaire may inadvertently check the wrong answer.

8. *Enumerator error*: When a household fails to return the mailed-out census questionnaire, a census enumerator may complete the questionnaire as a result of a visit to the household location. Enumerators may record information different from that supplied by the household respondent.

9. *Duplication error*: Some households provide multiple returns, either from the same household respondent or from different ones. Sometimes these duplicates are easy to catch, and sometimes not. This may be the result of geocoding or other types of error (see the following items).

10. *Coding and processing errors*: After a census questionnaire is completed and returned to the bureau, the information must be transferred to a computer file and subsequently processed and checked for consistency. Errors creep into the official files despite the new technologically based methods used in 1990 for data capture.

11. *Geocoding errors*: These errors occur at various stages in the process, from the compilation of initial mailing lists as part of the TIGER system all the way through coding. In 1990, complaints from local communities of missed housing units were attributed by the Census Bureau to geocoding problems; some of these, pre-

sumably, involve geocoding errors in census records. Despite all the "corrections" that occurred throughout the various forms of data review, residual geocoding errors place people in the wrong census blocks.

12. *Fabrication*: For every census there are anecdotal reports of enumerators "curbstoning," that is, fabricating questionnaires for real and often imaginary households. The bureau has a variety of methods to catch such fabrication, but inevitably a substantial number of fabricated questionnaires are included in the official census results.

13. *"Last resort" information*: Some completed census questionnaires go through an extensive review process and are edited for accuracy following reinterviews. Other questionnaires are actually filled out as a last resort by enumerators without their directly seeing or interviewing any household occupants. In such cases, enumerators use information from mail carriers, neighbors, or building managers that may be inaccurate, incomplete, or even intentionally false. Reports suggest that procedures used in 1990 produced many more questionnaires partially completed by enumerators based on last-resort information than in 1980.

14. *Parolees and Probationers*: The Census Bureau introduced a new coverage improvement program to count parolees and probationers using address information on file with state and local correction departments. A large proportion of the individuals added into the count by this program were not interviewed and might well have been living and already recorded in the census at addresses other than those on the lists used by the bureau for this program. The final "resident" population total released in December 1990 was just under three million more than the total released in August as the preliminary count. A substantial proportion of this increase was, according to statements by Bureau Director Barbara Bryant, based on the results of this program.

15. *Imputation*: In 1980, as in past censuses, the Census Bureau used various forms of statistical estimation (based either explicitly or implicitly on statistical models) to "fill in" missing data. This process of filling in is usually referred to as imputation. If the bureau had no information about the occupancy status of a housing unit (for example, one reported from last-resort methods), it imputed a status to it, that is, it categorized it as either occupied or vacant.

If a unit was imputed as occupied, or if the bureau otherwise believed it to be occupied, then it imputed a number of people to the household, as well as their characteristics. The current method of choice for imputation, known as the "sequential hot-deck" procedure, selects a housing unit proximate in processing as the donor of the characteristics. The statistical "model" underlying the imputation method is that the housing units are likely to be neighboring and have similar characteristics. In 1980, the bureau added 3.3 million people to the census through imputation. Of these, 762,000 were added into housing units for which the bureau had no knowledge, whether or not the units were occupied. Our understanding is that the numbers of imputed households and imputed individuals were much smaller in the 1990 census, in part because many of the units that would have undergone imputation were swept into the last-resort category.

These and other sources of error are usually grouped together into larger categories such as coverage error, nonresponse error, observational error, and data-processing error. Our central concern here is the impact of these sources of error on the coverage of the population. Some sources of error lead to omissions, and others to erroneous conclusions. The net error, omissions minus inclusions, is what we technically refer to as the undercount.

Judge Joseph M. McLaughlin's July 17, 1989, Stipulation and Agreement

The Settlement

The City of New York *et al.*, v. United States Department of Commerce, *et al.*, U.S. District Court Eastern District of New York, 88 Civ. 3474 (JMcL):

WHEREAS the Secretary of Commerce is vested by law with supervisory authority over the Bureau of the Census and the conduct of the Decennial Census and does not by anything said herein intend to relinquish any authority or decision-making power thereby duly vested in him, including without limitation the decision whether or not to adjust the 1990 Decennial Census; and

WHEREAS the Secretary of Commerce intends that the 1990 Decennial Census shall be conducted in conformity with all statutory and constitutional requirements including without limitation 13 U.S.C. §(b), (c) and in a manner designed to achieve the most accurate population counts practicable; and

WHEREAS the parties hereto at this time believe that the Census, including a post-enumeration survey and other adjustment-related operations, can and will be conducted in a manner that will result in the most accurate counts practicable, and no party has basis at this time

---

Appendixes B through I are verbatim extracts. For full citation information, please see the notes at the end of this volume.

to believe that the Census, including the PES and adjustment-related operations, cannot and will not be conducted in such a manner; and

WHEREAS the parties wish to avoid the burdens, costs, delays of unnecessary litigation.

NOW, THEREFORE, IT IS HEREBY STIPULATED AND AGREED, by and between the undersigned, that:

1. All pending motions, including plaintiffs' pending Motion for a Preliminary Injunction, are withdrawn.

2. Defendants agree and represent that, notwithstanding the decision by the Department of Commerce (the "Department") announced on October 30, 1987, that there would be no statistical adjustment or correction for undercount or overcount in the 1990 Decennial Census, and without conceding that that decision was incorrect, the decision is vacated, and the question of whether or not to carry out a statistical adjustment of the 1990 Decennial Census ("adjustment") shall be made by a thorough *de novo* reconsideration undertaken with an open mind, without any prejudgment, and consistent with the procedures set forth herein.

3. Defendants agree and undertake to conduct a post-enumeration survey ("PES") of not fewer than 150,000 households, a number defendants believe is sufficient for the purpose, and such other procedures or tests as they deem appropriate, as part of the 1990 Decennial Census in a manner calculated to ensure the possibility of using the PES, not solely for evaluation purposes, but to produce corrected counts usable for congressional and legislative reapportionment, redistricting and all other purposes for which the Bureau of the Census (the "Bureau") publishes data.

4. Defendants agree that the Department will promptly develop and adopt guidelines articulating what defendants believe are the relevant technical and nontechnical statistical and policy grounds for decision on whether to adjust the 1990 Decennial Census population counts. The Department's proposed guidelines shall be published in the *Federal Register* by December 10, 1989, with a request for comments. The guidelines shall be published in final form in the *Federal Register* by March 10, 1990.

5. Defendants shall determine whether an adjustment satisfies the guidelines specified in para. 4 hereof. If the Secretary determines to make an adjustment, defendants shall publish at the earliest

practicable date and, in all events, not later than July 15, 1991, a detailed statement of its grounds, including a detailed statement of which guidelines identified in para. 4 above were not met and in what respects such guidelines were not met.

6. Defendants intend to report census counts in accordance with the dates set forth in 13 U.S.C. §(b), (c). In the event that the Department releases or publishes any population counts from the 1990 Decennial Census prior to adjustment in accordance with para. 5 hereof, defendants agree that each such release or publication shall bear the following legend conspicuously on the first page:

> The population counts set forth herein are subject to possible correction for undercount or overcount. The United States Department of Commerce is considering whether to correct these accounts and will publish corrected counts, if any, not later than July 15, 1991.

7. Defendents shall establish as soon as practicable and, in all events, not later than September 30, 1989, an independent Special Advisory Panel (the "Panel") to advise the defendants on all matters relevant to the implementation of this Stipulation and, in particular, and without limitation, the guidelines identified in para. 4 above, the application and achievement of the guidelines, the expedition with which defendants are proceeding toward decision on adjustment, and plans and schedules for the implementation of the Census and the PES in a manner that will result in the most accurate final census data at the earliest practicable time. The Panel shall be composed of eight persons, none of whom shall be employed by any of the parties hereto, of such knowledge, judgment, and probity that their judgment and advice shall be entitled to the utmost respect by the defendants. All eight persons shall be appointed by the Secretary of Commerce. The Panel shall have two co-chairs from among their number appointed by the Secretary. Each member of the Panel shall submit his or her recommendations to the Secretary.

8. The members of the Panel shall be entitled to call for and shall receive the fullest cooperation from defendants, including access to all necessary or appropriate information and the opportunity to consult with any employee of the Bureau. Defendants shall take all steps necessary to give each member of the Panel reasonable access to all relevant records and information, including administering appropriate oaths of secrecy pursuant to 13 U.S.C. §9.

The Panel or any member thereof may make such disclosures, consistent with all applicable statutory requirements, as it or he deems appropriate. The Panel may adopt such rules for its governance as it deems appropriate.

9. The Department shall pay the members of the Panel a stipend of $284.80 per day for each day on which the Panel meets and such member is present and shall reimburse the members of the Panel for their reasonable and necessary expenses of travel and lodging in connection with the work of the Panel. The Department shall furnish the Panel with appropriate meeting and office facilities and clerical assistance. The Panel is entitled to retain appropriate assistants who shall be entitled to access to all materials made available to the Panel. Defendants shall make available to the Panel a fund of $500,000 against which each co-chair may draw, consistent with existing laws, rules, and regulations governing the expenditure of appropriated funds, for appropriate resources to ensure that Panel members can perform their mission.

10. The Panel shall dissolve on agreement of the parties that all of its functions pursuant to this Stipulation have been satisfied.

11. Except as expressly set forth herein, the parties reserve all their respective rights, claims, and defenses. Specifically, and not by way of limitation, plaintiffs reserve the right to challenge any of the guidelines, decisions, or procedures adopted, omitted, implemented, or announced in connection with or arising out of this Stipulation.

The 1989 Preliminary
Guidelines[1]

Each of the following guidelines is accompanied by a brief explanation or example of its intent. Following that explanation, a brief description of the empirical information directly bearing upon it is presented. The Census Bureau will implement the necessary technical operations to gather and evaluate this empirical information. The Bureau will use the highest level of professional judgment in implementing and evaluating these operations.

[1] The Census shall be considered the best count of the population of the United States unless an adjusted count is shown to be more accurate, within acceptable margins of statistical error, at the national, state, local, and census block levels.

Explanation: The Constitutional mandate of the Census Bureau is to enumerate the population, and the investment it makes in decennial census operations is to assure that the count is the best count of the population achievable given current methodology. The census is a standard. Other data collection activities are compared to census results to assess their quality. In the past, no sample survey has had as complete coverage as the decennial census, and no coverage measurement survey has produced data of better quality than the census. Strengths and weaknesses of the census are well known and extensively documented. The census is understood and because of its quality has wide acceptance and extensive use among policy makers and other users. Before replacing the census, we must be sure that the replacement is an improvement. The assumption that any effort involving less than an attempt to enumerate the entire population can lead to a more accurate enumeration calls into question the process that Census Bureau has developed over the past two hundred years. The enumeration is based on evidence that physical persons are in a particular location or block at a particular time. A set of adjusted counts would be based on a statistical inference that unaccounted for persons were present and that persons who were actually enumerated do not exist or were counted twice. Both determinations are based on a survey of a sample of similar blocks from locations across the country. To reiterate, there is no reason to adjust the census unless the adjusted count is shown to be better for all the uses to which the census counts are put. Thus, the evidence to be acceptable must show overwhelmingly that the count can be improved by statistical adjustment in order to overturn the premise that the actual enumeration is the best count possible.

Comparison of estimates of population size. The estimates of the size of the population from the original enumeration, the demographic analysis, and the post-enumeration-survey estimates will be compared to assess their consistency. The comparison will take into consideration the uncertainty inherent in the demographic analysis and post-enumeration-survey estimates. The original enumerations will be considered to be more accurate for all geographic areas unless contrary evidence is presented.

[1A] The post-enumeration survey is not to be considered as a substitute for the Census as a count of the population of the United States, any state, any locality, or any census block.

Explanation: The post-enumeration survey can provide an estimate of the total count of the population, based on techniques of survey sampling. It does not provide a substitute for that complete count. Its proper use is as an adjunct to the population count which provides an estimate of its completeness, within statistical limits of error. Thus, any adjustment of the population count, using post-enumeration-survey information, must be based on the enumeration.

[1B] Demographic analysis of the population is not to be considered as a substitute for the Census as a count of the population of the United States, any state, any locality, or any census block.

Explanation: Although demographic analysis can provide an alternative estimate of national population counts, it cannot be used to provide data at the subnational level required by the various uses to which census data are put. Demographic analysis is an estimate of the population principally based on administrative data sources. Although it could be considered a derived count of the population, it remains an alternative to the direct enumeration of the population, not a substitute for it. Thus any adjustment of the population using demographic analysis information must only be a supplement to the enumeration.

[1C] Any combination of the post-enumeration survey and demographic analysis of the population is not to be considered as a substitute for the Census as a count of population of the United States, any state, any locality, or any census block.

Explanation: This guideline affirms that any combination of the techniques referred to in the prior two guidelines remains an inadequate surrogate for the actual enumeration of the population.

[2] The size of any undercount or overcount inferred from demographic analysis of population subgroups shall be carefully scrutinized and fully described, and the degree to which the overcount or undercount is potentially an artifact of the assumption underlying the analysis shall be clearly presented.

Explanation: Estimates of the size of certain cohorts of the population are based on assumptions about or studies of the behavior of these population cohorts, rather than on administrative or other records. For some cohorts these assumptions alone have led to conclusions of undercounts or overcounts in several different censuses. The extent to which such conclusions result from specific assumptions must be expressly articulated. Moreover, the extent to which these assumptions are warranted, and the sensitivity of the conclusions to changes in these assumptions, must be assessed.

Evaluation of demographic analysis estimates. Demographic analysis of population estimates is susceptible to a variety of sources of error.

Numerous techniques will be used to evaluate the quality of the demographic analysis estimates. Among the potential sources of error in the demographic analysis are:

Birth registration completeness.

Net immigration of uncounted aliens.

White births, 1915–1935.

Black births, 1915–1935.

Foreign-born emigrants.

Population over age 65.

Models to translate historical birth-record racial classifications into 1990 self-reported census concepts.

The final analysis will discuss how these and other components cumulate into overall levels of error.

[3] The sources of any undercount or overcount of population subgroups inferred from the analysis of the post-enumeration survey conducted subsequent to the 1990 census shall be carefully scrutinized and fully described, and the degree to which the overcount or under-count is potentially an artifact of the assumptions underlying the anal-ysis or the methods inherent in the analysis shall be clearly presented.

Explanation: The capture-recapture method which lies at the heart of the post-enumeration-survey models for estimating population cov-erage deficiencies is not, as used in the decennial census, completely analogous to more conventional uses of the method in estimating pop-ulations of, say, fish or land-based fauna in a natural setting. Thus, it is imperative that the influence of this methodology on the under-count or overcount estimates be clearly explained. Moreover, the post-enumeration-survey adjustment mechanism relies on numerous as-sumptions. The extent to which these assumptions are warranted, and the sensitivity of the conclusions to changes in the assumptions, must be assessed.

Evaluations for post-enumeration-survey estimates. Numerous tech-niques will be used to evaluate the quality of the post-enumeration-survey estimates. Among the possible sources of error for the dual system estimate of population size based on the post-enumeration-survey and the census are:

Missing data.

Quality of the reported census day address.

Fabrication in the *P* sample.

Matching error.

Mismeasurement of erroneous enumerations.

Balancing the estimates of gross overcount and gross undercount.

Correlation bias.

Variance.

An analysis of how these and other component errors combine to produce an overall level of error will be discussed. Implicit in all eval-uations is that all analyses examine data for the population as a whole and within race, sex, Hispanic origin, and geographical detail.

[4] The 1990 Census may be adjusted only if the adjusted counts are consistent and complete across all jurisdictional level: national, state, local, and census block. Thus, for example, counts could not be adjusted at the state level and left unadjusted at the census block level. If any census block within a stratum is adjusted, then all census blocks within that same stratum must be adjusted. Any adjusted count must be arithmetically consistent across all levels of geography and with respect to age, race, Hispanic origin, and sex. This requirement does not apply when incorporating counts of military overseas into national totals for reapportionment purposes.

Explanation: If any adjusted count is to be used, it must be adjusted at every level at which census counts are used. Some strata, for which there is no conclusive evidence of an undercount, may not be adjusted. It must be arithmetically consistent to avoid unnecessary confusion and to avoid any efforts to choose among alternative sets of numbers to suit a particular purpose. It is unacceptable to conclude, for example, that one set of numbers at the level of individual states can be used for redistricting purposes, while another set could be used for apportionment purposes.

Evaluation of small area estimation. A synthetic estimation procedure might be used for adjustment. A synthetic adjustment assumes that the probability of being missed by the census is constant for each person within an age, race, Hispanic origin, and sex category in a geographical area. A synthetic adjustment is performed in two steps. First, the preferred adjustment factors are estimated for each age, race, Hispanic origin, and sex category for a post-enumeration-survey stratum. The same age, race, Hispanic origin, and sex categories may not be appropriate for every post-enumeration-survey stratum, in which case the categories will be combined as necessary. Then the adjusted estimate in each category for the census block is obtained by multiplying the unadjusted census estimate in that category by the adjustment factor. The adjusted census estimate for the census block is computed by adding the estimated adjustments for the age, race, Hispanic origin, and sex categories. Put simply, under adjustment each individual enumerated would receive a different relative weight in the adjusted population count according to his or her race, age, sex, ethnic background, and place of residence.

The coverage error may vary substantially within the post-enumeration-survey stratum, although the strata were drawn so as to be homogeneous with respect to expected coverage error. The goal of this analysis is to determine whether or not the assumptions underlying a synthetic adjustment of the census are valid and produce counts which are more accurate at all geographic levels at which census data are used.

[5] The 1990 Census may be adjusted only if statistical models of the adjustment process of comparable reliability lead to essentially similar conclusions or if a particular model is shown unequivocally to provide the best estimate. Ultimately, one statistical model must be chosen if adjustment is to be undertaken. It must be clear that this unique model yields the most accurate counts and that its selection should be based on the available information about relative accuracy of competing methods.

Explanation: This guideline is intended to deal with the ambiguous outcomes resulting from the application of different statistical models to the census, post-enumeration survey, and the demographic analysis. It acknowledges that individual judgment cannot be eliminated entirely from the reasoning leading to a conclusion related to the application of an adjustment. It would suggest, for example, that if all statistical models led to consistent statistical results that are all significant in one direction, the decision on adjustment would depend on the direction and the strength of the conclusions based on those results. If any one model were to be overwhelming in its accuracy, the results from this model could be accepted. In the latter instance, this guideline would require the strongest possible factual evidence to support such a conclusion. Whatever the case, however, statistical adjustment must ultimately use only one model that is shown to yield the most accurate counts.

Comparison of evaluations of the original enumeration. The demographic analysis and the post-enumeration-survey estimates provide evaluations of the original enumeration. The census coverage error rates from the demographic analysis and the post-enumeration-survey will be compared to assess the consistency of the evaluation.

[6] The 1990 Census may be adjusted only if the general rationale for the adjustment can be clearly and simply stated in a way that is understandable to the general public.

Explanation: The decennial Census is a public ceremony in which all usual residents of the United States are required to participate. If, for the first time in the history of the Census the count were statistically adjusted, and the adjustment was done in a way that is perceived to be out of the ordinary, the rationale for that action must be clearly and simply stated and understandable to the general public.

Documentation and reproducibility. The methods, assumptions, computer programs, and data used to prepare population estimates and adjustment factors will be fully documented. The documentation will be sufficiently complete for outside reviewers to reproduce the estimates. These standards apply to the post-enumeration-survey estimates, the demographic analysis estimates, and the small area estimates.

[7] The 1990 Census may be adjusted only if the resulting counts are of sufficient quality and level of detail to be usable for Congressional and legislative reapportionment, redistricting, and for all other purposes and at all levels, for which the Census Bureau publishes decennial Census data.

Explanation: The guideline recognizes that the population counts must be usable for all purposes for which the Census Bureau publishes data. Thus, the level of detail must be adequate to produce counts for all such purposes. The guideline also reinforces the fact that there can be, for the population at any one point in time, only *one* set of official government population figures. The guideline does not speak in any way to the issue of the timing of the release of adjusted figures, nor is it meant to preclude any adjustment solely on the basis of timing.

Evaluation of small area estimation. See the discussion under guideline [4], above.

[8] The 1990 Census may be adjusted only if the adjustment is fair and reasonable, and is not excessively disruptive to the orderly transfer of political representation.

Explanation: Any adjustment of the 1990 census should be fair and reasonable in its impact on the political process and on any allocation of economic resources that is based on the decennial population counts. This guideline is intended to ensure that the factor of disruption is explicitly taken into account as the decision whether or not to adjust the 1990 census is reached. It requires an explicit statement of the degree to which adjustment would be disruptive of the orderly transfer of political representation. It is not sufficient to simply state that disruption would or would not occur. Based on the empirical evidence and the recommended courses of action, the extent of disruption must be weighed against any benefits that might accrue from adjustment.

[9] The 1990 Census may be adjusted even though the differential overcount or undercount compares favorably with the results of the differential overcount and undercount in the 1980 census only if there are compelling statistical and policy reasons to do so.

Explanation: This guideline requires an examination of the results of the analysis of the adequacy of the 1980 count in terms of its comparison with the 1980 count. One fact of history is that, although there was an acknowledged undercount and overcount of population subgroups and of the entire population in 1980, the quality of the estimates of those deficiencies was not adequate to allow an adjustment of those figures. Should coverage deficiencies be no greater than they were in 1980, substantial documentation of the advantage of an adjustment in increasing the utility and accuracy of the Census count would be required to warrant a decision to adjust.

[10] Any decision whether or not to adjust the 1990 census must take into account the effects such a decision might have on future census efforts.

Explanation: The decennial census is an integral part of our democratic process. Participation in the Census must not be discouraged. Respect for the objectivity, accuracy, and confidentiality of the census process must be maintained. If an adjustment were to erode public confidence in the census or call into question the necessity of the population participating in future censuses, then that would weigh against adjustment. *The extent to* which adjustment or non-adjustment would be perceived as a politically motivated act, and thus would undermine the integrity of the census, should also be weighed in making any adjustment decisions.

[11] Any adjustment of the 1990 Census may not violate the United States Constitution or Federal statutes.

This guideline requires no explanation.

[12] There will be a determination whether or not to adjust the 1990 census only when sufficient data are available and analysis of the data is complete enough to make such a determination. If sufficient data and analysis of the data are not available in time to publish adjusted counts by July 15, 1991, a determination will be made not to adjust.

Explanation: It is inappropriate to decide to adjust without sufficient data and analysis. The Bureau will make every effort to ensure such data are available and analysis is complete in time for the Secretary to decide and publish adjusted data by July 15, 1991. If, however, sufficient data and analysis of the data are not available in time, a determination will be made not to adjust.

The 1990 Final Guidelines[1]

Introduction

Article I, *Section 2*, Clause 3, of the Constitution of the United States reads, in part:

> Representatives and direct Taxes shall be apportioned among the several States which may be included within the Union, according to their respective Numbers, which shall be determined by adding to the whole Number of free Persons, including those bound to Service for a Term of Years, and excluding Indians not taxed, three fifths of all other Persons. The actual Enumeration shall be made within three Years after the first Meeting of the Congress of the United States, and within every subsequent Term of ten Years, in such Manner as they shall by Law direct.

Amendment 14, *Section 2*, to the Constitution, reads in part:

> Representatives shall be apportioned among the several States according to their respective numbers, counting the whole number of persons in each State, excluding Indians not taxed.

The orderly redistribution of political representation, which in the ordinary course of events means transfer of political power, is effected on the basis of the decennial census. The decision on whether to adjust the 1990 census for net undercounts or net overcounts has substantial consequences. Whatever decision is made, it will affect the nation for at least the next ten years. It is not a simple technical decision: It is a momentous decision which will be made by the Secretary of Commerce, an official appointed by the President and confirmed by the Senate.

The basic decision the Secretary will face is whether the counts are made more accurate by adjustment or whether an adjustment would introduce more error into the census counts. He must also take account of other implications of his decision on the public. These guidelines are written to ensure that the counts produced from the 1990 census are the most accurate that can be practically produced. They are intended to provide a framework for a balanced consideration by the Secretary as to whether to adjust the census enumeration. In that framework, the quality of the census and the degree of accuracy of the census enumeration play fundamental roles.

Enumeration is the basic procedure for counting the population that is mandated by the Constitution. Accordingly, throughout its history the Census Bureau has developed, refined, and increased the precision of the methods involved in that procedure. Those refinements and the improvements in the count that they have brought about have given us great confidence in the basic census procedure. Thus, we view enumeration as the basis for the census counts, and require that statistical techniques used to modify the counts in an attempt to improve them be subject to close scrutiny. This is not a bias against adjusting the census for net undercount or net overcount. Rather, it is a prudent stance that requires that procedures that infer population counts be shown clearly to yield better counts, that is, counts subject to smaller errors than the enumeration procedures themselves. The true population may, in statistical theory, be inherently unknowable, but the enumeration must necessarily be considered closest to the true population count unless convincing evidence can be marshalled to show otherwise. Furthermore, this evidence must allow us to generate *better* counts—it cannot just show deficiencies in the enumeration. It must enable us to correct those deficiencies.

Much of the confusion that surrounded the proposed guidelines stemmed from differing visions of the census process. The census process is divided into several distinct phases. The first phase is the enumeration of the population. The second phase is the conduct of a post-enumeration survey, based on a probability sample of housing units. This sample provides data for three purposes: evaluation of the accuracy of the enumeration, assessment of the net overcount or undercount of basic enumeration subgroups using the capture-recapture methodology and, should it prove desirable, calculation of weights for the adjustment of the enumerated counts. The third phase of the census process is a determination of the adequacy of the post-enumeration survey as an evaluation and adjustment tool.

If a determination is made that the census enumeration counts are flawed, that the post-enumeration survey is adequate and accurate, and that the application of the weights generated by the post-enumeration survey would result in more accurate counts, then the census counts could be adjusted.

For these reasons, we view the census enumeration as an operation distinct and separable from the operations used to evaluate the enumeration. We, therefore, do not subscribe to an integrated view of the census, where enumeration and evaluation are inextricably bound together to produce counts. The enumeration produces counts which are subsequently evaluated. Should the evaluation show them deficient and correctable into more accurate counts, a decision can be made to adjust. Thus, sacrificing any parts of the enumeration and replacing them with evaluation activities is not appropriate. It is from this view of the census that the guidelines are drawn.

It is worth noting that the technical grounds for adjustment are contained in these guidelines in a manner that is intended to be understandable to the general public. The level of detail that some members of the public would desire is greater judging from the comments on the proposed guidelines. In consideration of this desire, the Department of Commerce will publish a detailed outline of technical operations and procedures. The Department of Commerce and the Bureau of the Census will keep the public informed as plans for implementing the procedures leading to an adjustment decision progress.

The guidelines will be weighed collectively. Not every consideration in each guideline need be completely satisfied or resolved in order to reach a decision. The issues of accuracy, fairness, disruption, and constitutionality must be addressed together in making the decision on whether an adjustment will increase the accuracy of the 1990 Census sufficiently to proceed with it.

The Department of Commerce will rely on the Bureau of the Census to implement the technical operations and procedures used in the decision making process. These include operations to evaluate the accuracy of the census enumeration and the proposed adjustments to the census enumeration, the reliability of statistical models used in the adjustment process and the quality of the resulting estimates. The Bureau of the Census will use the highest levels of professional standards in carrying out these operations, procedures and evaluations, and will document all their judgments in a way that allows the statistical community to evaluate them. Ultimately, however, the Secretary will, in the exercise of his sound discretion, determine whether to adjust the census.

Each of the following guidelines is accompanied by an explanation or example of its intent. Where appropriate, a brief description of the empirical information and technical operations bearing upon it is presented.

A treatment of substantive comments on the proposed guidelines is then presented. Favorable and unfavorable comments on each proposed guideline are both presented, followed by a summary analysis of the comments. Each subjective objection to each guideline is addressed individually. General comments on the proposed guidelines are presented and addressed last.

Guidelines

[1] The Census shall be considered the most accurate count of the population of the United States, at the national, state, and local level, unless an adjusted count is shown to be more accurate. The criteria for accuracy shall follow accepted statistical practice and shall require the highest level of professional judgment from the Bureau of the Census. No statistical or inferential procedure may be used as a substitute for the Census. Such procedures may only be used as supplements to Census.

Explanation: The mandate of the Census Bureau is to enumerate the population in a manner that assures that the count of the population is the best achievable given current methodology. As stated in the introduction, the assertion that a method involving statistical inference could lead to a more accurate enumeration warrants close scrutiny.

A set of adjusted counts would be based on a statistical inference that unaccounted-for persons were present and that persons who were actually enumerated do not exist or were counted twice. Both determinations are based on a survey of a sample of similar blocks from locations across the country. Thus, the evidence, to be acceptable, must show overwhelmingly that the count can be improved by statistical adjustment at national, state, and local levels. In making this assessment, we will examine the effects of the proposed adjustment on the accuracy of counts at all geographic levels.

Comparison of estimates of population size: The estimates of the size of the population from the original enumeration, the demographic analysis, and the post-enumeration-survey estimates will be compared to assess their consistency. The comparison will take into consideration the uncertainty inherent in the demographic analysis and post-enumeration-survey estimates. For the reason explained in the introduction, the original enumerations will be considered to be more accurate for all geographic areas unless the evidence from demographic analysis and the post-enumeration survey demonstrates convincingly that the dual-system estimate is more accurate.

Accordingly, the Bureau of the Census shall carefully scrutinize and fully describe the size of any net undercount or net overcount inferred from demographic analyses of population sub-groups and the sources of any net undercount or net overcount of population sub-groups inferred from the analysis of the post-enumeration survey.

[2] The 1990 Census may be adjusted if the adjusted counts are consistent and complete across all jurisdictional levels: national, state, local, and census block. The resulting counts must be of sufficient quality and level of detail to be *usable* for Congressional reapportionment and legislative redistricting, and for all other purposes and at all levels for which census counts are published.

Explanation: This guideline acknowledges that the population counts must be usable for all purposes for which the Census Bureau publishes data. The guideline also reinforces the fact that there can be, for the population at all geographic levels at any one point in time, only *one* set of official government population figures.

Thus, the level of detail must be adequate to produce counts for all such purposes. If the 1990 Census count is to be adjusted, it must be adjusted down to the census block level. It must be arithmetically consistent to eliminate confusion, and to prevent any efforts to choose among alternative sets of numbers to suit a particular purpose.

If the Census is to be adjusted, a process called synthetic adjustment will be used. A synthetic adjustment assumes that the probability of being missed by the census is constant for each person within an age, race, Hispanic origin, sex, and tenure category in a geographical area. A synthetic adjustment is performed in two steps. First, the preferred adjustment factors are estimated for a variety of post-strata defined by age, race, Hispanic origin, sex, and tenure within geographic areas. Then the adjusted estimate in each category for a census block is obtained by multiplying the unadjusted census estimate in that category by the adjustment factor. The adjusted census estimate for the census block is computed by adding the estimated adjustments for each post-strata cell of the block. Put simply, in an adjusted population count each individual enumerated will receive a relative weight according to his or her race, age, sex, ethnic background, tenure, and place of residence. The aggregate counts will then be built up from the weighted individuals to census block, local area, state and national counts. We will conduct evaluations of small area estimations to ensure that this process results in counts that are in fact more accurate.

Evaluations of small area estimation. Coverage error may vary substantially within the post-enumeration-survey post-strata, although the post-strata were drawn to be homogeneous with respect to expected coverage error. The goal of this analysis is to determine whether or not the assumptions underlying a synthetic adjustment of the census are valid and produce counts which are more accurate at all geographic levels at which census data are used. In particular, the within-strata block-to-block variance in characteristics and net overcounts or net undercounts will be analyzed.

[3] The 1990 census may be adjusted if the estimates generated from the pre-specified procedures that will lead to an adjustment decision are shown to be more accurate than the census enumeration. In particular, these estimates must be shown to be robust to variations in reasonable alternatives to the production procedures, and to variations in the statistical models used to generate the adjusted figures.

Explanation: The Bureau of the Census will determine the technical and operational procedures necessary for an adjustment decision before the results of the post-enumeration survey are known. This procedure shall be chosen to yield the most accurate adjusted counts that pre-census knowledge and judgment can provide. The Bureau of the Census will then assess the components of systematic and random error in the procedure and it will assess the robustness of the estimates generated from that procedure.

Various procedures and statistical models can be used to generate estimates of net overcounts and adjustment factors. This guideline specifies that a set of procedures for generating proposed adjusted counts will be determined in advance of receiving the 1990 post-enumeration-survey estimates. This guideline requires that these procedures be evaluated. These evaluations will identify other procedures and models that could be considered as reasonable alternatives to the chosen production process. These alternatives will be used to assess the accuracy and precision of the proposed adjusted counts. In addition they will be used to assess whether and by how much the adjusted counts could vary if alternative procedures were used.

[4] The decision whether or not to adjust the 1990 census should take into account the effects such a decision might have on future census efforts.

Explanation: The Decennial Census is an integral part of our democratic process. Participation in the census must be encouraged. Respect for the objectivity, accuracy, and confidentiality of the census process must be maintained. Accordingly, if evidence suggests that the adjustment would erode public confidence in the census or call into question the necessity of the population participating in future censuses, then that would weigh against adjustment. The extent to which adjustment or non-adjustment would be perceived as a politically motivated act, and thus would undermine the integrity of the census, should also be weighed in making any adjustment decision.

[5] Any adjustment of the 1990 Census may not violate the United States Constitution or Federal statutes.

If an adjustment would violate Article I, Section 2, Clause 3 of the U.S. Constitution, as amended by Amendment 14, Section 2, or 13 U.S.C. Section 195, or any other Constitutional provision, statute or later enacted legislation, it cannot be carried out.

[6] There will be a determination whether to adjust the 1990 census when sufficient data are available, and when analysis of the data are not available in time to publish adjusted counts by July 15, 1991, a determination will be made not to adjust the 1990 census.

Explanation: It is inappropriate to decide to adjust without sufficient data and analysis. The Bureau will make every effort to ensure that such data are available and that their analysis is complete in time for the Secretary to decide to adjust and to publish adjusted data at the earliest practicable date and, in all events, not later than July 15, 1991, as agreed to in the stipulation. Note, however, that the Department and the Bureau have consistently stated that this is the earliest possible date by which there is a 50 percent chance that an analysis could be completed on which a decision to adjust could be based. If, however, sufficient data and analysis of the data are not available in time, a determination will be made not to adjust the 1990 census. The coverage evaluation research program will continue until all technical operations and evaluation studies are completed. Any decisions whether to adjust other data series will be made after completion of those operations.

[7] The decision whether or not to adjust the 1990 Census shall take into account the potential disruption of the process of the orderly transfer of political representation likely to be caused by either course of action.

Explanation: This guideline is intended to ensure that the factor of disruption of the process of the orderly transfer of political representation is explicitly taken into account as the decision is reached. For example, many states have pointed to adjustment as being disruptive to their redistricting plans. Likewise, members of some communities that are believed to have been historically undercounted contend that if the census were not adjusted, this would disrupt the orderly and proper transfer of political representation to their communities. The inability to ensure accuracy of counts at local levels may result in politically disruptive challenges by localities to official census counts.

This guideline recognizes that the Decennial Census plays a pivotal role in the orderly distribution of political representation in our democratic republic. The process used to generate the required counts must not be arbitrary either in fact or appearance. The Secretary is thus obliged to consider the impact of his decision on the fairness and reasonableness of that redistribution to all those affected. This guideline requires an explicit statement of how and to what degree adjustment or non-adjustment would be disruptive. Even though these are concepts that are not easily quantifiable, they warrant serious consideration in order for the Secretary to make a prudent decision on an issue that profoundly affects public policy.

[8] The ability to articulate clearly the basis and implications of the decision whether or not to adjust shall be a factor in the decision. The *general rationale* for the decision will be clearly stated. The technical documentation lying behind the adjustment decision shall be in keeping with professional standards of the statistical community.

Explanation: It is the responsibility of the government to have its critical decisions understood by its citizens. We recognize, however, that the degree to which a decision can be understood cannot alone dictate an important policy decision.

The decennial census is a public ceremony in which all usual residents of the United States are required to participate. If the census count were statistically adjusted, the rationale for that action must be clearly stated and should be understandable to the general public. If the decision were made not to adjust, the elements of that decision must also be clearly stated in an understandable way. It will be the responsibility of the Department of Commerce and the Bureau of the Census to articulate the general rationale and implications of the decision in a way that is understandable to the general public.

This does not require the Bureau or the Department to explain in detail to the general public the complex statistical operations or inferences that could lead to a decision to adjust. But, as with any significant change in statistical policy, the government has the duty to explain to the public, in terms that most can understand, the reason for the change. If the decision is not to adjust, (that is, not to change) the public will be informed as well.

The last part of the guideline ensures that the methods, assumptions, computer programs, and data used to prepare population estimates and adjustment factors will be fully documented. The documentation will be sufficiently complete for an independent reviewer to reproduce the estimates. These standards apply to the post-enumeration survey estimates, the demographic analysis estimates, and the small area synthetic estimates.

Bureau of the Census Coverage Evaluation Reports, 1990 Census

Demographic Analysis Evaluation Project

D1. J. Gregory Robinson. 1991. "Error in the Birth Registration Completeness Estimates." Report 74.

D2. Karen A. Woodrow. 1991. "Preliminary Estimates of Undocumented Residents in 1990." Report 75.

D3. J. Gregory Robinson. 1991. "Uncertainty Intervals for Estimated White Births, 1915–1934." Report 76.

D4. J. Gregory Robinson. 1991. "Uncertainty Intervals for Estimated Black Births, 1915–1934." Report 77.

D5. Karen A. Woodrow. 1991. "Preliminary Estimates of Emigration Components." Report 78.

D6. J. Gregory Robinson. 1991. "Robustness of the Estimates of the Population Aged 65 and Over." Report 79.

D7. J. Gregory Robinson, Karen A. Woodrow, and Bashir Ahmed. 1991. "Uncertainty Measure for Other Components." Report 80.

D8. J. Gregory Robinson, David L. Word, and Gregory S. Spencer. 1991. "Uncertainty for Models to Translate 1990 Census Concepts into Historical Racial Classifications." Report 81.

D9. J. Gregory Robinson and Susan Lapham. 1991. "Inconsistencies in Race Classifications of the Demographic Estimates and the Census." Report 82.

D10. Bashir Ahmed and J. Gregory Robinson. 1991. "Differences Between Preliminary and Final Estimates of Percent Net Undercount." Report 83.

D11. Prithwis Das Gupta. 1991. "Models for Assessing Errors in Undercount Rates Based on Demographic Analysis." Report 84.

Postenumeration Survey Evaluation Project

P1. Stephen Mack, Eric Schindler, and Joe Schafer. 1991. "Analysis of Reasonable Alternatives." Report A-9.

P2. Philip M. Gbur. 1991. "Distribution of Missing Data Rates." Report B-4.

P3. Philip M. Gbur. 1991. "Evaluation of Imputation Methodology for Unresolved Match Status Cases." Report C-2.

P4. Kirsten K. West. 1991. "Quality of Reported Census Day Address." Report D-2.

P5. Antoinette Tremblay. 1991. "Analysis of PES P-Sample Fabrications from PES Quality Control Data." Report E-4.

P5a. Kirsten K. West. 1991. "Analysis of P-Sample Fabrication from Evaluation Followup Data." Report F-1.

P6. Kirsten K. West. 1991. "Fabrication in the P-Sample: Interviewer Effect." Report G-2.

P7. Mary C. Davis and Paul Biemer. 1991. "Estimates of P-Sample Clerical Matching Error from a Rematching Evaluation." Report H-2.

P8. Michael Ringwelski. 1991. "Matching Error: Estimates of Clerical Error from Quality Assurance Results." Report I-2.

P9. No author. 1991. "Accurate Measurement of Census Erroneous Enumerations." Report J-2.

P9a. Kirsten K. West. 1991. "Accurate Measurement of Census Erroneous Enumeration: Evaluation Follow-up." Report K-2.

P10. Mary C. Davis and Paul Biemer. 1991. "Measurement of the Census Erroneous Enumeration–Clerical Error Made in the Assignment of Enumeration Status." Report L-2.

P11. Randall Parmer. 1991. "Balancing Error Evaluation." Report M-2.

P12. Jay Kim. 1991. "Evaluation of Synthetic Assumption." Project N-4.

P13. William Bell. 1991. "Use of Alternative Dual-System Estimators to Measure Correlation Bias." Report O-3.

P14, pt. 1. Mary C. Davis. 1991. "Independence of the Census and the P-Sample: Comparison of Blocks." Report P-4.

P14, pt. 2. Kirsten K. West. 1991. "Independence of the Census and the P-Sample Field Debriefing Report." Report P-3.

P15. Kent Wurdeman. 1991. "Variances of Dual System Estimates." Report Q-2.

P16, pt. 1. Mary H. Mulry. 1991. "Total Error in PES Estimates by Evaluation Post Strata." Report R-6.

P16, pt. 2. Henry F. Woltman, Richard A. Griffin, Alfred Navarro, Lawrence Bates, and Mary H. Mulry. 1991. "Total Error Model: Loss Function Evaluation."

P17. Arjun Adlakha, Howard Hogan, and J. Gregory Robinson. 1991. "A Report on the Internal Consistency of the Post-Enumeration Survey Estimates." Report S-1.

P18. Nicholas Alberti. "The Evaluation of Late Census Data in the 1990 Post Enumeration Study." Report T-1.

Statement of Secretary Robert A. Mosbacher on Adjustment of the 1990 Census[1]

Reaching a decision on the adjustment of the 1990 census has been among the most difficult decisions I have ever made. There are strong equity arguments both for and against adjustment. But most importantly, the census counts are the basis for the political representation of every American, in every state, county, city, and block across the county.

If we change the counts by a computerized, statistical process, we abandon a two-hundred-year tradition of how we actually count people. Before we take a step of that magnitude, we must be certain that it would make the census better and the distribution of the population more accurate. After a thorough review, I find the evidence in support of an adjustment to be inconclusive and unconvincing. Therefore, I have decided that the 1990 census counts should not be changed by a statistical adjustment.

The 1990 census is one of the two best censuses ever taken in this country. We located about 98 percent of all the people living in the United States as well as U.S. military personnel living overseas, which is an extraordinary feat given the size, diversity and mobility of our population. But I am sad to report that despite the most aggressive outreach program in our nation's history, census participation and coverage was lower than average among certain segments of our population. Based on our estimates, Blacks appear to have been undercounted in the 1990 census by 4.8%, Hispanics by 5.2%, Asian-Pacific

Islanders by 3.1%, and American Indians by 5.0%, while non-Blacks appear to have been undercounted by 1.7%.

I am troubled by this problem of differential participation and undercount of minorities, and I regret that an adjustment does not address this phenomenon without adversely affecting the integrity of the census. Ultimately, I had to make the decision which was fairest for all Americans.

The 1990 census is not the vehicle to address the equity concerns raised by the undercount. Nonetheless, I am today requesting that the Census Bureau incorporate, as appropriate, information gleaned from the Post-Enumeration Survey into its intercensal estimates of the population. We should also seek other avenues for the Bush Administration and Congress to work together and address the impact of the differential undercount of minorities on federal programs.

In reaching the decision not to adjust the census, I have benefited from frank and open discussions of the full range of issues with my staff, with senior professionals from the Economics and Statistics Administration and the Census Bureau, with my Inspector General, and with statisticians and other experts. Throughout these discussions, there was a wide range of professional opinion and honest disagreement. The Department has tried to make the process leading to this decision as open as possible. In that spirit, we will provide the full record of the basis for our decisions as soon as it is available.

In reaching the decision, I looked to statistical science for the evidence on whether the adjusted estimates were more accurate than the census count. As I am not a statistician, I relied on the advice of the Director of the Census Bureau, the Associate Director for the Decennial Census and other career Bureau officials, and the Under Secretary for Economic Affairs and Administrator of the Economics and Statistics Administration. I was also fortunate to have the independent counsel of the eight members of my Special Advisory Panel. These eight experts and their dedicated staffs gave generously of their time and expertise, and I am grateful to them.

There was a diversity of opinion among my advisors. The Special Advisory Panel split evenly as to whether there was convincing evidence that the adjusted counts were more accurate. There was also disagreement among the professionals in the Commerce Department, which includes the Economics and Statistics Administration and the Census Bureau. This compounded the difficulty of the decision for me. Ultimately, I was compelled to conclude that we cannot proceed on unstable ground in such an important matter of public policy.

The experts have raised some fundamental questions about an adjustment. The Post-Enumeration Survey, which was designed to allow us to find people we had missed, also missed important segments of the population. The models used to infer populations across the nation depended heavily on assumptions, and the results changed in important ways when the assumptions changed. These problems don't disqualify the adjustment automatically—they mean we won't get a perfect count from an adjustment. The question is whether we will get better estimates of the population. But what does better mean?

First, we have to look at various levels of geography—whether the counts are better at national, state, local, and block levels. Secondly, we have to determine both whether the actual count is better and whether the share of states and cities within the total population is better. The paradox is that in attempting to make the actual count more accurate by an adjustment, we might be making the shares less accurate. The shares are very important because they determine how many congressional seats each state gets, how political representation is allocated within states, and how large a "slice of the pie" of federal funds goes to each city and state. Any upward adjustment of one share necessarily means a downward adjustment of another. Because there is a loser for every winner, we need solid ground to stand on in making any changes. I do not find solid enough ground to proceed with an adjustment.

To make comparisons between the accuracy of the census and the adjusted numbers, various types of statistical tests are used. There is general agreement that at the national level, the adjusted counts are better, though independent analysis shows that adjusted counts, too, suffer from serious flaws. Below the national level, however, the experts disagree with respect to the accuracy of the shares measured from an adjustment. The classical statistical tests of whether accuracy is improved by an adjustment at state and local levels show mixed results and depend critically on assessments of the amount of statistical variation in the survey. Some question the validity of these tests, and many believe more work is necessary before we are sure of the conclusions.

Based on the measurements so far completed, the Census Bureau estimated that the proportional share of about 29 states would be made more accurate and about 21 states would be made less accurate by adjustment. Looking at cities, the census appears more accurate in 11 of the 23 metropolitan areas with 500,000 or more persons: Phoenix, Washington, D.C., Jacksonville, Chicago, Baltimore, New York

City, Memphis, Dallas, El Paso, Houston, and San Antonio. Many large cities would appear to be less accurately treated under an adjustment. While these analyses indicated that more people live in jurisdictions where the adjusted counts appear more accurate, one third of the population lives in areas where the census appears more accurate. As the population units get smaller, including small and medium-sized cities, the adjusted figures become increasingly unreliable. When the Census Bureau made allowances for plausible estimates of factors not yet measured, these comparisons shifted toward favoring the accuracy of the census enumeration. Using this test, 28 or 29 states were estimated to be made less accurate if the adjustment were to be used.

What all these tests show, and no one disputes, is that the adjusted figures for some localities will be an improvement and for others the census counts will be better. While we know that some will fare better and some will fare worse under an adjustment, we don't really know how much better or how much worse. If the scientists cannot agree on these issues, how can we expect the losing cities and states as well as the American public to accept this change?

The evidence also raises questions about the stability of adjustment procedures. To calculate a nationwide adjustment from the survey, a series of statistical models are used which depend on simplifying assumptions. Changes in these assumptions result in different population estimates. Consider the results of two possible adjustment methods that were released by the Census Bureau on June 13, 1991. The technical differences are small, but the differences in results are significant. The apportionment of the House of Representatives under the selected scheme moved two seats relative to the apportionment implied by the census, whereas the modified method moved only one seat. One expert found that among five reasonable alternative methods of calculating adjustments, none of the resulting apportionments of the House were the same, and eleven different states either lost or gained a seat in at least one of the five methods. I recognize that the formulas for apportioning the House are responsive to small changes and some sensitivity should be expected. What is unsettling, however, is that the choice of the adjustment method selected by Bureau officials can make a difference in apportionment, and the political outcome of that choice can be known in advance. I am confident that political considerations played no role in the Census Bureau's choice of an adjustment model for the 1990 census. I am deeply concerned, however, that adjustment would open the door to political tampering with the census in the future. The outcome of the enumeration process cannot be directly affected in such a way.

My concerns about adjustment are compounded by the problems an adjustment might cause in the redistricting process, which is contentious and litigious enough without an adjustment. An adjusted set of numbers will certainly disrupt the political process and may create paralysis in the states that are working on redistricting or have completed it. Some people claim that they will be denied their rightful political representation without an adjustment. Those claims assume that the distribution of the population is improved by an adjustment. This conclusion is not warranted based on the evidence available.

I also have serious concerns about the effect an adjustment might have on future censuses. I am worried that an adjustment would remove the incentive of states and localities to join in the effort to get a full and complete count. The Census Bureau relies heavily on the active support of state and local leaders to encourage census participation in their communities. Because census counts are the basis for political representation and federal funding allocations, communities have a vital interest in achieving the highest possible participation rates. If civic leaders and local officials believe that an adjustment will rectify the failures in the census, they will be hard pressed to justify putting census outreach programs above the many other needs clamoring for their limited resources. Without the partnership of states and cities in creating public awareness and a sense of involvement in the census, the result is likely to be a further decline in participation.

In looking at the record of public comment on this issue, I am struck by the fact that many civic leaders are under the mistaken impression that an adjustment will fix a particular problem they have identified—for example, specific housing units or group quarters that they believe we missed. It does not do so. It is not a recount. What an adjustment would do is add over 6 million unidentified people to the census by duplicating the records of people already counted in the census while subtracting over 900,000 people who were actually identified and counted. The decisions about which places gain people and which lose people are based on statistical conclusions drawn from the same survey. The additions and deletions in any particular community are often based largely on data gathered from communities in other states.

The procedures that would be used to adjust the census are at the forefront of statistical methodology. Such research deserves and requires careful professional scrutiny before it is used to affect the allocation of political representation. Since the results of the evaluation studies of the survey were made available, several mistakes have been found which altered the certainty of some of the conclusions drawn by my advisors. The analysis continues, and new findings are likely. I am concerned that if an adjustment were made, it would be made on the basis of research conclusions that may well be reversed in the next several months.

It is important that research on this problem continue. We will also continue the open discussion of the quality of the census and the survey and will release additional data so that independent experts can analyze it. We must also look forward to the next census. Planning for the year 2000 has begun. A public advisory committee on the next census has been established and by early fall I will announce the membership of that committee. I have instructed the Census Bureau's Year 2000 task force to consider all options for the next census, including methods for achieving sound adjustment techniques.

I give heartfelt thanks to the many people who have devoted so much time and energy to this enterprise. The staff at the Census Bureau have demonstrated their professionalism at every turn through the last two difficult years. They executed a fine census and an excellent survey and then condensed a challenging research program into a few short months. I am deeply grateful for their help. Let me reiterate my sincere thanks to the Special Advisory Panel for their substantial contribution. The staff at the Department, especially those in the Economics and Statistics Administration, also deserve praise.

With this difficult decision behind us, we will commit ourselves anew to finding sound, fair and acceptable ways to continue to improve the census process. We welcome the leadership of Congress and other public officials, community groups, and technical experts in maximizing the effectiveness and minimizing the difficulties of the year 2000 census.

—July 15, 1991

Membership in House of Representatives by Region and State, 1790 to 1990

Region, Division, and State	1790	1800	1810	1820	1830	1840	1850	1860
U.S. Regions	106	142	186	213	242	232	237	243
Northeast	57	76	97	105	112	94	92	87
Midwest	—	1	8	19	32	50	59	75
South	49	65	81	89	98	86	83	76
West	—	—	—	—	—	2	3	5
New England	29	35	41	39	38	31	29	27
Maine	—	—	—	7	8	7	6	5
New Hampshire	4	5	6	6	5	4	3	3
Vermont	2	4	6	5	5	4	3	3
Massachusetts	14	17	20	13	12	10	11	10
Rhode Island	2	2	2	2	2	2	2	2
Connecticut	7	7	7	6	6	4	4	4
Mid-Atlantic	28	41	56	66	74	63	63	60
New York	10	17	27	34	40	34	33	31
New Jersey	5	6	6	6	6	5	5	5
Pennsylvania	13	18	23	26	28	24	25	24
East North Central	—	1	8	18	30	43	48	56
Ohio	—	1[a]	6	14	19	21	21	19
Indiana	—	—	1[a]	3	7	10	11	11
Illinois	—	—	1[a]	1	3	7	9	14
Michigan	—	—	—	—	1[a]	3	4	6
Wisconsin	—	—	—	—	—	2[a]	3	6
West North Central	—	—	—	1	2	7	11	19
Minnesota	—	—	—	—	—	—	2[a]	2
Iowa	—	—	—	—	—	2[a]	2	6
Missouri	—	—	—	1	2	5	7	9
North Dakota	—	—	—	—	—	—	—	—
South Dakota	—	—	—	—	—	—	—	—
Nebraska	—	—	—	—	—	—	—	1[a]
Kansas	—	—	—	—	—	—	—	1
South Atlantic	46	56	62	61	61	47	43	36
Delaware	1	1	2	1	1	1	1	1
Maryland	8	9	9	9	8	6	6	5
Virginia	19	22	23	22	21	15	13	11
West Virginia	—	—	—	—	—	—	—	—
North Carolina	10	12	13	13	13	9	8	7
South Carolina	6	8	9	9	9	7	6	4
Georgia	2	4	6	7	9	8	8	7
Florida	—	—	—	—	—	1[a]	1	1

1870	1880	1890	1900	1910	1930	1940	1950	1960	1970	1980	1990
293	332	357	391	435	435	435	437	435	435	435	435
95	95	99	108	123	122	120	115	108	104	95	88
98	117	128	136	143	137	131	129	125	121	113	105
93	107	112	126	136	133	135	134	133	134	142	149
7	13	18	21	33	43	49	59	69	76	85	93
28	26	27	29	32	29	28	28	25	25	24	23
5	4	4	4	4	3	3	3	2	2	2	2
3	2	2	2	2	2	2	2	2	2	2	2
3	2	2	2	2	1	1	1	1	1	1	1
11	12	13	14	16	15	14	14	12	12	11	10
2	2	2	2	3	2	2	2	2	2	2	2
4	4	4	5	5	6	6	6	6	6	6	6
67	69	72	79	91	93	92	87	83	79	71	65
33	34	34	37	43	45	45	43	41	39	34	31
7	7	8	10	12	14	14	14	15	15	14	13
27	28	30	32	36	34	33	30	27	25	23	21
69	74	78	82	86	90	87	87	88	86	80	74
20	21	21	21	22	24	23	23	24	23	21	19
13	13	13	13	13	12	11	11	11	11	10	10
19	20	22	25	27	27	26	25	24	24	22	20
9	11	12	12	13	17	17	18	19	19	18	16
8	9	10	11	11	10	10	10	10	9	9	9
29	43	50	54	57	47	44	42	37	35	33	31
3	5	7	9	10	9	9	9	8	8	8	8
9	11	11	11	11	9	8	8	7	6	6	5
13	14	15	16	16	13	13	11	10	10	9	9
—	1[a]	1	2	3	2	2	2	2	1	1	1
—	2[a]	2	2	3	2	2	2	2	2	1	1
1	3	6	6	6	5	4	4	3	3	3	3
3	7	8	8	8	7	6	6	5	5	5	4
43	49	50	53	56	54	56	60	63	65	69	75
1	1	1	1	1	1	1	1	1	1	1	1
6	6	6	6	6	6	6	7	8	8	8	8
9	10	10	10	10	9	9	10	10	10	10	11
3	4	4	5	6	6	6	6	5	4	4	3
8	9	9	10	10	11	12	12	11	11	11	12
5	7	7	7	7	6	6	6	6	6	6	6
9	10	11	11	12	10	10	10	10	10	10	11
2	2	2	3	4	5	6	8	12	15	19	23

(*Table continues on p. 272.*)

Region, Division, and State	1790	1800	1810	1820	1830	1840	1850	1860
East South Central	3	9	18	25	33	32	32	28
Kentucky	2	6	10	12	13	10	10	9
Tennessee	1^a	3	6	9	13	11	10	8
Alabama	—	—	1^a	3	5	7	7	6
Mississippi	—	—	1^a	1	2	4	5	5
West South Central	—	—	1	3	4	7	8	12
Arkansas	—	—	—	—	1^a	1	2	3
Louisiana	—	—	1^a	3	3	4	4	5
Oklahoma	—	—	—	—	—	—	—	—
Texas	—	—	—	—	—	2^a	2	4
Mountain	—	—	—	—	—	—	—	1
Montana	—	—	—	—	—	—	—	—
Idaho	—	—	—	—	—	—	—	—
Wyoming	—	—	—	—	—	—	—	—
Colorado	—	—	—	—	—	—	—	—
New Mexico	—	—	—	—	—	—	—	—
Arizona	—	—	—	—	—	—	—	—
Utah	—	—	—	—	—	—	—	—
Nevada	—	—	—	—	—	—	—	1^a
Pacific	—	—	—	—	—	2	3	4
Washington	—	—	—	—	—	—	—	—
Oregon	—	—	—	—	—	—	1^a	1
California	—	—	—	—	—	2^a	2	3
Alaska	—	—	—	—	—	—	—	—
Hawaii	—	—	—	—	—	—	—	—

Source: U.S. Bureau of the Census, *Statistical Abstract of the United States, 1985* (Washington, DC: Government Printing Office, 1984), p. 242, and U.S. Bureau of the Census, *Statistical Abstract of the United States, 1997* (Washington, D.C.: Government Printing Office, 1997), p. 276–79.

^{a}Assigned after appointment.

^{b}Included in apportionment act in anticipation of statehood.

1870	1880	1890	1900	1910	1930	1940	1950	1960	1970	1980	1990
34	36	37	38	39	34	35	32	29	27	28	27
10	11	11	11	11	9	9	8	7	7	7	6
10	10	10	10	10	9	10	9	9	8	9	9
8	8	9	9	10	9	9	9	8	7	7	7
6	7	7	8	8	7	7	6	5	5	5	5
16	22	25	35	41	45	44	42	41	42	45	47
4	5	6	7	7	7	7	6	4	4	4	4
6	6	6	7	8	8	8	8	8	8	8	7
—	—	—	5[a]	8	9	8	6	6	6	6	6
6	11	13	16	18	21	21	22	23	24	27	30
2	5	7	8	14	14	16	16	17	19	24	24
—	1[a]	1	1	2	2	2	2	2	2	2	1
—	1[a]	1	1	2	2	2	2	2	2	2	2
—	1[a]	1	1	1	1	1	1	1	1	1	1
1[a]	1	2	3	4	4	4	4	4	5	6	6
—	—	—	—	1[b]	1	2	2	2	2	3	3
—	—	—	—	1[b]	1	2	2	3	4	5	6
—	—	1[a]	1	2	2	2	2	2	2	3	3
1	1	1	1	1	1	1	1	1	1	2	2
5	8	11	13	19	29	33	43	52	57	61	69
—	1[a]	2	3	5	6	6	7	7	7	8	9
1	1	2	2	3	3	4	4	4	4	5	5
4	6	7	8	11	20	23	30	38	43	45	52
—	—	—	—	—	—	—	1[a]	1	1	1	1
—	—	—	—	—	—	—	1[a]	2	2	2	2

Office of Management and Budget Statistical Policy Directive 15 Revisions to Standards for the Classification of Federal Data on Race and Ethnicity

Standards for Maintaining, Collecting, and Presenting Federal Data on Race and Ethnicity

This classification provides a minimum standard for maintaining, collecting, and presenting data on race and ethnicity for all Federal reporting purposes. The categories in this classification are social-political constructs and should not be interpreted as being scientific or anthropological in nature. They are not to be used as determinants of eligibility for participation in any Federal program. The standards have been developed to provide a common language for uniformity and comparability in the collection and use of data on race and ethnicity by Federal agencies. The standards have five categories for data on race: American Indian or Alaska Native, Asian, Black or African American, Native Hawaiian or Other Pacific Islander, and White. There are two categories for data on ethnicity: "Hispanic or Latino," and "Not Hispanic or Latino."

Categories and Definitions

The minimum categories for data on race and ethnicity for Federal statistics, program administrative reporting, and civil rights compliance reporting are defined as follows:

American Indian or Alaska Native. A person having origins in any of the original peoples of North and South America (including Central America), and who maintains tribal affiliation or community attachment.

Asian. A person having origins in any of the original peoples of the Far East, Southeast Asia, or the Indian subcontinent including, for example, Cambodia, China, India, Japan, Korea, Malaysia, Pakistan, the Philippine Islands, Thailand, and Vietnam.

Black or African American. A person having origins in any of the black racial groups of Africa. Terms such as "Haitian" or "Negro" can be used in addition to "Black or African American."

Hispanic or Latino. A person of Cuban, Mexican, Puerto Rican, South or Central American, or other Spanish culture or origin, regardless of race. The term, "Spanish origin," can be used in addition to "Hispanic or Latino."

Native Hawaiian or Other Pacific Islander. A person having origins in any of the original peoples of Hawaii, Guam, Samoa, or other Pacific Islands.

White. A person having origins in any of the original peoples of Europe, the Middle East, or North Africa.

Respondents shall be offered the option of selecting one or more racial designations. Recommended forms for the instruction accompanying the multiple response question are "Mark one or more" and "Select one or more."

Data Formats

The standards provide two formats that may be used for data on race and ethnicity. Self-reporting or self-identification using two separate questions is the preferred method for collecting data on race and ethnicity. In situations where self-reporting is not practicable or feasible, the combined format may be used.

In no case shall the provisions of the standards be construed to limit the collection of data to the categories described above. The collection of greater detail is encouraged; however, any collection that uses more detail shall be organized in such a way that the additional categories can be aggregated into these minimum categories for data on race and ethnicity.

With respect to tabulation, the procedures used by Federal agencies shall result in the production of as much detailed information on race and ethnicity as possible. However, Federal agencies shall not present data on detailed categories if doing so would compromise data quality or confidentiality standards.

a. Two-question format:

To provide flexibility and ensure data quality, separate questions shall be used wherever feasible for reporting race and ethnicity. When race and ethnicity are collected separately, ethnicity shall be collected first. If race and ethnicity are collected separately, the minimum designations are:

Race:
- American Indian or Alaska Native
- Asian
- Black or African American
- Native Hawaiian or Other Pacific Islander
- White

Ethnicity:
- Hispanic or Latino
- Not Hispanic or Latino

When data on race and ethnicity are collected separately, provision shall be made to report the number of respondents in each racial category who are Hispanic or Latino. When aggregate data are presented, data producers shall provide the number of respondents who marked (or selected) only one category, separately for each of the five racial categories. In addition to these numbers, data producers are strongly encouraged to provide the detailed distributions, including all possible combinations, of multiple responses to the race question. If data on multiple responses are collapsed, at a minimum the total number of respondents reporting "more than one race" shall be made available.

b. Combined format:

The combined format may be used, if necessary, for observer-collected data on race and ethnicity. Both race (including multiple responses) and ethnicity shall be collected when appropriate and feasible, although the selection of one category in the combined format is acceptable. If a combined format is used, there are six minimum categories:

- American Indian or Alaska Native
- Asian
- Black or African American
- Hispanic or Latino
- Native Hawaiian or Other Pacific Islander
- White

When aggregate data are presented, data producers shall provide the number of respondents who marked (or selected) only one category, separately for each of the six categories. In addition to these numbers, data producers are strongly encouraged to provide the detailed distributions, including all possible combinations, of multiple responses. In cases where data on multiple responses are collapsed, the total number of respondents reporting "Hispanic or Latino and one or more races" and the total number of respondents reporting "more than one race" (regardless of ethnicity) shall be provided.

Use of the Standards for Record Keeping and Reporting

The minimum standard categories shall be used for reporting as follows:

a. Statistical reporting
These standards shall be used at a minimum for all federally sponsored statistical data collections that include data on race and/or ethnicity, except when the collection involves a sample of such size that the data on the smaller categories would be unreliable, or when the collection effort focuses on a specific racial or ethnic group. Any other variation will have to be specifically authorized by the Office of Management and Budget (OMB) through the information collection clearance process. In those cases where the data collection is not subject to the information collection clearance process, a direct request for a variance shall be made to OMB.

b. General program administrative and grant reporting
These standards shall be used for all Federal administrative reporting or record keeping requirements that include data on race and

ethnicity. Agencies that cannot follow these standards must request a variance from OMB. Variances will be considered if the agency can demonstrate that it is not reasonable for the primary reporter to determine racial or ethnic background in terms of the specified categories, that determination of racial or ethnic background is not critical to the administration of the program in question, or that the specific program is directed to only one or a limited number of racial or ethnic groups.

c. Civil rights and other compliance reporting:

These standards shall be used by all Federal agencies in either the separate or combined format for civil rights and other compliance reporting from the public and private sectors and all levels of government. Any variation requiring less detailed data or data which cannot be aggregated into the basic categories must be specifically approved by OMB for executive agencies. More detailed reporting which can be aggregated to the basic categories may be used at the agencies' discretion.

Presentation of Data on Race and Ethnicity

Displays of statistical, administrative, and compliance data on race and ethnicity shall use the categories listed above. The term "nonwhite" is not acceptable for use in the presentation of Federal Government data. It shall not be used in any publication or in the text of any report.

In cases where the standard categories are considered inappropriate for presentation of data on particular programs or for particular regional areas, the sponsoring agency may use:

a. The designations "Black or African American and Other Races" or "All Other Races" as collective descriptions of minority races when the most summary distinction between the majority and minority races is appropriate;

b. The designations "White," "Black or African American," and "All Other Races" when the distinction among the majority race, the principal minority race, and other races is appropriate; or

c. The designation of a particular minority race or races, and the inclusion of "Whites" with "All Other Races" when such a collective description is appropriate. In displaying detailed information that represents a combination of race and ethnicity, the description of the data being displayed shall clearly indicate that both bases of classification are being used.

When the primary focus of a report is on two or more specific identifiable groups in the population, one or more of which is racial or ethnic, it is acceptable to display data for each of the particular groups separately and to describe data relating to the remainder of the population by an appropriate collective description.

Effective Date

The provisions of these standards are effective immediately for all new and revised record keeping or reporting requirements that include racial and/or ethnic information. All existing record keeping or reporting requirements shall be made consistent with these standards at the time they are submitted for extension, or not later than January 1, 2003.

Committee Report:
U.S. House of Representatives
105-405

M aking Appropriations for the Departments of Commerce, Justice, and State, the Judiciary, and Related Agencies for the Fiscal Year Ending September 30, 1998, and for Other Purposes

General Provisions—Department of Commerce

Sec. 209.

(a) Congress finds that—

    (1) it is the constitutional duty of the Congress to ensure that the decennial enumeration of the population is conducted in a manner consistent with the Constitution and laws of the United States;

    (2) the sole constitutional purpose of the decennial enumeration of the population is the apportionment of Representatives in Congress among the several States;

    (3) section 2 of the 14th article of amendment to the Constitution clearly states that Representatives are to be "apportioned among the several States according to their respective numbers, counting the whole number of persons in each State";

    (4) article I, section 2, clause 3 of the Constitution clearly requires an "actual Enumeration" of the population, and section 195 of title 13, United States Code, clearly provides "Except

for the determination of population for purposes of apportionment of Representatives in Congress among the several
States, the Secretary shall, if he considers it feasible, authorize
the use of the statistical method known as "sampling" in carrying out the provisions of this title.";

(5) the decennial enumeration of the population is one of the
most critical constitutional functions our Federal Government
performs;

(6) it is essential that the decennial enumeration of the population be as accurate as possible, consistent with the Constitution and laws of the United States;

(7) the use of statistical sampling or statistical adjustment in conjunction with an actual enumeration to carry out the census
with respect to any segment of the population poses the risk
of an inaccurate, invalid, and unconstitutional census;

(8) the decennial enumeration of the population is a complex and
vast undertaking, and if such enumeration is conducted in a
manner that does not comply with the requirements of the
Constitution or laws of the United States, it would be imprac-
ticable for the States to obtain, and the courts of the United
States to provide, meaningful relief after such enumeration
has been conducted; and

(9) Congress is committed to providing the level of funding that
is required to perform the entire range of constitutional census activities, with a particular emphasis on accurately enumerating all individuals who have historically been undercounted, and toward this end, Congress expects—

(A) aggressive and innovative promotion and outreach campaigns in hard-to-count communities;

(B) the hiring of enumerators from within those communities;

(C) continued cooperation with local government on address
list development; and

(D) maximized census employment opportunities for individuals seeking to make the transition from welfare to
work.

(b) Any person aggrieved by the use of any statistical method in violation of the Constitution or any provision of law (other than this

Act), in connection with the 2000 or any later decennial census, to determine the population for purposes of the apportionment or redistricting of members in Congress, may in a civil action obtain declaratory, injunctive, and any other appropriate relief against the use of such method.

(c) For purposes of this section—

    (1) the use of any statistical method as part of a dress rehearsal or other simulation of a census in preparation for the use of such method, in a decennial census, to determine the population for purposes of the apportionment or redistricting of members in Congress shall be considered the use of such method in connection with that census; and

    (2) the report ordered by title VIII of Public Law 105-18 and the Census 2000 Operational Plan shall be deemed to constitute final agency action regarding the use of statistical methods in the 2000 decennial census, thus making the question of their use in such census sufficiently concrete and final to now be reviewable in a judicial proceeding.

(d) For purposes of this section, an aggrieved person (described in subsection (b)) includes—

    (1) any resident of a State whose congressional representation or district could be changed as a result of the use of a statistical method challenged in the civil action;

    (2) any Representative or Senator in Congress; and

    (3) either House of Congress.

(e)

    (1) Any action brought under this section shall be heard and determined by a district court of three judges in accordance with section 2284 of title 28, United States Code. The chief judge of the United States court of appeals for each circuit shall, to the extent practicable and consistent with the avoidance of unnecessary delay, consolidate, for all purposes, in one district court within that circuit, all actions pending in that circuit under this section. Any party to an action under this section shall be precluded from seeking any consolidation of that action other than is provided in this paragraph. In selecting the district court in which to consolidate such actions, the chief judge shall consider the convenience of the parties and

witnesses and efficient conduct of such actions. Any final order or injunction of a United States district court that is issued pursuant to an action brought under this section shall be reviewable by appeal directly to the Supreme Court of the United States. Any such appeal shall be taken by a notice of appeal filed within 10 days after such order is entered; and the jurisdictional statement shall be filed within 30 days after such order is entered. No stay of an order issued pursuant to an action brought under this section may be issued by a single Justice of the Supreme Court.

(2) It shall be the duty of a United States district court hearing an action brought under this section and the Supreme Court of the United States to advance on the docket and to expedite to the greatest possible extent the disposition of any such matter.

(f) Any agency or entity within the executive branch having authority with respect to the carrying out of a decennial census may in a civil action obtain a declaratory judgment respecting whether or not the use of a statistical method, in connection with such census, to determine the population for the purposes of the apportionment or redistricting of members in Congress is forbidden by the Constitution and laws of the United States.

(g) The Speaker of the House of Representatives or the Speaker's designee or designees may commence or join in a civil action, for and on behalf of the House of Representatives, under any applicable law, to prevent the use of any statistical method, in connection with the decennial census, to determine the population for purposes of the apportionment or redistricting of members in Congress. It shall be the duty of the Office of the General Counsel of the House of Representatives to represent the House in such civil action, according to the directions of the Speaker. The Office of the General Counsel of the House of Representatives may employ the services of outside counsel and other experts for this purpose.

(h) For purposes of this section and section 210–

(1) the term "statistical method" means an activity related to the design, planning, testing, or implementation of the use of representative sampling, or any other statistical procedure, including statistical adjustment, to add or subtract counts to or from the enumeration of the population as a result of statistical inference; and

(2) the term "census" or "decennial census" means a decennial enumeration of the population.

(i) Nothing in this Act shall be construed to authorize the use of any statistical method, in connection with a decennial census, for the apportionment or redistricting of members in Congress.

(j) Sufficient funds appropriated under this Act or under any other Act for purposes of the 2000 decennial census shall be used by the Bureau of the Census to plan, test, and become prepared to implement a 2000 decennial census, without using statistical methods, which shall result in the percentage of the total population actually enumerated being as close to 100 percent as possible. In both the 2000 decennial census, and any dress rehearsal or other simulation made in preparation for the 2000 decennial census, the number of persons enumerated without using statistical methods must be publicly available for all levels of census geography which are being released by the Bureau of the Census for (1) all data releases before January 1, 2001, (2) the data contained in the 2000 decennial census Public Law 94-171 data file released for use in redistricting, (3) the Summary Tabulation File One (STF-1) for the 2000 decennial census, and (4) the official populations of the States transmitted from the Secretary of Commerce through the President to the Clerk of the House used to reapportion the districts of the House among the States as a result of the 2000 decennial census. Simultaneously with any other release or reporting of any of the information described in the preceding sentence through other means, such information shall be made available to the public on the Internet. These files of the Bureau of the Census shall be available concurrently to the release of the original files to the same recipients, on identical media, and at a comparable price. They shall contain the number of persons enumerated without using statistical methods and any additions or subtractions thereto. These files shall be based on data gathered and generated by the Bureau of the Census in its official capacity.

(k) This section shall apply in fiscal year 1998 and succeeding fiscal years.

Sec. 210.

(a) There shall be established a board to be known as the Census Monitoring Board (hereinafter in this section referred to as the "Board").

(b) The function of the Board shall be to observe and monitor all aspects of the preparation and implementation of the 2000 decennial census (including all dress rehearsals and other simulations of a census in preparation therefor).

(c)

    (1) The Board shall be composed of 8 members as follows:

        (A) 2 individuals appointed by the majority leader of the Senate.

        (B) 2 individuals appointed by the Speaker of the House of Representatives.

        (C) 4 individuals appointed by the President, of whom–

            (i) 1 shall be on the recommendation of the minority leader of the Senate; and

            (ii) 1 shall be on the recommendation of the minority leader of the House of Representatives.

All members of the Board shall be appointed within 60 days after the date of enactment of this Act. A vacancy in the Board shall be filled in the manner in which the original appointment was made.

    (2) Members shall not be entitled to any pay by reason of their service on the Board, but shall receive travel expenses, including per diem in lieu of subsistence, in accordance with sections 5702 and 5703 of title 5, United States Code.

    (3) The Board shall have—

        (A) a co-chairman who shall be appointed jointly by the members under subsection (c)(1)(A) and (B), and

        (B) a co-chairman who shall be appointed jointly by the members under subsection (c)(1)(C).

    (4) The Board shall meet at the call of either co-chairman.

    (5) A quorum shall consist of 5 members of the Board.

    (6) The Board may promulgate any regulations necessary to carry out its duties.

(d)

    (1) The Board shall have—

        (A) an executive director who shall be appointed jointly by the members under subsection (c)(1)(A) and (B), and

    (B) an executive director who shall be appointed jointly by the members under subsection (c)(1)(C),

each of whom shall be paid at a rate not to exceed level IV of the Executive Schedule.

(2) Subject to such rules as the Board may prescribe, each executive director—

    (A) may appoint and fix the pay of such additional personnel as that executive director considers appropriate; and

    (B) may procure temporary and intermittent services under section 3109(b) of title 5, United States Code, but at rates for individuals not to exceed the daily equivalent of the maximum annual rate of pay payable for grade GS-15 of the General Schedule.

Such rules shall include provisions to ensure an equitable division or sharing of resources, as appropriate, between the respective staff of the Board.

(3) The staff of the Board shall be appointed without regard to the provisions of title 5, United States Code, governing appointments in the competitive service, and shall be paid without regard to the provisions of chapter 51 and subchapter III of chapter 53 of such title (relating to classification and General Schedule pay rates).

(4) The Administrator of the General Services Administration, in coordination with the Secretary of Commerce, shall locate suitable office space for the operation of the Board in the W. Edwards Deming Building in Suitland, Maryland. The facilities shall serve as the headquarters of the Board and shall include all necessary equipment and incidentals required for the proper functioning of the Board.

(e)

(1) For the purpose of carrying out its duties, the Board may hold such hearings (at the call of either co-chairman) and undertake such other activities as the Board determines to be necessary to carry out its duties.

(2) The Board may authorize any member of the Board or of its staff to take any action which the Board is authorized to take by this subsection.

(3)

    (A) Each co-chairman of the Board and any members of the staff who may be designated by the Board under this paragraph shall be granted access to any data, files, information, or other matters maintained by the Bureau of the Census (or received by it in the course of conducting a decennial census of population) which they may request, subject to such regulations as the Board may prescribe in consultation with the Secretary of Commerce.

    (B) The Board or the co-chairmen acting jointly may secure directly from any other Federal agency, including the White House, all information that the Board considers necessary to enable the Board to carry out its duties. Upon request of the Board or both co-chairmen, the head of that agency (or other person duly designated for purposes of this paragraph) shall furnish that information to the Board.

(4) The Board shall prescribe regulations under which any member of the Board or of its staff, and any person whose services are procured under subsection (d)(2)(B), who gains access to any information or other matter pursuant to this subsection shall, to the extent that any provisions of section 9 or 214 of title 13, United States Code, would apply with respect to such matter in the case of an employee of the Department of Commerce, be subject to such provisions.

(5) Upon the request of the Board, the head of any Federal agency is authorized to detail, without reimbursement, any of the personnel of such agency to the Board to assist the Board in carrying out its duties. Any such detail shall not interrupt or otherwise affect the civil service status or privileges of the Federal employee.

(6) Upon the request of the Board, the head of a Federal agency shall provide such technical assistance to the Board as the Board determines to be necessary to carry out its duties.

(7) The Board may use the United States mails in the same manner and under the same conditions as Federal agencies and shall, for purposes of the frank, be considered a commission of Congress as described in section 3215 of title 39, United States Code.

(8) Upon request of the Board, the Administrator of General Services shall provide to the Board on a reimbursable basis such administrative support services as the Board may request.

(9) For purposes of costs relating to printing and binding, including the cost of personnel detailed from the Government Printing Office, the Board shall be deemed to be a committee of the Congress.

(f)

(1) The Board shall transmit to the Congress—

(A) interim reports, with the first such report due by April 1, 1998;

(B) additional reports, the first of which shall be due by February 1, 1999, the second of which shall be due by April 1, 1999, and subsequent reports at least semiannually thereafter;

(C) a final report which shall be due by September 1, 2001; and

(D) any other reports which the Board considers appropriate.

The final report shall contain a detailed statement of the findings and conclusions of the Board with respect to the matters described in subsection (b).

(2) In addition to any matter otherwise required under this subsection, each such report shall address, with respect to the period covered by such report–

(A) the degree to which efforts of the Bureau of the Census to prepare to conduct the 2000 census—

(i) shall achieve maximum possible accuracy at every level of geography;

(ii) shall be taken by means of an enumeration process designed to count every individual possible; and

(iii) shall be free from political bias and arbitrary decisions; and

(B) efforts by the Bureau of the Census intended to contribute to enumeration improvement, specifically, in connection with—

(i) computer modernization and the appropriate use of automation;

(ii) address list development;

(iii) outreach and promotion efforts at all levels designed to maximize response rates, especially among groups that have historically been undercounted (including measures undertaken in conjunction with local government and community and other groups);

(iv) establishment and operation of field offices; and

(v) efforts relating to the recruitment, hiring, and training of enumerators.

(3) Any data or other information obtained by the Board under this section shall be made available to any committee or subcommittee of Congress of appropriate jurisdiction upon request of the chairman or ranking minority member of such committee or subcommittee. No such committee or subcommittee, or member thereof, shall disclose any information obtained under this paragraph which is submitted to it on a confidential basis unless the full committee determines that the withholding of that information is contrary to the national interest.

(4) The Board shall study and submit to Congress, as part of its first report under paragraph (1)(A), its findings and recommendations as to the feasibility and desirability of using postal personnel or private contractors to help carry out the decennial census.

(g) There is authorized to be appropriated $4,000,000 for each of fiscal years 1998 through 2001 to carry out this section.

(h) To the extent practicable, members of the Board shall work to promote the most accurate and complete census possible by using their positions to publicize the need for full and timely responses to census questionnaires.

(i)

(1) No individual described in paragraph (2) shall be eligible—

(A) to be appointed or to continue serving as a member of the Board or as a member of the staff thereof; or

(B) to enter into any contract with the Board.

(2) This subsection applies with respect to any individual who is serving or who has ever served—

(A) as the Director of the Census; or

(B) with any committee or subcommittee of either House of Congress, having jurisdiction over any aspect of the decennial census, as—

(i) a Member of Congress; or

(ii) a congressional employee.

(j) The Board shall cease to exist on September 30, 2001.

(k) Section 9(a) of title 13, United States Code, is amended in the matter before paragraph (1) thereof by striking "of this title—" and inserting "of this title or section 210 of the Departments of Commerce, Justice, and State, the Judiciary, and Related Agencies Appropriations Act, 1998—".

November 13, 1997: Conference report House Report 105-405 filed in House. House agreed to Conference Report by the Yeas and Nays: 282 to 110 (Roll 640). Senate agreed to conference report by unanimous consent. November 26, 1997: Signed by President. Became Public Law no. 105-119.

Notes

Chapter 1

1. Memorandum for Plaintiff in Support of its Motion for Summary Judgment, *U.S. House of Representatives et al. v. Dept. of Commerce et al.*, April 6, 1998, p. 1. A note on cited legal documents is in order here. The unpublished court filings are in the possession of the authors. There are two major sets of briefs, memoranda, depositions, trial exhibits, and transcripts. The first are from the 1990 census undercount lawsuit, *City of New York v. Dept. of Commerce*, 822 F. Supp. 906 (EDNY 1993); 34 F.3d 1114 (2d Cir 1994); and the continuation of the case before the Supreme Court, *Wisconsin v. City of New York*, 517 U.S. 1. The second set are from the litigation challenging the plans for the 2000 census, filed by the Speaker of the House of Representatives and Matthew Glavin against the Department of Commerce and the president, *U.S. House v. Dept. of Commerce*, 11 F. Supp. 2d 76 (DC 1998); *Glavin v. Clinton*, 19 F. Supp. 2d 543 (ED VA, 1998); and the appeals to the Supreme Court, *Dept. of Commerce v. U.S. House* and *Clinton v. Glavin*, 98-404, 98-564, __U.S. __ (1999). Endnotes include a description of the unpublished document and the case to which it refers. The reference list cites the court opinion.

2. Memorandum of Law in Support of Plaintiffs Motion for Summary Judgment, *Glavin, Barr et al. v. Clinton et al.*, April 6, 1998, p.1.

3. Drew Days, solicitor general of the United States, statement from January 10, 1996, oral argument before the United States Supreme Court in *Wisconsin v. New York* (1996), the 1990 Census adjustment lawsuit.

4. Memorandum for Plaintiff in Support of its Motion for Summary Judgment, *U.S. House et al. v. Dept. of Commerce et al.*, April 6, 1998, p. 1.

5. *Human Events*, August 22, 1997.

6. Rep. Dennis Hastert (Rep.-Ill.), quoted in Associated Press report, July 14, 1997.

7. William Safire, *New York Times*, December 7, 1997.

8. Memorandum for Plaintiff in Support of its Motion for Summary Judgment, *U.S. House et al., v. U.S. Dept. of Commerce et al.*, April 6, 1998, p. 12.

9. "Will you be Counted in 2000? Census Plans to Sample May Lead to Big Errors," *Investor's Business Daily*, July 8, 1998, pp. 1, 32.

10. David Freedman (1993).

11. Memorandum for Plaintiff in Support of its Motion for Summary Judgment, *U.S. House et al. v. U.S. Dept. of Commerce et al.*, April 6, 1998, pp. 13–14.

Chapter 2

1. The overview of census history in this chapter is taken primarily from Anderson 1988. See also Rakove (1996) on the constitutional history; Choldin (1994); Magnuson (1995a, 1995b); Magnuson and King (1995).
2. Demographic data taken from Bureau of the Census (1996c).
3. For the administrative history of the bureau in the late nineteenth and early twentieth centuries, see Wright and Hunt (1900); Holt (1929).

Chapter 3

1. *New York Times*, Dec. 1, 1970. The 1970 resident population, which included the fifty states and the District of Columbia, was 203.2 million. The apportionment population, which included selected groups of Americans abroad and excluded residents of the District of Columbia, was 204 million (Bureau of the Census 1976, 1–15).
2. See Advisory Committee (1971, 57–58), for quotes and 57–98, for the research proposed.
3. The final published figures (see Fay et al. 1988) differ somewhat from these preliminary ones, but the basic facts regarding the size of the differential undercount remain.

Chapter 4

1. Actually, there are alternative versions of the estimates of the numbers of omissions and erroneous enumerations, and the ones that add up to the gross error of 8 percent cited in the text are viewed by many as being conservative. The General Accounting Office, for example, has said that the level of gross error in the 1990 census was somewhere in the range of 10 to 12 percent, corresponding to more than twenty-five million errors. For further details, see, for example, U.S. General Accounting Office (1991); Ericksen and Defonso (1993, 14, 38–43).
2. With apologies to one of our favorite authors, Dr. Seuss (1960).

Chapter 5

1. Benjamin King, letter to John G. Keane, May 26, 1987, Plaintiffs' Admitted Trial Exhibit No. 5 (*City of New York v. Dept. of Commerce* 1993).
2. *City of New York v. Dept. of Commerce* 1993, plaintiffs' trial exhibit no. 574.

Chapter 6

1. Table 6.1 is also presented in Fienberg (1990a, 34); see also U.S. Bureau of the Census (1993a, ch. 6, 45–46, 54).

Chapter 7

1. Rolph subsequently reviewed his testimony in Rolph (1993).
2. An overview of this testimony appears in Fienberg (1993b).

3. The testimony Breiman was about to give was excluded from evidence and thus did not have an impact on the trial court's decision. It did subsequently confuse the overall understanding of the quality of the 1990 census and the PES, however, when it was published in revised form (Breiman 1994)—so much so that it is the evidentiary base of part of Myth 10 in chapter 1. In chapter 10, we return to the issues Breiman raised.

4. For his own overview of this testimony, see Wachter (1993b).

5. Wachter's more extensive views on both smoothing and loss functions subsequently appeared in joint papers with David Freedman and others (see Freedman et al. 1993, 1994).

6. For his own overview of this testimony, see Freedman (1993).

7. The report supporting this testimony was subsequently published in revised form as Freedman et al. (1993).

8. The background report linked to this testimony on loss functions was subsequently published as Freedman et al. (1994).

9. Petitioner State of Oklahoma's Brief on the Merits, November 9, 1995, 7; Brief of Petitioner State of Wisconsin, pp. 19ff; Brief for the Federal Petitioners, November 1995, p. 50; Respondents' Brief, December 8, 1995 (*Wisconsin v. City of New York* 1996).

Chapter 8

1. The classification scheme for race and ethnicity in the Post Enumeration Survey and the census enumeration is different from that associated with vital statistics, however. Mapping categories from the census form to those from the demographic method requires the researcher to assign all births and immigration data to specific racial groups. How this is done can change the results of the undercount methods in important ways. For a general description of the methods and comparisons, see Robinson et al. (1993), and, especially, the discussion by Jeffrey Passel (1993).

2. For further details on this and other subsequent tests of question wording, see Martin, DeMaio, and Campanelli (1990); Bates et al. (1994).

3. See, for example, U.S. Bureau of the Census (1993b); Lieberson and Waters (1988); Rodriguez and Cordero-Guzman (1992). For demographic analysis, those responding "yes" to the other category on the race question must be assigned to a racial group that can be linked to the classifications emanating from vital statistics data. See Passel (1993, 1076).

4. www.naacp.org/president/releases/archives/1997/categor.htm.

5. Other countries, such as Canada, also have differential undercounts, but they are not so neatly identified with racial or ethnic groups. As a consequence, the Canadian decision to adjust intercensal estimates for undercount went essentially unnoticed and unchallenged. (See *Toronto Globe and Mail*, March 27, 1993.)

6. See the description of this procedural history in the *Federal Register* announcement by the Office of Management and Budget in Office of Informa-

tion and Regulatory Affairs (1997b), and the summary of the research in Office of Information and Regulatory Affairs (1997a).

Chapter 9

1. And when the census is actually in progress, the bureau works on three censuses: past, present, and future.
2. Transcript of Mosbacher press conference, July 15, 1991, Plaintiff's Admitted Trial Exhibit no. 678, (*City of New York v. Department of Commerce* 1993).
3. Those advocating the use of continuous measurement at the bureau did so as a replacement for the census sample long form, but many related proposals in the past suggest that such a rolling survey might well be used in lieu of a decennial census (see, for example, Kish 1981, 1983, 1989, 1990a, 1990b; Kish and Verma 1986).
4. The authors were members of the Requirements Panel.
5. Many believed that the PES in 1990 was adequate to be used for adjustment, but a major source of criticism in 1990 was the "small" sample size and the need to use data across state boundaries. For example, Secretary Mosbacher referred to this problem in his July 15, 1991, decision (see appendix F).
6. Ericksen and DeFonso (1993) describe this phenomena using data from the 1990 census.
7. This is the same "one-number census" notion that originated in the planning initiated by former Census Bureau Director Barbara Bryant.
8. The 1997 Emergency Supplemental Appropriations Act for Recovery from Natural Disasters, and for Overseas Peacekeeping Efforts, Including Those in Bosnia.
9. As Ericksen and DeFonso (1993) and the General Accounting Office (1991) argued following the 1990 census, if the overcount and undercount would not cancel each other out at relevant low levels of geography, then the best estimate of census error would be the sum of the overcount and undercount, rather than their difference, or net census error. See also the discussion of this point in Fienberg (1993b) and in Ericksen, Fienberg, and Kadane (1994).
10. The coefficient of variation (*cv*) is the standard deviation divided by the mean. The *cv* is often used in the sampling literature to compare the accuracy of estimators of quantities with widely varying magnitudes. Thus, the coefficient of variation of a small error rate can be doubly large, once because of a high standard error owing to small sample sizes and a second time because of the small value being estimated.

Chapter 10

1. These cases are now described as *Department of Commerce v. House of Representatives*, 98-404, and *Clinton v. Glavin*, 98-564.
2. Darga has now amplified on his testimony and the memorandum he submitted for the subcommittee record, and he has reorganized the material somewhat in the form of a book (Darga 1999). The material here performs no new analyses of error, quotes extensively from Breiman (1994), in particular (and

in the process corrects one of Breiman's most egregious reporting errors), and presents some highly misleading "reanalyses" of 1990 PES results in an attempt to argue against the use of the PES for adjustment. This volume does not touch upon the role of sampling for nonresponse follow-up or any of the changes in the design of the ICM sampling and analysis plan vis-à-vis the PES plan from 1990.

3. The formal papers associated with these presentations were Thompson and Fay 1998, and Waite and Hogan 1998.

4. Koyak is an assistant professor of operations research at the Naval Postgraduate School and formerly worked for the Justice Department, where he assisted in the defense of the New York City 1991 lawsuit over adjustment.

5. Other evaluations of the PES do not accept Breiman's characterization. See, for example, Hogan 1993, Mulry and Spencer 1988, Belin and Rolph 1994a and 1994b, and Ericksen, Fienberg, and Kadane 1994. Furthermore, even were the statement a correct and proper interpretation of the known data, it would be effectively irrelevant to the usefulness of the DSE approach. The net national undercount, which is the difference between omissions and erroneous enumerations, is not the reason the Census Bureau carried out the PES and did DSE. The closer the estimates for omissions and erroneous enumerations come to balancing out, the closer the net undercount estimate is to zero and the bigger the impact of "errors." If there were a zero net estimated undercount, a single error would account for it all. Because omission and erroneous enumerations are not distributed in the same way across states and lower levels of geography, however, the effect of errors diminishes as one moves to comparisons of interest. Thus, the seemingly explosive statement may be of little importance when we come to understand the improved accuracy from using PES-adjusted data. See also Anderson and Fienberg 1999 on this issue.

6. http://tier2.census/gov/CGI-WIN/pl94-171/PL94-171.EXE.

Appendix C

1. Materials excerpted from "Request for Comments on the Proposed Guidelines for Considering whether or Not a Statistical Adjustment for the 1990 Decennial Census of Population and Housing Should Be Made for Coverage Deficiencies Resulting in an Overcount or Undercount of the Population" (F.R. Doc. 89-29003, Dec. 7, 1989).

Appendix D

1. Material excerpted from "Final guidelines for Considering Whether or Not a Statistical Adjustment of the 1990 Decennial Census of Population and Housing Should Be Made for Coverage Deficiencies Resulting in an Overcount or Undercount of the Population" (F.R. Doc. 90–91282, March 15, 1990).

Appendix F

1. Department of Commerce, Office of the Secretary. "Decision on Whether or Not a Statistical Adjustment of the 1990 Decennial Census of Population Should Be Made for Coverage Deficiencies Resulting in an Overcount or Undercount of the Population; Explanation" (1-1–1-7).

Appendix H

1. See *Federal Register* 62 (210): 58788-90, October 30, 1997. These revisions appear at the end of a longer *Federal Register* document that includes extensive background on the changes.

References

Advisory Committee on Problems of Census Enumeration. 1971. *America's Uncounted People*. Washington, D.C.: National Academy of Sciences.

Allen, Theodore. 1994. *The Invention of the White Race*. New York: Verso.

American Anthropological Association. 1997. "Response to OMB Directive 15; Release/OMB 15; Fact Sheet/OMB Directive 15. http://www.ameranthassn.org/ombnews.htm, September 8.

American Statistical Association. 1996. Statement of Blue-Ribbon Panel on the 2000 Census, http://www.amstat.org/outreach/ExecSummary.htm/.

Anderson, Margo. 1988. *The American Census: A Social History*. New Haven, Conn.: Yale University Press.

Anderson, Margo, and Stephen E. Fienberg. 1995. "Black, White, and Shades of Gray (and Brown and Yellow)." *Chance* 8(1): 15–18.

———. 1996. "An Adjusted Census in 1990?: The Supreme Court Decides." *Chance* 9(3): 1–5.

———. 1997. "Who Counts: The Politics of Census Taking." *Society/Transaction* 34(3): 19–26.

———. 1999. "To Sample or Not to Sample: The 2000 Census Controversy." *Journal of Interdisciplinary History* 30(1): 1–35.

Arthur, John, and Amy Shapiro. 1996. *Color Class Identity: The New Politics of Race*. Boulder, Colo.: Westview Press.

Baker v Carr. 1962. 369 U.S. 182.

Balinski, Michel, and H. Peyton Young. 1982. *Fair Representation: Meeting the Ideal of One Man, One Vote*. New Haven, Conn.: Yale University Press.

Bates, Nancy A., Manuel de la Puente, Theresa J. DeMaio, and Elizabeth A. Martin. 1994. "Research on Race and Ethnicity: Results from Questionnaire Design Tests." (disc: P160-166). In *Proceedings of the Bureau of the Census Annual Research Conference*.

Belin, Thomas R., and John E. Rolph. 1994a. "Can We Reach Consensus on Census Adjustment?" *Statistical Science* 9(4): 486–508.

———. 1994b. Rejoinder to "Can We Reach Consensus on Census Adjustment?" *Statistical Science* 9(4): 520–21.

Bell, William R. 1993. "Using Information from Demographic Analysis in Post-enumeration Survey Estimation." *Journal of the American Statistical Association* 88(September): 1106–18.

Bishop, Yvonne M. M., Stephen E. Fienberg, and Paul H. Holland. 1975. *Discrete Multivariate Analysis: Theory and Practice*. Cambridge, Mass.: MIT Press.

"Black America and Tiger's Dilemma." 1997. *Ebony*, July 28–34, 138.

Breiman, Leo. 1994. "The 1991 Census Adjustment: Undercount or Bad Data?" *Statistical Science* 9(4): 458–75.

———. 1998. Testimony before House Subcommittee on the Census, Statisticians Opposed to Sampling Hearing, Sept. 17. 105th Congress, 2d Sess.

Brown, Lawrence D., Morris L. Eaton, David A. Freedman, Stephen P. Klein, Richard A. Olshen, Kenneth W. Wachter, Martin T. Wells, and Donald Ylvisaker. 1998. "Statistical Controversies in Census 2000." Technical Report 357, Department of Statistics, University of California, Berkeley (October).

Bryant, Barbara, and William Dunn. 1995. *Moving Money and Power: The Politics of Census Taking.* Ithaca, N.Y.: New Strategist Publications.

Bulletin Broadfaxing Network. 1998. "The Bulletin's Frontrunner." December 1.

The Census and You. 1992. 27(November): 16.

Chandra Sekar, C., and W. E. Deming. 1949. "On a Method of Estimating Birth and Death Rates and the Extent of Registration." *Journal of the American Statistical Association* 44(March): 101–15.

Choi, C. Y., D. G. Steel, and T. J. Skinner. 1988. "Adjusting the 1986 Australian Census Count for Underenumeration." *Survey Methodology* 14: 173–89.

Choldin, Harvey. 1994. *Looking for the Last Percent: The Controversy over Census Undercounts.* New Brunswick, N.J.: Rutgers University Press.

Citro, Constance F., and Michael L. Cohen, eds. 1985. *The Bicentennial Census: New Directions for Methodology in 1990.* Committee on National Statistics, National Research Council. Washington, D.C.: National Academy Press.

City of New York v. U.S. Department of Commerce. 1993. 822 F. Supp. 906 (Eastern District, New York).

City of New York v. U.S. Department of Commerce. 1994. 34 F.3d 1114.

Clinton v. Glavin. 1999. No. 98-564. _U.S._.

Coale, Ansley. 1955. "The Population of the United States in 1950 by Age, Sex, and Color: A Revision of the Census Figures." *Journal of the American Statistical Association* 50(March): 16–54.

Cohen, Patricia C. 1982. *A Calculating People: The Spread of Numeracy in Early America.* Chicago: University of Chicago Press.

Cowan, Charles D., and Donald J. Malec. 1986. "Capture-Recapture Models When Both Sources Have Clustered Observations." *Journal of the American Statistical Association* 81(June): 347–53.

Cuomo v. Baldrige. 1987. 674 F. Supp. 1089 (Southern District, New York).

Daniels, Roger. 1990. *Coming to America: A History of Immigration and Ethnicity in American Life.* New York: HarperCollins.

Darga, Kenneth. 1999. *Sampling and the Census: A Case Against the Proposed Adjustments for Undercount.* Washington, D.C.: American Enterprise Institute.

Darroch, John N, Stephen E. Fienberg, Gary F. V. Glonek, and Brian W. Junker. 1993. "A Three-Sample Multiple-Recapture Approach to Census Population Estimation, with Heterogeneous Catchability." *Journal of the American Statistical Association* 88(September): 1137–48.

Davis, F. James. 1991. *Who Is Black?: One Nation's Definition.* University Park: Pennsylvania State University Press.

Diffendal, Gregg J. 1988. "The 1986 Test of Adjustment-Related Operations in Central Los Angeles County." *Survey Methodology* 14: 71–86.

Duncan, Joseph, and William Shelton. 1978. *Revolution in United States Government Statistics, 1926–1976.* Washington, D.C.: Government Printing Office.

Eastland, Terry, and William J. Bennett. 1979. *Counting by Race: Equality from the Founding Fathers to Bakke and Weber.* New York: Basic Books.

Eckler, A. Ross. 1972. *The Bureau of the Census.* New York: Praeger.

Editorial. 1969. *Ebony*, January, 102.

Economics and U.S. Department of Commerce Statistics Administration, Office of the Under Secretary. 1991. *U.S. Department of Commerce News*, October 15.

Edmonston, Barry, Joshua Goldstein, and Juanita Tamayo Lott. 1996. *Spotlight on Heterogeneity: The Federal Standards for Racial and Ethnic Classification, Summary of a Workshop.* Committee on National Statistics, National Research Council. Washington, D.C.: National Academy Press.

Edmonston, Barry, and Charles Schultze, eds. 1995. *Modernizing the U.S. Census: Panel on Census Requirements in the Year 2000 and Beyond.* Committee on National Statistics, National Research Council. Washington, D.C.: National Academy Press.

Elving, Ronald. 1991. "Census Credibility: A Gap Too Wide." *Congressional Quarterly Weekly Report* 49(September 9).

Ericksen, Eugene P., and Teresa K. DeFonso. 1993. "Beyond the Net Undercount: How to Measure Census Error." *Chance* 6(4): 38–43.

Ericksen, Eugene P., Stephen E. Fienberg, and Joseph B. Kadane. 1994. "Comment on Three Papers on Census Adjustment." *Statistical Science* 9(4): 511–15.

Ericksen, Eugene P., and Joseph B. Kadane. 1985. "Estimating the Population in a Census Year: 1980 and Beyond (with Discussion)." *Journal of the American Statistical Association* 80(March): 98–131.

Ericksen, Eugene P., Joseph B. Kadane, and John W. Tukey. 1989. "Adjusting the 1980 Census of Population and Housing." *Journal of the American Statistical Association* 84(December): 927–44.

Evinger, Suzann. 1995. "How Shall We Measure Our Nation's Diversity?" *Chance* 8(1): 7–14.

Fay, Robert E., Jeffrey S. Passel, J. Gregory Robinson, and Charles D. Cowan. 1988. *The Coverage of the Population in the 1980 Census, Bureau of the Census.* Washington, D.C.: U.S. Department of Commerce.

Fienberg, Stephen E. 1972. "The Multiple-Recapture Census for Closed Populations and the 2^k Incomplete Contingency Table." *Biometrika* 59: 591–603.

———. 1989. "An Adjusted Census in 1990?" *Chance* 2(3): 23–25.

———. 1990a. "An Adjusted Census in 1990?: An Interim Report." *Chance* 3(1): 19–21.

———. 1990b. "An Adjusted Census in 1990?: Back to Court Again." *Chance* 3(2): 32–35.

———. 1990c. "An Adjusted Census in 1990?: The Judge Rules and the PES Begins." *Chance* 3(3): 33–36.

———. 1991a. "An Adjusted Census in 1990?: Commerce Says 'No.'" *Chance* 4(3): 44–51.

———. 1991b. "An Adjusted Census in 1990?: A Full-Scale Judicial Review Approaches." *Chance* 4(4): 22–24.

———. 1992a. "An Adjusted Census in 1990?: The Trial." *Chance* 5(3–4): 28–38.

———. 1992b. "Bibliography on Capture-Recapture Modelling with Application to Census Undercount Adjustment." *Survey Methodology* 18(1): 143–54.

———. 1993a. "Ethical and Modelling Considerations in Correcting the Results of the 1990 Census." In *Ethics in Modelling*, ed. W. A. Wallace. New York: Plenum.

———. 1993b. "The New York City Census Adjustment Trial: Witness for the Plaintiffs." *Jurimetrics Journal* 34: 65–83.

———. 1994. "An Adjusted Census in 1990?: Trial Judgement Set Aside." *Chance* 7(4): 31–32.

Fisher, Christy. 1998. "It's All in the Details." *American Demographics* 20(April): 45.

Freedman, David A. 1991. "Policy Forum: Adjusting the 1990 Census." *Science* 252: 1233–36.

———. 1993. "Adjusting the Census of 1990." *Jurimetrics Journal* 34: 99–106.

Freedman, David A., and William C. Navidi. 1986. "Regression Models for Adjusting the 1980 Census (with Discussion)." *Statistical Science* 1(1): 3–39.

———. 1992. "Should We Have Adjusted the U.S. Census of 1980? (with Discussion)." *Survey Methodology* 18: 3–24.

Freedman, David A., Kenneth W. Wachter, Daniel C. Coster, D. Richard Cutler, and Stephen P. Klein. 1993. "Adjusting the Census of 1990: The Smoothing Model." *Evaluation Review* 17: 371–443.

Freedman, David A., Kenneth W. Wachter, D. Richard Cutler, and Stephen P. Klein. 1994. "Adjusting the U.S. Census of 1990: Loss Functions." *Evaluation Review* 18: 243–80.

Funderburg, Lisa. 1994. *Black, White, Other: Biracial Americans Talk About Race and Identity*. New York: William Morrow.

Glavin, Barr, et al. v. Clinton et al. 1998. 19 F.Supp. 2d 543 (Eastern District, Virginia).

Graham, Hugh D. 1990. *The Civil Rights Era: Origins and Development of National Policy, 1960–1972*. New York: Oxford University Press.

Gregory, Steven, and Roger Sanjek. 1994. *Race*. New Brunswick, N.J.: Rutgers University Press.

Hacker, Andrew. 1995. *Two Nations: Black and White, Separate, Hostile, Unequal*. New York: Ballantine Books.

Haney Lopez, Ian F. 1996. *White by Law: The Legal Construction of Race*. New York: New York University Press.

Hansen, Morris, and William Hurwitz. 1942a. "On the Theory of Sampling from Finate Populations." *Annals of Mathematical Statistics* 14: 333–62.

———. 1942b. "Relative Efficiencies of Various Sampling Units in Population Inquiries." *Journal of the American Statistical Association* 37(March): 89–94.

Heer, David. 1967. *Social Statistics and the City.* Cambridge, Mass.: Joint Center for Urban Studies of Harvard and MIT.

Herrnstein, Richard, and Charles Murray. 1994. *The Bell Curve: Intelligence and Class Structure in American Life.* New York: Free Press.

Hogan, Howard. 1993. "The 1990 Postenumeration Survey: Operations and Results." *Journal of the American Statistical Association* 88(September): 1047–60.

Hogan, Howard, and Kirk M. Wolter. 1988. "Measuring Accuracy in a Postenumeration Survey." *Survey Methodology* 14: 99–116.

Holt, W. Stull. 1929. *The Bureau of the Census: Its History, Activities, and Organization.* Washington, D.C.: Brookings Institution.

Ignatiev, Noel. 1995. *How the Irish Became White.* New York: Routledge.

Isaki, Corey T., L. K. Schultz, J. G. Diffendal, and E. T. Huang. 1988. "On Estimating Census Undercount in Small Areas." *Journal of Official Statistics* 4: 95–112.

Jaro, Matthew. 1989. "Advances in Record-Linkage Methodology as Applied to Matching the 1985 Test Census of Tampa, Florida." *Journal of the American Statistical Association* 84(June): 414–20.

Kadane, Joseph B., Michael M. Meyer, and John W. Tukey. 1992. "Correlation Bias in the Presence of Stratum Heterogeneity." An expanded and revised version will appear in *Journal of the American Statistical Association* (1999).

Kish, Leslie. 1981. "Population Counts from Cumulated Samples." In *Using Cumulated Rolling Samples to Integrate Census and Survey Operations of the Census Bureau*, ed. Congressional Research Service. Washington, D.C.: Government Printing Office. Prepared for the Subcommittee on Census and Population, Committee on Post Office and Civil Service, House of Representatives.

———. 1983. "Data Collection for Details over Space and Time." In *Statistical Methods and the Improvement of Data Quality*, edited by Tommy Wright. New York: Academic.

———. 1989. "Unique Features and Problems of Rolling Samples." In *Statistics Canada Symposium.*

———. 1990a. Reply to "Rolling Samples and Censuses." *Survey Methodology* 16: 93–94.

———. 1990b. "Rolling Samples and Censuses (with Discussion)." *Survey Methodology* 16: 63–78.

Kish, Leslie, and Vijay Verma. 1986. "Complete Censuses and Samples." *Journal of Official Statistics* 2: 381–95.

Kromkowski, Charles A., and John A. Kromkowski. 1991. "Why 435?: A Question of Political Arithmetic." *Polity* 24(Fall): 129–45.

———. 1992. "Beyond Administrative Apportionment: Rediscovering the Constitutional Calculus of Representative Government." *Polity* 24(Spring): 495–97.

Krótki, Karol J., ed. 1978. *Developments in Dual-System Estimation of Population Size and Growth.* Edmonton: University of Alberta Press.

Lieberson, Stanley, and Mary C. Waters. 1988. *From Many Strands: Ethnic and Racial Groups in Contemporary America.* New York: Russell Sage Foundation.

Lubiano, Wahneema. 1997. *The House That Race Built: Black Americans, U.S. Terrain.* New York: Pantheon Books.

Magnuson, Diana. 1995a. "The Making of a Modern Census: The United States Census of Population, 1790–1940." Ph.D. diss., University of Minnesota.

———. 1995b. "Who and What Determined the Content of the U.S. Population Schedule over Time." *Historical Methods* 28(Winter):11–27.

Magnuson, Diana, and Miriam King. 1995. "Comparability of the Public-Use Microdata Samples: Enumeration Procedures." *Historical Methods* 28(Winter): 27–33.

Martin, Elizabeth, Theresa J. DeMaio, and Pamela C. Campanelli. 1990. "Context Effects for Census Measures of Race and Hispanic Origin." *Public Opinion Quarterly* 54: 551–66.

Mencke, John G. 1978. *Mulattoes and Race Mixture: American Attitudes and Images, 1865–1918.* Ann Arbor, Mich: UMI Research Press.

Meyer, Michael M., and Joseph B. Kadane. 1992. "Reconstructing the Adjusted Census for Florida: A Case Study in Data Examination." *Journal of Computational and Graphical Statistics* 1:287–300.

Miskura, Susan. 1992. "Why the United States Might Modify Its Decennial Census, 1992." Paper included in background materials book for the first meeting of the Panel on Census Requirements, Committee on National Statistics, Washington, D.C. (June).

Mitroff, Ian, Richard O. Mason, and Vincent Barabba. 1983. *The 1980 Census: Policymaking amid Turbulence.* Lexington, Mass.: Lexington Books.

Mulry, Mary H., and Bruce D. Spencer. 1988. "Total Error in the Dual-System Estimator: The 1986 Census of Los Angeles County." *Survey Methodology* 14: 241–63.

———. 1991. "Total Error in PES Estimates of Population (with discussion)." *Journal of the American Statistical Association* 81(September): 839–63.

———. 1993. "Accuracy of the 1990 Census and Undercount Adjustments." *Journal of the American Statistical Association* 88(September): 1080–92.

Nash, Gary B. 1974. *Red, White, and Black: The Peoples of Early America.* Englewood Cliffs, N.J.: Prentice Hall.

Numbers News. 1989. December 6, 1989.

Oberby, L. Martin. 1992. "Apportionment, Politics, and Political Science: A Response to Kromkowski and Kromkowski." *Polity* 24(Spring): 483–94.

Office of Information and Regulatory Affairs. 1997a. "Recommendations from the Interagency Committee for the Review of the Racial and Ethnic Standards to the Office of Management and Budget Concerning Changes to the Standards for the Classification of Federal Data on Race and Ethnicity." *Federal Register* 62(131): 36874–946 (July 9).

———. 1997b. "Revisions to the Standards for the Classification of Federal Data on Race and Ethnicity." *Federal Register* 62(21): 58782–90 (October 30).

O'Hare, William. 1998. "Managing Multiple-Race Data." *American Demographics* 20(April): 42.

Omi, Michael, and Howard Winant. 1994. *Racial Formation in the United States: From the 1960s to the 1990s.* 2d ed. New York: Routledge.

Panel on Decennial Census Plans. 1978. *Counting the People in 1980: An Appraisal of Census Plans.* Committee on National Statistics, National Research Council. Washington, D.C.: National Academy of Sciences.

Passel, Jeffrey S. 1993. "Comment on Robinson, Ahmed, Das Gupta, and Woodrow." *Journal of the American Statistical Association* 88(September): 1074–77.

Peterson, Paul. 1995. *Classifying by Race.* Princeton, N.J.: Princeton University Press.

Price, Daniel O. 1947. "A Check on Underenumeration in the 1940 Census." *American Sociological Review* 12(February): 44–49.

Pritzker, Leon, and Naomi D. Rothwell. 1968. "Procedural Difficulties in Taking Past Censuses in Predominantly Negro, Puerto Rican, and Mexican Areas." In *Social Statistics and the City* edited by David Heer. Cambridge, Mass.: Joint Center for Urban Studies of MIT and Harvard University.

Rakove, Jack. 1979. *The Beginning of National Politics: An Interpretive History of the Continental Congress.* New York: Knopf.

———. 1996. *Original Meanings: Politics and Ideas in the Making of the Constitution.* New York: Knopf.

Reader, Scott. 1994. "One Person, One Vote Revisited: Choosing a Population Basis to Form Political Districts." *Harvard Journal of Law and Public Policy* 17(2): 521–66.

Robinson, J. Gregory, Bashir Ahmed, Prithwis DasGupta, and Karen A. Woodrow. 1993. "Estimation of Population Coverage in the 1990 United States Census, Based on Demographic Analysis (with Discussion)." *Journal of the American Statistical Association* 88(September): 1061–79.

Rodriguez, Clara E., and J. M. Cordero-Guzman. 1992. "Placing Race in Context." *Ethnic and Racial Studies* 15: 523–43.

Rolph, John E. 1993. "The Census Adjustment Trial: Reflections of a Witness for the Plaintiffs." *Jurimetrics Journal* 34: 85–98.

Schenker, Nathaniel. 1988. "Handling Missing Data in Coverage Estimation, with Application to the 1986 Test of Adjustment-Related Operations." *Survey Methodology* 14: 87–98.

Schirm, A. L. 1991. "The Effects of Census Undercount Adjustment on Congressional Apportionment." *Journal of the American Statistical Association* 86(June): 526–41.

Seuss, Dr. (Theodore Geisel). 1960. *One Fish Two Fish Red Fish Blue Fish.* New York: Random House.

Shapiro, S. 1949. "Estimating Birth Registration Completeness." *Journal of the American Statistical Association* 45(June): 261–64.

———. 1954. "Recent Testing of Birth Registration Completeness in the United States." *Population Studies* 8: 3–21.

Shoemaker, Nancy. 1997. "How Indians Got to Be Red." *American Historical Review* 102(3): 625–44.

Skrentny, John D. 1996. *The Ironies of Affirmative Action: Politics, Culture, and Justice in America.* Chicago: University of Chicago Press.

Smedley, Audrey. 1993. *Race in North America: Origin and Evolution of a Worldview.* Boulder, Colo.: Westview Press.

Steffey, D. L., and N. M. Bradburn, eds. 1994. *Counting People in the Information Age*. Committee on National Statistics, National Research Council. Washington, D.C.: National Academy Press.

Taagepera, Rein, and Matthew S. Shugart. 1989. *Seats and Votes: The Effects and Determinants of Electoral Systems*. New Haven, Conn.: Yale University Press.

Takaki, Ronald. 1993. *A Different Mirror: A History of Multicultural America*. Boston: Little, Brown.

Thernstrom, Stephan, and Abigail Thernstrom. 1997. *America in Black and White: One Nation, Indivisible*. New York: Simon and Schuster.

Thompson, John H., and Robert E. Fay. 1998. "Census 2000: The Statistical Issues." In *Proceedings of the Survey Research Methods Section*. Alexandria, Va: American Statistical Association.

Tracy, W. R. 1941. *Fertility of the Population of Canada*. Ottawa: Cloutier.

Tucker, Clyde, Ruth McKay, Brian Kojetin, R. Harrison, Manuel de la Puente, L. Stinson, and E. Robinson. 1996. "Testing Methods of Collecting Racial and Ethnic Information: Results of the Current Population Survey Supplement on Race and Ethnicity." Technical Report 40. Bureau of Labor Statistics Statistical Notes. Washington, D.C.: Bureau of the Labor Statistics.

U.S. Bureau of the Census. 1976. *U.S. Census of Population and Housing: 1970 Procedural History*. Washington, D.C.: U.S. Government Printing Office.

————. 1979. *Twenty Censuses: Population and Housing Questions, 1790–1980*. Washington, D.C.: U.S. Government Printing Office.

————. 1980. *Conference on Census Undercount*. Washington, D.C.: U.S. Government Printing Office.

————. 1986a. *Census of Population and Housing, 1980: History*. Part A, PHC80-R-2A. Washington, D.C.: U.S. Government Printing Office.

————. 1986b. *Census of Population and Housing, 1980: History*. Part B, PHC80-R-2B. Washington, D.C.: U.S. Government Printing Office.

————. 1986c. *Census of Population and Housing, 1980: History*. Part C, PHC80-R-2C. Washington, D.C.: U.S. Government Printing Office.

————. 1989a. *Census of Population and Housing, 1980: History*. Part D, PHC80-R-2D. Washington, D.C.: U.S. Government Printing Office.

————. 1989b. *Census of Population and Housing, 1980: History*. Part E, PHC80-R-2E. Washington, D.C.: U.S. Government Printing Office.

————. 1991. Press release, June 13.

————. 1992a. "Assessment of Accuracy of Adjusted Versus Unadjusted 1990 Census Base for Use in Intercensal Estimates, 1992." Report of the Committee on Adjustment of Postcensal Estimates (August 7).

————. 1992b. "2000 Census Research and Development Program and Plans, March 31, 1992." Paper included in background-materials book for the first meeting of the Panel on Census Requirements (June).

————. 1993a. *1990 Census of Population and Housing: History*. Part A, 1990CPH-R-2A. Washington, D.C.: U.S. Government Printing Office.

————. 1993b. *Challenges of Measuring an Ethnic World*. Washington, D.C.: U.S. Government Printing Office.

———. 1995a. *1990 Census of Population and Housing: History.* Part B, 1990CPH-R-2B. Washington, D.C.: U.S. Government Printing Office.

———. 1995b. *1990 Census of Population and Housing: History.* Part C, 1990CPH-R-2C. Washington, D.C.: U.S. Government Printing Office.

———. 1995c. "The Reengineered Census." Draft (May 19).

———. 1996a. *1990 Census of Population and Housing: History.* Part D, 1990CPH-R-2D. Washington, D.C.: U.S. Government Printing Office.

———. 1996b. "The Plan for Census 2000." Revised and Reissued. Typescript (Feb 28).

———. 1996c. *Statistical Abstract of the United States, 1996.* Washington, D.C.: Government Printing Office.

———. 1997. "Report to Congress: The Plan for Census 2000." Washington, D.C.: U.S. Government Printing Office.

U.S. Civil Rights Commisssion. 1974. *Counting the Forgotten: The 1970 Census Count of Persons of Spanish-Speaking Background in the United States.* Washington, D.C.: U.S. Government Printing Office.

U.S. Department of Commerce. 1989. "Preliminary PES Guidelines." *Federal Register* 54(236): 51002–5. Docket no. 91282-8282.

———. 1991. Press release, October 15.

U.S. Department of Commerce v. U.S. House of Representatives. 1999. 98-404, _U.S._.

U.S. General Accounting Office. 1991. *1990 Census: Reported Net Undercount Obscured Magnitude of Error.* GAO/GGD-91-113. Washington, D.C.: U.S. Government Printing Office.

U.S. House of Representatives. 1970. Committee on Post Office and Civil Service. Subcommittee on Census and Statistics. *Accuracy of 1970 Census Enumeration and Related Matters.* 91st Cong., 2d sess. Serial 91-30.

———. 1982. Committee on Post Office and Civil Service. Subcommittee on Census and Population. *Impact of Budget Cuts on Federal Statistical Programs.* 97th Cong., 2d sess. Serial 97-41.

———. 1988. Committee on Post Office and Civil Service. Subcommittee on Census and Population. *The Decennial Census Improvement Act: Hearing Before the Subcommittee on Census and Population of the Subcommittee on Post Office and Civil Service.* 100th Cong., 2d sess. Serial 100-51.

———. 1996. Committee on Government Reform and Oversight. *Sampling and Statistical Adjustment in the Decennial Census: Fundamental Flaws.* 104th Cong., 2d sess. Serial 104-821.

———. 1997. H.R. 1469. Flood Relief Bill.

U.S. House of Representatives et al. v. U.S. Department of Commerce et al. 1998. 11 F.Supp. 2d 76 (D.C. circuit).

U.S. Senate. 1997. Committee on Governmental Affairs. Serial 105-233. Full Committee Hearing on Census 2000.

Vacca, E. Ann, Mary Mulry, and Ruth A. Killion. 1996. "The 1995 Census Test: A Compilation of Results and Decisions." Memorandum 46. Paper presented at the ASA/PAA Subcommittee of the Census Advisory Committee of Professional Associations (April 25–26).

Wachter, Kenneth W. 1993. "The Census Adjustment Trial: An Exchange." *Jurimetrics Journal* 34: 107–15.

Waite, Preston J., and Howard Hogan. 1998. "Statistical Methodologies for Census 2000: Decisions, Issues, and Preliminary Results." In *Proceedings of the Survey Research Methods Section.* Alexandria, Va.: American Statistical Association.

White, Andrew A., and Keith F. Rust, eds. 1997. *Preparing for the 2000 Census: Interim Report II.* Committee on National Statistics, National Research Council. Washington, D.C.: National Academy Press.

————. 1999. *Measuring a Changing Nation: Modern Methods for the 2000 Census.* Committee on National Statistics, National Research Council. Washington, D.C.: National Academy Press.

Williamson, Joel. 1980. *New People: Miscegenation and Mulattoes in the United States.* New York: Free Press.

Wisconsin v. City of New York. 1996. 517 U.S. 1.

Wolter, Kirk M. 1986. "Some Coverage Error Models for Census Data." *Journal of the American Statistical Association* 81: 338–346.

————. 1990. "Capture-Recapture Estimation in the Presence of a Known Sex Ratio." *Biometrics* 46: 157–62.

————. 1991. "Policy Forum: Accounting for America's Uncounted and Miscounted." *Science* 253: 12–15.

Wright, Carroll, and William C. Hunt. 1900. *History and Growth of the United States Census.* Washington, D.C.: U.S. Government Printing Office.

Wright, L. 1994. "Annals of Politics: One Drop of Blood." *New Yorker,* July 25, 46–56.

Zaslavsky, A. M., and G. S. Wolfgang. 1990. "Triple-System Modeling of Census, Postenumeration Survey, and Administrative List Data." In *Proceedings of the Section on Survey Research, American Statistical Association.* Alexandria, Va.: American Statistical Association.

About the Authors

MARGO J. ANDERSON is a professor of history and urban studies at the University of Wisconsin–Milwaukee.

STEPHEN E. FIENBERG is Maurice Falk University Professor of Statistics and Social Science at Carnegie Mellon University.

Index

Adams, John Quincy, 20
adjustment
    constitutionality of (McLaughlin),
        114
adjustment methodology
    arguments of opponents related to
        minority undercount, 169–74
    for 1990 census, 78–85
    decision of Secretary of Commerce
        not to use (1991), 127–31,
        261–66
    introduction of sampling-based sur-
        vey designs, 158
    PES design for 1990 census,
        95–99
    statistical improvements (1980s), 52
    Test of Adjustment-Related Opera-
        tions (TARO), 81–83
    See also dual-systems estimation
        (DSE); postenumeration survey
        (PES); undercount
advertising
    by Bureau of the Census, 16, 48
Advisory Committee (to Census Bu-
    reau). See Bureau of the Census
American Anthropological Association
    (AAA), 173–74
American Statistical Association (ASA)
    Blue-Ribbon Panel on the 2000
        census, 205
    Census Advisory Committee, 83
    Technical Panel on the Census
        Undercount, 77
apportionment
    census-based, 17, 226–29
    different methods of Jefferson and
        Hamilton, 18
    formulas used for, 7

"one man, one vote" concept, 32
    population as measure of, 13–14
    Supreme Court rulings about malap-
        portionment and reapportionment
        (1962), 32
    using population count to apportion
        political power, 14
    See also reapportionment
ASA. See American Statistical Associa-
    tion (ASA)
Austin, William Lane, 27

Bailar, Barbara, 52, 82, 84–85, 87–89,
    91–92, 140, 145, 153, 200
Baker v. Carr (1962), 32
Barabba, Vincent, 45–46, 49, 50, 51,
    145
Betts, Jackson, 37
Bounpane, Peter, 146–47
Bradburn, Norman, 192
Breiman, Leo, 148, 218
Brown, George, 38, 40, 42
Brown, Lawrence, 206–7, 218
Brown, Ronald, 155, 195
Bryant, Barbara Everitt, 94, 104,
    106–7, 127, 155, 160, 191, 194,
    218
Bureau of Labor Statistics (BLS)
    sampling-based adjustment in
        survey designs, 158
    statistical programs, 24–25
Bureau of the Census
    advertising after 1980 census,
        48
    advertising campaign after 1990
        census, 116
    Advisory Committee to, 25–26
    Census of Distribution, 26

309